Gehry draws

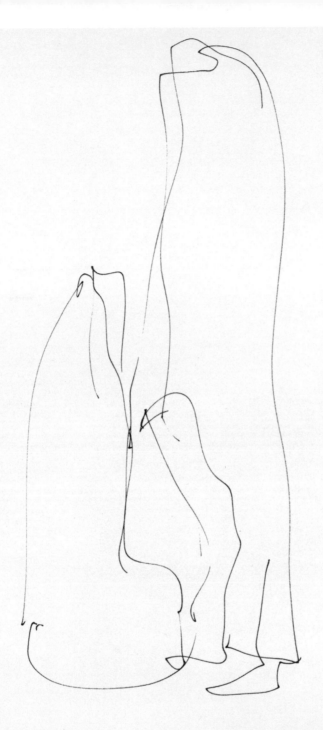

Gehry draws

**Essays by Horst Bredekamp,
Rene Daalder, and Mark Rappolt**

**Commentary by Frank Gehry,
Edwin Chan, and Craig Webb**

Edited by Mark Rappolt
and Robert Violette

The MIT Press, Cambridge, Massachusetts
in association with
Violette Editions, London

First published in 2004 in North and South America
by The MIT Press, Cambridge, Massachusetts,
in association with Violette Editions, London

MIT Press books may be purchased at special quantity
discounts for business or sales promotional use. For
information, please email special_sales@mitpress.mit.edu
or write to Special Sales Department, The MIT Press,
5 Cambridge Center, Cambridge, MA 02142.

Edited by Mark Rappolt and Robert Violette

Gehry Partners architectural models photographed by
Whit Preston, with additional photographs by Tom Bonner,
Joshua White, and Brian S. Yov

Designed by Peter B. Willberg and Paulus Dreibholz
at Clarendon Road Studio, London
Printed and bound in Slovenia

Frontispiece: drawing by Frank Gehry for the unbuilt
Astor Place Hotel, New York (see Project 26)

Library of Congress Control Number: 2004109220

ISBN: 0-262-18241-6

10 9 8 7 6 5 4 3 2 1

Contents

Editors' Note

MARK RAPPOLT AND ROBERT VIOLETTE

"I came at architecture through fine arts, and painting is still a fascination to me. Paintings are a way of training the eye. You see how people compose a canvas. The way Bruegel composes a canvas, or Jasper Johns. I learned about composition from their canvases. I picked up all those visual connections and ideas. And I find myself using them sometimes. The ideas of space through paintings, through the Pinturicchio paintings in Siena, which are just beautiful, huge, spatial experiences. They are about cities. And Lorenzetti, Gentile Bellini, Carpaccio. All of these paintings are about space and cities. Pict Mondrian has inspired the window and wall elevations of many buildings from Gropius to Le Corbusier. I have been fortunate to have had support from living painters and sculptors, and I have always felt that artists and architects do similar things. That there is a moment of truth in which you decide what color, what size, what composition. How you get to that moment of truth is different and the end result is different. There is a point where I have to make a decision, take a direction. There are a lot of them in a building. It's essentially what makes a building look like it does." FRANK GEHRY

In the 42 years that he has practiced as an architect, Frank Gehry's work has become the subject of an ever-increasing number of exhibitions, magazine articles, books, and monographs. And during that time, a succession of works, including Gehry's own residence, the Guggenheim Museum in Bilbao, and, most recently, the Walt Disney Concert Hall in Los Angeles, have become iconic examples of the architecture of their age. But while these and other buildings designed by Gehry are instantly familiar, the processes that led to their creation are not.

At the heart of his design process, Gehry draws. Indeed, he refers to his drawings as his means of "thinking aloud," one of the ways in which he arrives at those moments of truth of creation. This book, which contains over 360 drawings (most of which are previously unpublished), selected from Gehry's archive of thousands, offers a unique insight into these "thoughts" and the ways in which Gehry's design propositions morph in tandem with the intensive development of scale models.

Gehry Draws documents 29 major projects, starting from the Winton Guest House (1983–1987), during which Gehry evolved the drawing style for which he is now well known, and continuing with a series of ongoing projects that are in various stages of development and construction. Although drawing is an important part of Gehry's daily practice as an architect and informs his work on buildings from planning stages through to completion, there is no strict method to its use; for some projects Gehry makes only a few drawings and for others dozens. The selection and particular arrangement of drawings for this publication were made in collaboration with Keith Mendenhall and others at Gehry Partners in Venice, California, including, of course, the architect himself. This book is not meant to represent a wholly inclusive retrospective of drawings for every architectural project undertaken by Gehry in the last 20 years. Neither does this book aim at documenting or portraying Gehry's design process as a chronological progression from drawing to model to finished building, with literal, marked-out connections between them. Rather, it seeks to present Gehry's drawings as a form of communication, as the visual language by which he works his way through challenges inherent in each commission—large and small—and translates his ideas into form. In keeping with Gehry's description of his drawings as a way of "thinking aloud," or communicating, this book includes commentaries by Gehry himself and by Edwin Chan and Craig Webb, Project Designers and Partners, who interpret Gehry's visual language in quite different ways as they help transform his drawings into three-dimensional structures.

Gehry's drawings are placed in context by three introductory essays. Art historian Horst Bredekamp analyzes Gehry's unique drawing style and its links to a tradition of drawing, which he traces back to Dürer and sixteenth-century preoccupations with line and representation.

Bredekamp also takes us through a detailed demonstration by Gehry on how he draws and how one might "read" his line. As a counterpoint, virtual-reality filmmaker Rene Daalder looks at the way Gehry's combined use of drawings and computers anticipates new directions for architects in the twenty-first century. Mark Rappolt takes a look at the drawings in the context of the potentials and freedoms they offer architectural design, through the interplay of gesture, personality, and objective design.

The remainder of this book is left to the drawings themselves, reproduced uncropped showing their original paper supports, as naturalistically as possible and nearly actual size. They are presented in roughly chronological order, but sometimes in groups where the drawings themselves address specific aspects of an individual design. Select stages of model development are also illustrated alongside the drawings from time to time, to emphasize key progressions or experiments in design. The dates of these models refer to the date they were photographed, not necessarily to the precise date they were created (usually they are near enough the same). Most of the drawings were dated in Gehry's own hand in the moment they were drawn. For the most part, the drawings could be described as plans, elevations, or details; as this is evident from the drawings themselves, they have not been labelled as such. However, models and drawings are identified individually, from left to right on the page, top to bottom, for example, as "M01.01" and "D01.01"; the first pair of digits refer to the project number and the second pair to the individual model or drawing. The original drawings measure 9 × 12 inches, and with few exceptions have been drawn in black ink on the same uncoated off-white wove paper. As most of the projects in *Gehry Draws* are not yet built, we have used only one establishing shot of each building that does exist. This is not a book about Gehry's completed work.

We would like to express our grateful thanks first to Frank Gehry himself for opening up his drawing archive for more than three years. This book could not have been produced also without the intensive and always generous collaboration of Keith Mendenhall and others at Gehry Partners, including Edwin Chan, Craig Webb, Laura Stella, and Whit Preston. For additional help, we should also like to thank Abner Stein, Sandy Violette, Sophie Calle, Francesco Vezzoli, Ruth McNeil, Sara Cochran, Peter Willberg, Paulus Dreibholz, Horst Bredekamp, Rene Daalder, Steven Lindberg, Kyoko Tachibana, Vanessa Mitchell, Andrea Rutchick, Michael Hodgson, Roger Conover, Anjay Patel, Danilo Goriup, Boris Uran, Elena Sironi, Greg Lynn, Tom Emerson, Stephanie MacDonald, Sharon Gallagher, and Nancy Allan.

London, June 2004

En la que tabla rasa tanto excede,
que uee todas las cosas en potencia,
solo elpinçel consoberana ciencia,
reducir lapotencia al acto puede.

Fig. 1. Vicente Carducho (1576–1638), from *Dialogos de la pintura*
(Madrid: Martinez, 1633).

Frank Gehry and the Art of Drawing

HORST BREDEKAMP

The First Move

It is well known that the design phases of Frank Gehry's architectural projects are worked out through numerous models constructed from a wealth of materials, such as paper, cardboard, Styrofoam, and wood. And it is equally well known that it would be impossible to construct the complex spatial bodies that result from that process without calculations made by computers.[1] It is less well known, however, that Gehry draws incessantly.

This is not unusual. There are twentieth-century architects who have produced great and most diverse drawings, but others, like Walter Gropius, for example, neither wanted nor were able to draw.[2] Drawing and architecture do not necessarily go hand in hand. In Gehry's case, the use of drawing is not a question of ability, nor really a conscious decision at all. Rather, in its interplay of thinking and hand movements, drawing is the creative ferment of his goals, so that drawing should be considered as much a part of his calling as architecture and sculpture.

When Gehry was awarded the Pritzker Prize in 1989, he confessed: 'In trying to find the essence of my own expression, I fantasized the artist standing before the white canvas deciding what was the first move. I called it the moment of truth.'[3] In paying homage to the application of the first line to a blank surface, Gehry was employing one of the oldest metaphors for the creative process. Countless treatises on painting— Carducho's *Dialogos de la pintura,* published in Madrid (fig. 1) for example—discuss the approach to that crucial first stroke. A symbol of a self-referential art, which conceals within itself every conceivable formal possibility, the brush paints its own shadow falling downward to the left, an action triggering a decision that determines all the subsequent steps.[4]

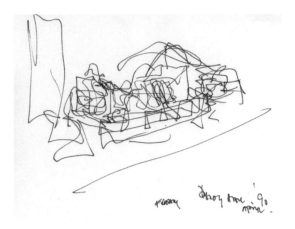

Fig. 2. Frank Gehry, drawing for Walt Disney Concert Hall, Los Angeles, ink on paper, see Project 19.

Fig. 3. Frank Gehry, drawing for Walt Disney Concert Hall, Los Angeles, ink on paper, see Project 19.

Subsequent versions of drawings by Gehry isolate or integrate the crucial fundamental lines [*Grundlinie*], as Gehry builds the tension between the white sheet, the first stroke, and the lines that follow. For example, one of the sketches for the Walt Disney Concert Hall in Los Angeles (fig. 2) programmatically reveals the initial line to be a liberated S shape. In another sketch for this project (fig. 3), three somewhat less isolated fundamental lines transform themselves by way of protrusions, wave shapes, and sharp bends into the curving, angular shapes—free in two dimensions, yet spatial in their cross-hatching. In one of the drawings for Der Neue Zollhof in Düsseldorf (fig. 4), these fundamental lines—horizontal forms that swing back and forth to open up into narrow surfaces—are connected to the building. Finally, the h-shape that leans diagonally to the left in a sketch of the Lewis Residence (fig. 5) is a form-constituting fundamental line integrated into a shape that not only suggests a landscape or a geological situation determining the ground plan but also evokes a mobile.

Tracing these variations on the "first move" of painting make it tempting to evaluate Gehry's drawings in terms of the degree to which they are freed from an operative purpose.[5] From the work of Giambattista Piranesi to the early Daniel Libeskind there has indeed repeatedly been a separation of architectural drawings from concrete building tasks. For example, Erich Mendelsohn, who may be considered one of Gehry's most important inspirations, produced "architectural psychographs," sometimes based on impressions derived from classical music, that lacked any reference to specific architectural projects.[6]

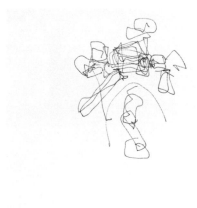

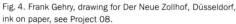

Fig. 4. Frank Gehry, drawing for Der Neue Zollhof, Düsseldorf, ink on paper, see Project 08.

Fig. 5. Frank Gehry, drawing for the Lewis Residence (unbuilt), ink on paper, see Project 05.

Nevertheless, detaching Gehry's drawings from the Hell of Purposes to make them products of the Heaven of Freedom would be a fundamental mistake. After years of experience with construction drawings and perspective views, the conditioning factors of terrain, of statics, and of means come so naturally to him that they are already integrated, even if they are not obvious at first glance. If the "first move" of painting formulates the primal conflict between constraint and freedom, it represents in a general form that which characterizes architecture in a particularly pointed way. In this respect, Gehry's drawings are intertwined with every planning stage.[7] From the first moment through the final state, and afterward as a reminder of the built complex, they help to fix still unfamiliar ideas, to grasp the essence of the stages of modeling, to free them from ossification, and to formulate new alternatives.

Gehry's drawings are therefore a fully valid part of the history of the art of drawing, not because they have been freed from their architectural calling, but because they embody this tension between constraint and freedom. And Gehry's confession that at the outset he is always like a painter before a white canvas should be understood in this sense.

The Framed Image

In 2002, in order to elucidate his drawing technique, Gehry made a sample sheet: he drew two sketches in black felt-tip pen on the same thin white card that he has used for years for his drafts and studies (fig. 6). Differences in placement and technique make the two drawings so crucially distinct that they clarify not only characteristics of Gehry's

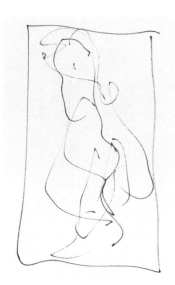

Fig. 6. Frank Gehry, sample drawing for the author, ink on paper, March 2002.

Fig. 7. Frank Gehry, drawing after Michelangelo's *Rebellious Slave,* detail of fig. 6.

Fig.8. Michelangelo Buonarroti (1475–1564), *Rebellious Slave*, Musée du Louvre, Paris.

own manner of drawing but also the fundamental motivations of architectural drawing in general.

One difference between the sample sheet's two shapes that immediately strikes the eye is that the form on the left is placed on the ground without a frame or base, and thus seems to be an undefined, atopic presence, whereas the one on the right has a frame and is thus defined as a picture. The framed sketch (fig. 7) relates to Michelangelo's *Rebellious Slave,* which is now in the Musée du Louvre (fig. 8). With its lines of different length, each starting anew, this sketch has its source in a free motion in which the whole arm participates, creating an impression of oscillation. Filling out the space to the upper and right edges, the diagonal orientation of the upper part emphasizes the inclination of the compact upper torso of the sculpture. The line that runs diagonally from chest to back is tangled, to suggest the fetters against which the body presses. An arc that curves back at lower right suggest the buttocks, while the curving lines in front indicate the drapery over the genitals and the balanced poise of the legs.

Drawn from memory and intended to capture the essence of the sculpture, these eight lines, running parallel or intersecting and playing with one another, exploit that fundamental principle of drawing according to which no mark is made until pressure is put on the pen, but without movement all that remains is a single point.[8] Gehry's individual lines range from those that have a powerful density to frail, diluted dots. Thus the sketch also elucidates the speed at which the lines were applied. Drawings are executed according to a rhythm that cannot be planned, alternating between acceleration and deceleration, rapidity and hesitating

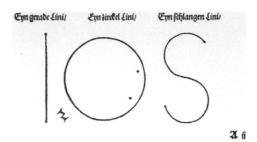

Fig. 9. Frank Gehry, drawing for Walt Disney Concert Hall, Los Angeles, ink on paper, see Project 19.

Fig. 10. Albrecht Dürer (1471–1528), three fundamental lines from Dürer, *Unterweysung der Messung* (Nuremberg, 1525).

control, followed by pentimenti.[9] Gehry's eight lines are not corrected anywhere, and their smooth flow illustrates the constant speed with which they were drawn. Consequently they are products of an unprogrammed way of thinking whose statements, as unmistakable as handwriting, are inimitable.

The Universal Line

Even more revealing are the composition and style of the eight lines, which pass through eleven more or less well defined S curves, characterized, as if by *mottoes*, by the lines sketched in the upper left and lower right corners. These S forms, which are only one element of Gehry's highly complex arsenal of drawing techniques, can be taken as an example of the semantic wealth that is encapsulated even in seemingly unspectacular motifs. These curving lines offer themselves all the more as an example of Gehry's manner since they run through his entire *oeuvre* of drawings. In contrast to the sketch for the Walt Disney Concert Hall, which isolated this form within the drawing (fig. 2), another drawing of this same project (fig. 9) plants the S shape in the middle of the building, as if it were at once its heart and its springy hinge.

These lines are part of a chain of efforts, stretching far into the past, to obtain a single pictorial formula for movements in nature and in thought. The naturalness with which Gehry uses this formula is the result of centuries-old reflection on this problem (not just in art but in philosophy and science as well) that informs this shape.

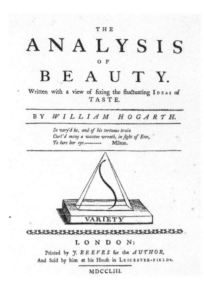

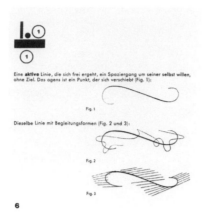

Fig. 12. Paul Klee (1879–1940), the active line, from *Pädagogisches Skizzenbuch* (Munich: Bauhausbücher, 1925).

Fig. 11. William Hogarth (1697–1764), title page from *The Analysis of Beauty* (London, 1753).

The idea of the serpentine line can be traced back to Leon Battista Alberti (1404–1472), who compared the movement of hair to that of flames and snakes.[10] This image was so suggestive that both the serpentine form and the flame became symbols of the creative line that stimulates the imagination. For example, in his *Unterweysung der Messung* of 1525 Albrecht Dürer asserted that the serpentine line perfectly embodied the dual purpose of drawing—both pointing back to nature and revealing the mind—because it could be pulled back and forth 'according to one's wishes' (fig. 10).[11] After a series of analogous applications, in 1753 William Hogarth fixed the serpentine 'variety' within a prism as the symbol of the summa of all forms of movement and depiction (fig. 11).[12] And a good hundred years after Hogarth's line of perfection the chemist August Kekulé picked up the topos of the serpentine line as art theory's image of mobile nature and applied it to the sciences as well.[13] Even the abstract model of the double helix created in 1953 by the artist Odile Crick seems to feed on the tradition of the S line.[14]

The validity of the *linea serpentinata* has not gone undisputed, and there have been repeated efforts to turn contour into the atmospheric effect of zones of spatial and misty light found in Impressionism. Because an art form without contours lacks the line's double quality of being extremely precise as a line in motion while still permitting freedom, the artists of Expressionism and Fauvism, to say nothing of Art Nouveau, rehabilitated the contour line. Paul Klee assigned the serpentine line in particular to the highest rank of motoric energy for subsidiary lines, hatching, and self-twisting: "An *active* line on a walk, moving freely, without goal. A walk for a walk's sake. The mobility agent is a point, shifting its position"

Fig. 13. Frank Gehry, drawing for the Museum of
Tolerance, Jerusalem, Center for Human Dignity,
a Project of the Simon Wiesenthal Center, ink
on paper, detail of fig. 6, see Project 24.

(fig. 12).[15] Developing Klee's idea, Gilles Deleuze[16] characterized the folds
of the baroque and Klee's serpentine lines as the essence of creative
thought—an observation that had an enormous influence on architectural
theory in the 1990s.[17]

This return demonstrates the power of a universal form that Gehry
developed independently, reflecting on the early drawings of Erich
Mendelsohn, for example, which the latter first exhibited in Paul Cassirer's
gallery in Berlin and then pursued in his *Dune Architectures*.[18] The sketches
by the architect Hermann Finsterlin also stand in a tradition that Gehry's
draftsman-like, imaginative intelligence brought to a unique and
unmistakable stage in the shaping of internal and external movement.[19]

The Model of the Museum of Tolerance, Jerusalem

In contrast to the rather planar sketch of Michelangelo's *Rebellious
Slave,* the figure on the left side of the sample sheet (fig. 13) has a stronger
spatial presence. The impression of depth is the result of applying the
strokes in a single uninterrupted gesture, within the radius of a supported
elbow, through a series of circling and spiraling movements. The unfold-
ing of this form reveals the spatial quality of Gehry's touch, which
gives the form depth by continually circling and curving anew, bringing
the elements of the S form into an organic continuum.

With no external borders or foundations, the shape floats in space
without referent. Although the two loops at lower left that point outward
might suggest a shadow falling on a plane, the dominant impression is
of a two-tier form rising up without being tied to any ground. Above a

Fig. 14. Detail of fig. 13.

Fig. 15. Detail of fig. 13.

cylindrical pedestal looms a tower that seems, at first, to be lashing itself in and is hardly less articulated and folded than the lower story. This is a sketch for the Museum of Tolerance in Jerusalem.

The uninterrupted line of the architectural model has its starting and ending points at the far right of the lower story (fig. 14). The curving, circling, scythe-like bending, eddying, meandering, and above all snaking lines produce a plexus in the interior (fig. 15), but their cumulative effect suggests vibrating, pulsing forms. This contrast reveals the crucial nature of architectural drawing.

The idea of "architecture as image" evolved from Ferdinando Bibiena's stage designs and the *architecture parlante* of French architects.[20] By contrast, Carl Linfert's still unsurpassed theory of architectural drawing—without which Walter Benjamin's conception of "distraction" would scarcely have been conceivable[21]—resolutely emphasized that the physical shape of architecture can only be revealed successively; it cannot be assimilated in the single image alone.[22] Interactions between architecture and bodily movements yield sensory events whose contingency eludes both static images and images that permit a simulated walk-through. This determination also defines the limits of central perspective, which relates the work of architecture to a single possible viewpoint. Perspective, which almost immediately came to dominate the construction of images in two dimensions, was employed in architecture far more hesitantly; even the Bauhaus rejected vanishing-point perspective in favor of axonometric renderings, so that buildings would not be fixed according to a particular point of view.[23] Working against this sort of objective alienation, Gehry's drawings do not attempt to tailor

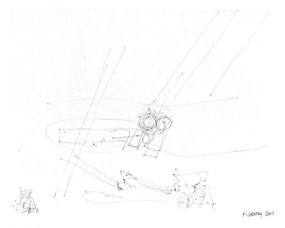

Fig. 16. Frank Gehry, drawing for the Guggenheim Museum, Bilbao, ink on paper, see Project 06.

the building to the subjective viewer but instead try to conceive the autonomous objectivity of the building in the viewer's imagination as a sum of possibilities. Hence his drawings avoid contours to which the lines projected from vanishing points could attach.

In a second drawing from 2002, a side view of the museum in Bilbao appears below an aerial view (fig. 16). Above the fundamental line of the lower figure is a single stroke that unfolds a continuous movement through Euclidean space, connecting the side and ground planes and rotating them into the third dimension. This quite commonplace method of projecting a side view and a top view into a single plane takes on an unusual quality in Gehry's work: although each shape is connected to the other by two lines, the side view is shifted to the right relative to the top view, by about a third of its length. This not only tips the building on its side toward the viewer but also makes it seem to spiral in space.

In their combination of different points of view and in their groundless and frameless indeterminacy, Gehry's figures conform astonishingly well to Linfert's call for an "unconstrained indifference of the foil" that avoids locating the building pictorially.[24] If parchment—which has no fixed ground and whose translucent appearance seems to sublate the underlying surface, as it were—is the appropriate foil for architectural drawing, as, for example, Bramante's magnificent floor plan for Saint Peter's in Rome demonstrates,[25] then Gehry's drawings appear as though they had been sketched on parchment. Offering neither the certainty of the mathematical point of view nor the pictorial fixing of a ground, they show the models as the motoric imagining of the building's entire complex. The sketch for the Museum of Tolerance

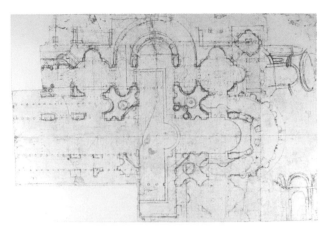

Fig. 17. Donato Bramante (1444–1514), sketch for New Saint Peter's, Rome; Uffizi, Florence.

(fig. 13) is exemplary in this sense because it avoids not only the simplifications of perspective but also the deficiencies of the visual. As an atopic dream shape, it imagines an architecture in a form that attempts to sublate pictorial reduction.

By juxtaposing on the sample sheet the framed image with the liberated architectural model (fig. 6), Gehry complies with the divergent agendas of two- and three-dimensional shapes. On the right, a sculpture is brought within the plane of a drawing by means of eight variations on the serpentine form; in the shape on the left, the single uninterrupted line creates an imaginary space out of circles and spirals, leading to the objective self-representation of architecture as the dream shape of the thinking hand.

Composition

The arrangement of the two figures on the first sheet makes it evident, thanks to its clear compositional principle, that Gehry is employing the transition from the image to the haptic imagination as a structural principle in all his drawings. Axially aligned, the figures appear in calm isolation, and because they are shifted slightly into the upper half of the sheet and displaced a touch to the left, the signature at lower right offers an optical point of orientation. Analogously, in the sketch for the Bilbao museum (fig. 16) a convulsion of lines is added at lower right to establish a *contrapposto* with the signature and thus balance the overall composition.

The history of drawn architectural models is filled with ground plans and perspective details that overlap and start again anew, as can be seen

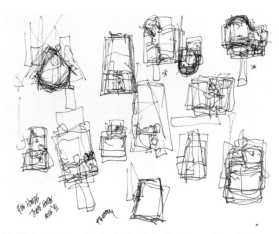

Fig. 18. Frank Gehry, drawing for the Gehry Residence, Santa Monica, California, ink on paper, see Project 02.

from one of the most enigmatic of examples: Bramante's Uffizi-20A-plan for New Saint Peter's in Rome (fig. 17). But even when his drawings fill the entire space, as with this sketch for the his own house (fig. 18), Gehry allows the individual motifs to speak in isolation, permitting him to capture the self-determination of every architectural model in its totality, which transcends the image. In terms of composition his sketches retain a visual equilibrium, which lends a gentle rhythm to the tension between abundance and emptiness. In populating his sheets Gehry shows respect for the individual value of even the tiniest details. Each of his figures retains a halo of respect, protecting the presence of the building from the overlapping that becomes possible in its image. Thus Gehry's compositions also illustrate an effort to preserve in the image architecture's ability to transcend the pictorial.

The Line's Autonomous Course

Gehry's principle of positioning the imagination in order to allow it to wander freely is also evident in the first sample sheet (fig. 6), where both figures move along the border between abstraction and recognizable motif. This is because, while the overall form may permit us to discern a purpose, the activity of the lines follows its own inclination, which obeys inherent, independent laws and energies. Both figures give the impression that the draftsman was observing himself in the act of drawing. He becomes the object of their autonomous course.

This is the principle of the ceaseless scribbling, sketching activity of the hand, which Leonardo da Vinci, as an obsessive, was probably the

Fig. 19. Albrecht Dürer, marginal drawing from *Das Gebetbuch Kaiser Maximilians I.,* 1515; Munich, Staatsbibliothek, fol. 42, verso.

first to employ. The pleasure Parmigianino took in allowing the stroke of his pen to be guided by the curving line, until the lines broke free of the content and began to oscillate freely, also helped to establish this tradition.[26]

Dürer, however, gave it a particular stamp. The marginal drawings in *Das Gebetbuch Kaiser Maximilians I* of 1515 are among the most valuable objects in the art of drawing, because here Dürer is at play, toying with ornaments, letters, and figures; he forsakes all semantics and embraces the principle that the creative imagination propels itself. Along the image's upper edge are perpetual metamorphoses of vertical or horizontal S lines that, because of their indomitable mutability and interpretability, form an organ of the creative urge (fig. 19).[27] It is as if they had taken Lucretius's immortal evocation of the constantly mutating form of clouds and translated it into drawings: "Forming themselves in many ways, aloft, / Changing incessantly, fluent, volatile."[28] To the extent that nature itself is the generator of the images, it is one model for Dürer's protean gesture: the theme enunciated by his highly artistic shapes is the stochastic effect of forms that seem to come arbitrarily from outside.

The courses of Gehry's dynamic lines, which come together into an overall form seemingly against their will, offer a cosmos of related webs: this becomes clear, for example, if one superimposes one of the drawings for the Walt Disney Concert Hall (fig. 20) with the cross-hatching of a sketch for Der Neue Zollhof in Düsseldorf (fig. 21). Gehry belongs to a line of outstanding draftsmen for whom the creative principle does not involve, for example, the artist revealing himself as the lord of his creation: instead he controls the course of his imagination's motor

Fig. 20. Frank Gehry, drawing for Walt Disney Concert Hall,
Los Angeles, ink on paper, see Project 19.

Fig. 21. Frank Gehry, drawing for Der Neue Zollhof, Düsseldorf,
ink on paper, see Project 08.

activity as if from the perspective of an observer. His drawings remain
tied to construction, but they push us into regions devoid of articulated
ideas. Therein lies what is perhaps their most important calling:
not to obey their creator but to astonish him. In contrast to the great
architectural drawings of Zaha Hadid, for example, who develops her
shapes by means of a highly geometric, constructivist, and—for all their
splintering—Ciceronian gesture, Gehry's drawings are subtly Epicurean,
as it were: they yield to the ideas and circumstances that affect a form.
In contrast to a constructivism that turns perspectival or axonometric
forms into brilliantly constrained shapes, Gehry's figures preserve a subtle
joy in a metamorphic dynamics.

Chance as a Principle of Form

Chance is also part of this motor activity, offering, in nature and in
everyday life, an inexhaustible source for the powers of the imagination.
In accordance with ancient theories of chance sources of inspiration,[29]
Alberti associated the artistic imagination with the ability to perceive
lines, *lineamenta,* in irregular objects, like clumps of earth, which by
means of slight alterations could then be endowed with a form, their
shape perfect and complete.[30] In mere spots on the wall Leonardo saw
entire cosmoses of designs for paintings,[31] indeed he endorsed Botticelli's
method of throwing a sponge soaked with different paints at the wall
in order to obtain spots as a source of inspiration for landscapes, and
even extended it to every other conceivable subject, such as battles, seas,
clouds, and forests.[32] By way of Alexander Cozens, who called his

landscapes "a production of chance, with a small degree of design," this principle continued to have an effect through such aleatoric artists of twentieth-century art as Hans Arp and John Cage.[33]

Gehry took it up in his own way. He takes chance not as an absolute principle but as an opening that frees him to react to unintentional forms of both the quotidian and associative arrangements, as well as the uncontrolled movements of one's own thoughts. Already in Dürer's marginal drawings, whose very value neutralizes the hierarchy of main and subordinate theme, there is a nonhierarchical mechanism at work that liberates the imagination from the strict meaning of the motifs. The theory of chance images applies this method to the sources for the artistic imagination.

Gehry's drawings correspond to the curves of Dürer's marginal lines as well as to Alberti's systems of clumps and Leonardo's sponges tossed against walls. As architectural drawings, they are never free of an awareness of the possibility of their realization. They do not constitute an immediate means of translation but instead an artistically created primal matter that stimulates the imagination like a gift from nature.

Drawings, like every form of art, must be understood in terms of their historical period,[34] but they possess a dense, almost anthropological proximity to the ideas that formed them, so that they have an inherent, timeless modernity. When faced with drawings by Bosch, Callot, Tiepolo, Menzel, or Mendelsohn, viewers are so astonished by their immediacy that for a moment they forget these works derive from other ages and cultures. Gehry's drawings belong to this same sphere.

The Problem of Drawing

Drawings are among the ephemeral products of the visual arts, but the frailty of their physical constitution is not a shortcoming; rather, their reduced materiality possesses a force that drives the imagination, which itself can overcome possible inhibitions. Among the strangest aspects of the human capability to perceive and process is the power of drawings, at times more powerful than stone. Onofrio Panvinio recounted the story of Bramante persuading Pope Julius II to tear down the Constantinian basilica of Saint Peter's, an act as incomprehensible in 1505 as it is now: 'He showed the Pope now ground plans, now some other drawings of the building, never ceasing to plead with him, ensuring that the project would bring him supreme fame.'[35] The enormous late antique church was knocked down, because the imagination could not bear seeing its drawings go unrealized.

Describing this phenomenon in the language of art theory, Giorgio Vasari (1511–1574) extols the superiority of the line over the building:

"The designs for the latter [architecture] are composed entirely of lines, which for the architect is nothing less than the beginning and end of this art, for what remains to be communicated by models in wood, derived from these lines, is nothing but the work of stonecutters and masons."[36] The Neoplatonic, antimaterial basis of this argument would be alien to Gehry, but he would underscore the high regard for drawing in terms no less resolute.

Recent decades have been filled with a technical euphoria that has led some commentators, and even architects, to speak of the end of craft skills and all forms that are not technically mediated. Since, from the initial stages, the computer helps to lend ideas material form by calculating the spaces and statics and since it also makes sculptural models consistent by means of scanning processes, it has in fact taken over or replaced many of the functions of drawing. In its indispensable importance, the computer has become, in the spirit of the *mathesis universalis,* the generator of forms it produces of its own accord.[37]

The inwardly curving spatial bodies of Gehry's Guggenheim Museum in Bilbao could scarcely have been conceived and built if they had not been simulated and calculated using a computer program designed for the aviation industry.[38] However, the possibility of imagining spaces that go beyond the limits of the human imagination is, for Gehry, irrevocably based on the drawing hand. From the earliest planning stages to the digital CATIA, *disegno* is placed within an extended continuum, and the "first move" of the hand remains the metaphor for the ur-line that determines all the processes to come.

The choice between computer and drawing is thus wrongly put. The drawing hand and the modeling hand can only be eliminated at the cost of losing the body's direct input in the process of forming the model. There are new opportunities there but also impoverishments so clear that we should not expect drawing—an instrument of thinking tied to the body—to be eliminated, even over the long term. Rather, there is an interaction with the most advanced technologies that obtains its productivity precisely by means of sharpening the distinctions between drawing and the digital line. The events of recent times have not meant the end of *disegno* but rather its perpetuation on two planes: as a product and a medium of both craft skill and technology. Gehry's communication of technological possibilities by means of the motoric potential of the thinking hand, using every mechanical innovation, but not neglecting any manual technique that might aid the imagination, was and is, in its imperturbable freedom, the embodiment of the more sophisticated avant-garde.

The magic of architectural drawing led Vasari to consider it more enduring than stones. Gehry's *oeuvre* is an exemplary case of the mysterious validity of this conclusion.

Notes

1. William J. Mitchell, "Roll Over Euclid: How Frank Gehry Designs and Builds," in J. Fiona Ragheb, ed., *Frank Gehry, Architect,* exh. cat. (New York: Guggenheim Museum, 2001), 353–63.

2. Winfried Nerdinger, *The Architect Walter Gropius: Drawings, Prints, and Photographs from the Busch-Reisinger Museum, Harvard University Art Museums, Cambridge, Mass., and from Bauhaus-Archiv, Berlin,* trans. Andreas Solbach and the Busch-Reisinger Museum (Berlin: Gebr. Mann, 1985), 29; Jürgen Paul, "Der Architekturentwurf im 20. Jahrhundert als kunsthistorisches Arbeitsfeld," in Stefan Kummer and Georg Satzinger, eds., *Studien zur Künstlererziehung: Klaus Schwager zum 65.Geburtstag* (Stuttgart: Hatje, 1990), 308–21, esp. 313. An excellent survey may be found in Matilda McQuaid, ed., *Envisioning Architecture: Drawings from the Museum of Modern Art* (New York: Museum of Modern Art, 2002).

3. *The Pritzker Architecture Prize 1989, Presented to Frank Owen Gehry, Sponsored by the Hyatt Foundation* (Los Angeles: The Foundation, 1990), unpaginated.

4. Vicente Carducho, *Dialogos de la pintura* (Madrid: Martinez, 1633), final image; see Victor I. Stoichita, *A Short History of the Shadow,* trans. Anne-Marie Glasheen (London: Reaktion,1997), 95–98.

5. On the history of the emancipation of models as autonomous works, see Irving Lavin, "Bozzetti and Modelli: Notes on Sculptural Procedure from the Early Renaissance through Bernini," in *Stil und Überlieferung in der Kunst des Abendlandes: Akten des 21. Internationalen Kongresses für Kunstgeschichte in Bonn, 1964* (Berlin: Gebr. Mann, 1967), 100–1, and more recently, Michael Wiemers, *Bildform und Werkgenese: Studien zur zeichnerischen Bildvorbereitung in der italienischen Malerei zwischen 1450 und 1490* (Munich: Deutscher Kunstverlag, 1996). This sifting out of pure drawings from the cosmos of sketches made for a specific purpose—including architectural drawings—was encouraged by, among other things, Arthur Drexler's introduction to *Visionary Architecture,* exh. cat. (New York: Museum of Modern Art, 1960).

6. Winfried Nerdinger with Florian Zimmermann, eds., *Die Architekturzeichnung: Vom barocken Idealplan zur Axonometrie,* exh. cat. (Munich: Prestel, 1986), 176.

7. See the exemplary chronology in Coosje van Bruggen, *Frank O. Gehry: Guggenheim Museum Bilbao* (New York: Guggenheim Museum, 1997).

8. Alexander Perrig, *Michelangelo's Drawings: The Science of Attribution* (New Haven: Yale Univ. Press, 1991), 15–16.

9. Ibid., 19.

10. Leon Battista Alberti, *On Painting,* trans. John R. Spencer (Westwood, CT: Greenwood Press, 1976), 81: "waves in the air like flames, twines around itself like a serpent"; Leon Battista Alberti, "De pictura," in idem, *Das Standbild, Die Malkunst, Grundlagen der Malerei,* ed. and trans. Oskar Bätschmann et al. (Darmstadt: Wissenschaftliche Buchgesellschaft, 2000), 278 (sec. 45): "atque undent in aera flammas imitantes, modoque sub aliis crinibus serpant."

11. Albrecht Dürer, *The Painter's Manual: A Manual of Measurement . . . ,* trans. Walter L. Strass (New York: Abaris, 1977), 41; Albrecht Dürer, *Unterweysung der Messung / mit dem Zirkel und richtscheyt. . . .* (Nördlingen: Uhl, 1983; facsimile of Nuremberg, 1525), A2: "wie man will."

12. William Hogarth, *The Analysis of Beauty,* ed. Joseph Burke (Oxford: Clarendon Press, 1955; originally published London, 1753). See David Bindman, *Hogarth and His Times,* exh. cat. (London: British Museum Press, 1997), 168. On the tradition of the serpentine line as an ur-element in aesthetics from Dürer to Hogarth, see Peter Gerlach, "Zur zeichnerischen Simulation von Natur und natürlicher Lebendigkeit," *Zeitschrift für Ästhetik und Allgemeine Kunstwissenschaft* 34, no. 2 (1989): 243–79.

13. Richard Anschütz, *August Kekulé,* 2 vols. (Berlin: Chemie, 1929), 2:942: "Alles in Bewegung, schlangenartig sich windend und drehend" (Everything in motion, winding snakelike and turning).

14. J. D. Watson and F. H. Crick, "Molecular Structure of Nucleic Acids: A Structure for

Deoxyribose Nucleic Acid," *Nature,* April 25, 1953, 737.

15. Paul Klee, *Pedagogical Sketchbook,* trans. Sibyl Moholy-Nagy (New York: Frederick A. Praeger, 1953), 16; Paul Klee, *Pädagogisches Skizzenbuch,* Bauhausbücher 2 (Munich: Bauhausbücher, 1925), 6: "Eine aktive Linie, die sich frei ergeht, ein Spaziergang um seiner selbst willen, ohne Ziel. Das agens ist ein Punkt, der sich verschiebt."

16. Gilles Deleuze, *Le pli: Leibniz et le baroque* (Paris: Minuit, 1988), 5–54.

17. See, for example, Anthony Vidler, *Warped Space: Art, Architecture, and Anxiety in Modern Culture* (Cambridge, MA: MIT Press, 2000), 219–33.

18. Susan King, *The Drawings of Eric Mendelsohn,* exh. cat. (Berkeley: University Art Museum, 1969), 30.

19. See, example, the architectural sketches in Reinhard Döhl, *Hermann Finsterlin: Eine Annäherung,* exh. cat. (Stuttgart: Hatje, 1988), 262. With the dominance of the Neues Bauen (Modern building) movement, this tendency was continued less in architecture than in abstract expressionist painting of and above all in the curvy forms of Art Informel and the "antiobjects" of groups such as Geflecht; see *Geflecht: Bachmeyer, Heller, Köhler, Nanjoks, Rieger, Sturm, Zimmer; Antiobjekte, 1965–1966,* exh. cat. ([Munich]: Galerie Loo, [1966]).

20. Bruno Reudenbach, *G. B. Piranesi, Architektur als Bild: Der Wandel in der Architekturauffassung des achtzehnten Jahrhunderts* (Munich: Prestel, 1979).

21. Walter Benjamin, "Strenge Kunstwissenschaft: Zum ersten Band der 'Kunstwissenschaftliche Forschungen,'" in idem, *Gesammelte Schriften,* ed. Rolf Tiedemann and Hermann Schweppenhäuser, vol. 3, *Kritiken und Rezensionen,* ed. Hella Tiedemann-Bartels (Frankfurt am Main: Suhrkamp, 1972), 367–69, 373–74, 652–58; Walter Benjamin, "The Rigorous Study of Art: On the First Volume of the *Kunstwissenschaftliche Forschungen,*" trans. Thomas Y. Levin, in idem, *Selected Writings, 1927–34,* ed. Michael W. Jennings, Howard Eiland, and Gary Smith (Cambridge, MA: Belknap Press, 1999), 669–70. See also the correspondence between Walter Benjamin and Carl Linfert on architectural drawing, in Walter Benjamin, *Gesammelte Briefe,* vol. 4, ed. Christoph Gödde and Henri Lonitz (Frankfurt am Main: Suhrkamp, 1998), 42, 261. Benjamin made use of Linfert's view of architecture in his "Work of Art" essay, but, probably in order to protect him, did not cite him; see Walter Benjamin, "Das Kunstwerk im Zeitalter seiner technischen Reproduzierbarkeit," in idem, *Gesammelte Schriften,* ed. Rolf Tiedemann and Hermann Schweppenhäuser, vol. 7.1, ed. Christoph Gödde, Henri Lonitz, and Gary Smith (Frankfurt am Main: Suhrkamp, 1989), 380–81; Walter Benjamin, "The Work of Art in the Age of Its Technological Reproducibility" trans. Edmund Jephcott and Harry Zohn, in idem, *Selected Writings, 1927–34,* ed. Michael W. Jennings, Howard Eiland, and Gary Smith (Cambridge, MA: Belknap Press, 1999), 119–20.

22. Carl Linfert, "Die Grundlagen der Architekturzeichnung, mit einem Versuch über französische Architekturzeichnungen des 18. Jahrhunderts," in *Kunstwissenschaftliche Forschungen,* vol. 1 (Berlin : Frankfurter Verlags-Anstalt, 1931), 133–246.

23. Walter Gropius, "The Theory and Organization of the Bauhaus," in Herbert Bayer, Walter Gropius, and Ise Gropius, eds., *Bauhaus, 1919–1928* (Boston: C. T. Branford, 1952), 20–29, esp. 27. To the history of axonometry, see: Yve-Alain Bois, "Metamorphoses of Axonometry," in *De Stijl,* exh. cat. (The Hague: Gemeentemuseum, 1983), 146–61.

24. Linfert, "Die Grundlagen der Architekturzeichnung" (note 22), 152.

25. Christof Thoenes, "Neue Beobachtungen an Bramantes St.-Peter-Entwürfen," *Münchner Jahrbuch der bildenden Kunst* 45 (1994): 109–32, esp. 118–19. See also Olaf Klodt, "Bramantes Entwürfe für die Peterskirche in Rom: Die Metamorphose des Zentralbaus," in *Festschrift für Fritz Jacobs zum 60. Geburtstag,* ed. Olaf Klodt et al. (Münster: Lit, 1996), 119–52, esp. 127–29,

and Linfert, "Die Grundlagen der Architekturzeichnung" (note 22), 152–53.

26. Konrad Oberhuber, "Parmigianino als Zeichner," in *Parmigianino und der europäische Manierismus,* ed. Sylvia Ferino-Pagden and Lucia Fornari Schianchi (Vienna: Kunsthistorisches Museum, 2003), 97–107, esp. 99–100.

27. Friedrich Teja Bach, *Struktur und Erscheinung: Untersuchungen zu Dürers graphischer Kunst* (Berlin: Gebr. Mann, 1996), 172, fig. 194.

28. Lucretius, *The Way Things Are: The De Rerum Natura of Titus Lucretius Carus,* trans. Rolfe Humphries (Bloomington: Indiana Univ. Press, [1968]), 122–23; Titus Lucretius Carus, *De rerum natura / Welt aus Atomen,* ed. and trans. Karl Büchner (Stuttgart: Reclam, 1977), 262–63 (4.141 –42): "ut nubes facile inter dum concrescere in alto / cernimus et mundi speciem violare serenam / aëra mulcentes motu."

29. Pliny the Elder, *Historia naturalis,* 2.61.152; H. W. Janson, "Chance Images," in *Dictionary of the History of Ideas: Studies of Selected Pivotal Ideas,* ed. Philip Wiener, 5 vols. (New York: Scribner, 1973–74), 1:340–53, esp. 340–42.

30. Leon Battista Alberti, *On Painting and On Sculpture: The Latin Texts of De Pictura and De Statua,* ed. and trans. Cecil Grayson ([London]: Phaidon, [1972]), 121: "They [who attempt to create images and likenesses from bodies produced by Nature] probably occasionally observed in a tree-trunk or clod of earth and other similar inanimate objects certain outlines in which, with slight alterations, something very similar to the real faces of Nature was represented. They began, therefore, by diligently observing and studying such things, to try to see whether they could not add, take away or otherwise supply whatever seemed lacking to effect and complete the true likeness"; ibid., 120: "nam ex trunco glebave et huiusmodi mutis corporibus fortassis aliquando intuebantur lineamenta nonnulla, quibus paululum immutatis persimile quidpiam veris naturae vultibus redderetur. Coepere id igitur animo advertentes atque adnotantes adhibita diligentia tentare conarique possentne illic adiungere adimereve atque perfinire quod ad veram simulacri speciem comprehendendam absolvendamque deesse videretur."

31. *The Literary Works of Leonardo da Vinci,* ed. Jean Paul Richter, trans. R. C. Bell, 2 vols. (London: S. Low, Marston, Searle, & Rivington, 1883), 1:254.

32. Leonardo da Vinci, *Treatise on Painting,* trans. A. Philip McMahon, 2 vols. (Princeton, NJ: Princeton Univ. Press, 1956), 1:59.

33. Alexander Cozens, quoted in H. W. Janson, "The 'Image Made by Chance' in Renaissance Thought," in *De Artibus Opuscula XL: Essays in Honor of Erwin Panofsky,* ed. Millard Meiss, 2 vols. (New York: New York University, 1961), 1:264. See Bernhard Holeczek and Lida von Mengden, eds., *Zufall als Prinzip: Spielwelt, Methode und System der Kunst des 20. Jahrhunderts,* exh. cat. (Heidelberg: Braus, 1992).

34. Francis Ames-Lewis, *Drawing in Early Renaissance Italy* (New Haven: Yale Univ. Press, 2000). See, above all, Wolfgang Kemp, review of *Michelangelostudien,* by Alexander Perrig, *Kritische Berichte* 5, no. 1 (1977): 34–42.

35. Onofrio Panvinio, *De rebus antiquis memorabilibus basilicae sancti Petri apostolorum principis vaticanae libri VII,* ms. Vatican Library, quoted in Christoph Luitpold Frommel, "Die Peterskirche unter Papst Julius I. im Licht neuer Dokumente," *Römisches Jahrbuch für Kunstgeschichte* 16 (1976): 57–136, esp. 90–91.

36. Giorgio Vasari, *Le vite de' più eccellenti pittori scultori ed architettori,* ed. Gaetano Milanesi, 9 vols., (Florence: G. C. Sansoni, 1906), 1:170: "i disegni di quella [architettura] non son composti se non di linee: il che non è altro, quanto all' architettore, che il principio e la fine di quell' arte, perchè il restante, mediante i modelli di legname tratti dalle dette linee, non è altro che opera di scarpellini e muratori."

37. Greg Lynn, *Animate Form* (Princeton, NJ: Princeton Univ. Press, 1998).

38. Francesco Dal Co, Kurt Forster, and Hadley Arnold, *Frank O. Gehry: The Complete Works* (New York: Monacelli, 1998), 488.

Frank Gehry:
Foreshadowing the Twenty-first Century

RENE DAALDER

In a recent conversation with Frank Gehry about the drawings that are the subject of this book I was reminded of my mother, a well-known graphologist in the Netherlands, who proved to me that every stroke of the pen and every written gesture opened up a whole world to the experienced handwriting expert. I told Gehry that my mother once analyzed the writing of my oldest friend, Rem Koolhaas, and predicted that he would in the course of his life be involved with museums, libraries, and other such cultural institutions. This was many years before Rem deserted our joint filmmaking efforts to study architecture, and subsequently take on the world's museums and libraries, just like my mother said he would.

When I first looked at Gehry's drawings my mind instantly connected his artistic scribbles to the computer as the perfect medium to analyze and translate his inimitable gestures into architecture. When a trained handwriting expert can analyze the highly personal flourishes of the human hand to the extent described above, then it seems entirely reasonable to suggest that a computer can translate and interpret them just as well. In fact, this is a task that millions of computers perform every day, checking the authenticity of credit card signatures and performing all kinds of handwriting recognition tasks for intelligence agencies across the globe.

As should be obvious by now, I am neither an architect, nor an art historian. The focus of my contribution to this book will be to establish Frank Gehry's importance as a trailblazer for the digital age. When we met, however, I was surprised at how reluctant he was to consider himself a digital pioneer. Although he did credit the computer for playing a major role in his organizational process, providing him with the upper hand in the often-contentious relationship between architects and "parental" developers, he looked at the computer primarily as a number-crunching machine rather than an active participant in his creative process.

I told him that on an intuitive level he may be much more connected to the computer's digital intelligence than he thinks and that the popular perception of his work as computer-driven architecture may indeed be more to the point than his own attitude towards the technology suggests. Even though Gehry was willing to listen, he wasn't quite prepared to accept the visionary mantle he so clearly deserves, leaving it up to me to articulate his importance for the digital era regardless of his own day-to-day relationship with the computer. In any case, that is ultimately irrelevant. After all, it is a well-published fact that the writer William Gibson has only a perfunctory knowledge of computers and invented the term "cyberspace" while working on an IBM Selectric typewriter, and that hasn't prevented anyone from heralding him as one of the most visionary authors articulating the digital age. In the case of Gehry, it is interesting to note that every architectural expert who writes about his creative process focuses on the fact that the computer is merely a stepping stone. The cover copy of the book *Gehry Talks* even goes out of its way to proclaim that "the computer is a tool, not a partner, an instrument for catching the curve, not for inventing it." As I will demonstrate, however, the general public has a distinctly different impression.

The appreciation of Gehry's work by his peers often doesn't seem to measure up to his tremendous popular success. In the course of writing this chapter I came across considerable criticism heaped upon Gehry from within the architectural community. One writer I know described the Walt Disney Concert Hall in Los Angeles (Project 19) as a stack of tissues thrown away by someone with a head cold, while a prominent young Dutch architect's reluctant visit to the building only produced the disdainful comment that the stainless-steel surfaces were sloppily applied. A quick poll among architecture students at Sci-Arc in LA had equally lukewarm results, although, in light of the above, the suggestion that Frank Gehry might at least "save us from the Dutch" did stand out. Around the same time, former *New York Times* architecture critic and sometime Gehry fan Herbert Muschamp, saw fit to describe Gehry's Experience Music Project building in Seattle (Project 09) as "something that crawled out of the sea, rolled over, and died."

By contrast, an arbitrary sampling of the public's response to the Disney Concert Hall showed that people outside of the profession have a much deeper connection to the building than to most other architecture they ever encountered. During the building's official unveiling its reception was positively ecstatic. One sophisticated connoisseur of art I know admitted that she cried upon coming face to face with the

Fig. 1. Guggenheim Museum, Bilbao
(photo: David Heald © SRGF, New York).

Fig. 2. Walt Disney Concert Hall, Los Angeles (photo: Grant Mudford).

strikingly different architecture, while a talented young screenwriter of my acquaintance went so far as to break down the most important milestones in the history of architecture as follows: "First there was pyramid builder Imhotep, next came the Renaissance architect Palladio, and now, at the dawn of the Digital Age, we have Frank Gehry."

Whatever we might think of these opinions, one thing stands out within the public's reaction to Gehry's work: they appear to be most affected by those buildings that represent the biggest departure from the Modernist aesthetic, such as the Guggenheim Museum in Bilbao (Project 06) and Disney Concert Hall, both of which are perceived as somehow strongly associated with the computer. Clearly, the notion of the "computer" in this context evokes something much bigger than the utilitarian devices people stare at every day at work. It is as if the people beholding the complex shape of Gehry's buildings are infused with a deep sense of longing for the future.

Similarly, my use of the term "computer" in this essay implies a much larger context than the common connotation of a physical box, loaded with circuit boards and software applications. In our networked world that box is gradually reduced to being just an interface that gives us access to the internet, which increasingly manifests itself as an all-encompassing intelligence freed of all boundaries of time and space. The box itself, to the extent there will even be one in the future, no longer needs to be encumbered by onboard software or data taxing its limited memory. Instead, all information processing will increasingly take place on servers, providing the online users with "intelligence on tap." Any serious computing will automatically be outsourced to "invisible" processors whose

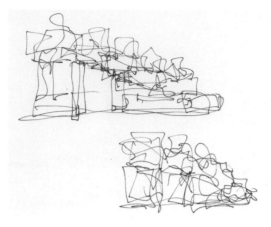

Fig. 3. Frank Gehry, drawing for the Samsung Museum of Modern Art (unbuilt), Seoul, Korea, ink on paper, see Project 17.

Fig. 4. Rene Daalder, computer-generated image of a suburban house for Daalder's film *Habitat* (1997).

geographic location has become completely inconsequential to the end user as the tasks he needs to be performed are constantly in transit throughout the global network. Thanks to today's wireless communication technologies, digital intelligence is rapidly becoming all-pervasive to the point where it literally surrounds us like a man-made atmosphere. If the zeitgeist is something we can access because, as the saying goes, it is "in the air," then it can be no surprise that a highly receptive individual like Gehry is capable of picking up on the far-reaching implications of this "techno sphere" and articulating his connection with its transformative powers in creative terms.

Given that line of thought, it may be appropriate to look at Frank Gehry as a defining architect of our historical moment, a man who is intuitively in touch with the future as it is implied by the present. To put this suggestion in its historical perspective, it may be useful to look beyond Gehry's own references to the art of his contemporaries as a seminal influence on his work. We might consider instead the fact that the digital age that is now upon us was instigated by individuals informed by the 1960s ethos of breaking down boundaries, of promoting connection and fluidity over the separation and the rigidity of the existing "straight" society. These pioneers of computer technology set into motion an evolutionary process that would eventually do away with the prevailing man/machine dialectic among architects who, in the course of the last century, have been favoring the functional pragmatism of the machine over more humanistic "soft" impulses. As it turns out, in the digital age the "machine" itself has thrown these Modernist attitudes for a loop by proving that computers are imminently adept at embracing

Fig. 5. Gehry Partners, model for the Lewis Residence (unbuilt), Lyndhurst, Ohio, see Project 05.

Fig. 6. Gehry Partners, model for the Lewis Residence (unbuilt), Lyndhurst, Ohio, see Project 05.

more "humanistic" tendencies and indeed tend towards a biomorphic expressiveness that has been considered anathema for most of the last century until the computer validated it.

In the early 1990s I worked at the seminal Computer Graphics Lab of the New York Institute of Technology in Long Island. It was the Parc Xerox of imaging technologies, whose alumni would give birth to Silicon Graphics computers, George Lucas's Industrial Light and Magic, and Steve Jobs' Pixar. The challenge at the time was to create simulated reality for the motion picture industry, which amounted to reinventing the real world in the digital domain, from *particle systems* that imitated the behavior of flocking birds or schools of fish, to the early versions of *texture maps* that would provide the skins for *Jurassic Park* dinosaurs. A parallel universe evolved from pixels, one step at a time, recreating all natural processes, from the rippling of water to the twisting fury of tornadoes, until ultimately everything that constitutes reality could be manipulated in the digital domain. In the process of doing this, the notion took hold that the more we would be able to migrate the physical world into the computer, the more we would be able to set it free and reconsider "reality" from an entirely different perspective.

During that period I was working closely with programmer Tom Brigham who would go on to win an Academy Award for his contributions to the invention of *morphing*. The challenge we had set for ourselves was to make a suburban house come alive for my movie *Habitat*, which due to a lack of funds ended up being released minus the amazing special effects we created. The images that evolved from our custom software showed amazing biomorphic transformations of what started out as a standard craftsman house. In the process of letting the various algorithms loose on the digital timber we witnessed one example after another of the computer's astonishing capabilities to seemingly return the man-made wooden structure to its original "natural" shapes of twisted branches and gnarly roots.

Looking recently at images of Frank Gehry's shape-shifting iterations of the Lewis residence, I noticed many remarkably similar forms that strongly suggested that, even though in Gehry's case there was hardly any intervention by the computer, many of his most effective forms can only be described as *morph-shapes*, showing such a prodigious kinship with the transformative power of the computer's algorithms that one has to come to the conclusion that the computer and the architect are somehow possessed of matching sensibilities.

Writing about the computer as a design tool, the architectural thinker Marcus Novak, who coined the phrase *liquid architecture*, came to the conclusion that "music seem(s) to explain everything …; it is the metaphor with which it all begins and ends." Undoubtedly a frustrated musician like so many of us working in less intuitive disciplines, Novak is onto something. In order to learn how software design develops over time in more complex media like movies and architecture, we can gain a lot of insight from the evolution of electronic music.

First there was a whole generation of electronic instruments, starting with Moog synthesizers, that were able to generate synthetic sounds from purely electronic sources like waveform oscillators—a technology that was exemplified by the work of musicians like Wendy Carlos, Morton Subotnick, and Terry Riley. Today's generation of computer-based architects, who are struggling to come into their own, have learned to work directly within the digital environment, in a manner that is similar to electronic music when it still revolved exclusively around synthesis. This has led to some remarkable designs, most of which will most likely never be built, but nevertheless have been of critical importance in paving the way for the next generation of computer-based architecture.

In music, the real breakthrough came about when a very different instrument called the sampler superseded the synthesizer as the musicians' tool of choice. Samplers allowed musicians to conjure up sounds from their keyboards, sounds derived from a vast library of sampled audio sources, ranging from every possible natural and industrial sound to all known musical instruments. Thus, as it turned out, electronic music started conquering the world with the help of real world input. Today, the early synthesizer music, which once seemed groundbreaking, tends to sound dated, whereas, for example, the early work with tape-loops of German musician Holger Czukay, which foreshadowed the sampling technology, continues to have a profound influence on almost every contemporary musical genre around.

Fig. 8. Gehry Partners, model (detail) for the Lewis Residence (unbuilt), Lyndhurst, Ohio, see Project 05.

Fig. 7. Claus Sluter [Werve] (c. 1380–1439), *Mourner from the Tomb of Philip the Bold, Duke of Burgundy*, Vizille alabaster, 16 ½ in high; © The Cleveland Museum of Art, bequest of Leonard C. Hanna, Jr., 1958.66.

In the much more computer intensive visual environment of the movies things happen much later than in music, but ultimately both media are subject to the same trends: keyframe animation, in which a computer operator defines movement by setting parameters for which the computer does the "in-betweening," has been greatly enhanced by motion capture, a technique that transfers actual human body language directly onto digital characters. Similarly, cyber-scans allow for real-life actors to migrate their likeness into the digital realm. As happened with music, this hybridization of digital and analog expressions is now revolutionizing the motion picture industry. As a rule, real world input is the next logical step beyond digital synthesis, regardless of the medium.

In this respect as well Frank Gehry has managed intuitively to stay ahead of the game. From his spontaneous sketches to the folds and creases of waxed cloth, the architect has been introducing elements from the actual into the virtual realm all along. Ironically, the critic who compared the Disney Concert Hall to a stack of discarded tissues was unwittingly voicing his appreciation of Gehry's sampling techniques.

Such transactions between art and the real world are of course not unprecedented. In order to create the vaulted shapes of his buildings, Gaudi, for example, hung chains from his ceiling and copied their reflection from carefully positioned mirrors. Drawing a parallel with today, we might look at the computer as a twenty-first-century mirror that not only captures the real world, but proposes an exchange between the virtual and the real that allows the architect to go as far beyond the looking glass as he desires, while still helping him to implement his vision in the real world by turning data into matter.

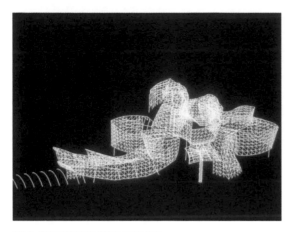

Fig. 9. Gehry Partners, CATIA rendering
for the Guggenheim Museum, Bilbao.

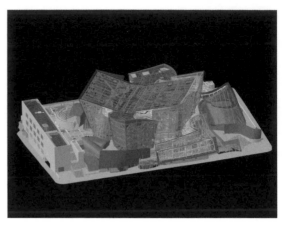

Fig. 10. Gehry Partners, CATIA rendering
for the Walt Disney Concert Hall, Los Angeles.

As mentioned before, Gehry acknowledges his debt to the computer
to the extent that it allows him always to be a few steps ahead of the
developers by knowing far in advance what it will take to deliver his
buildings on time and on budget. This has had a tremendously liberating
effect on him and has been the key to his current productivity, unparal-
leled by anyone of his stature today. But architects will soon be able
to do much better. From the earliest stages of their design process, the
computer will be able to support their efforts through instantly accessible
knowledge of real-world conditions and the characteristics of all known
materials in the physical world. Computer programs will be able to render
digitally, manipulate and edit three-dimensional representations of their
buildings in real time. A virtual replica of the construction site can be
mapped into the computer allowing architects to work on the design in
its actual context; and through immersion they will be able to experience
their buildings interactively from an interior perspective as well. Thanks
to these new design tools, the creative mind will, to an ever-larger
extent, be freed from the restrictions imposed by non-intuitive processes.
All the architects will have to do, as Marcus Novak puts it, is "to learn
designing by algorithms, then learn to design the algorithms themselves,
and finally learn how to let algorithms design themselves." Which is
another way of saying that in order to push the envelope beyond today's
limitations, architects need to get involved in the development of their
own software.

Recently, Gehry Partners, under the guidance of Partner and systems
expert James M. Glymph, has embarked on a co-venture with Dassault
Systemes, the French company whose CATIA software (originally

Fig. 11. Greg Lynn FORM, computer rendering of Ark of the World, Costa Rica, 2002 (courtesy Greg Lynn FORM, Venice, California).

designed for the aerospace industry) they have been using, to develop new tools for architectural purposes. Once again Gehry has confirmed his talent to opportunistically move ahead, while many of his younger colleagues are still wholly dependent on off-the-shelf software that is not specific to their trade. In fact, the creative output of a whole generation of architects today is threatened by the ubiquitous Maya software which has resulted in the severely limited aesthetic that characterizes most of their work, not unlike the early practitioners of synthesizer music whose once groundbreaking efforts were mentioned before. Following Gehry's example, this generation will have to involve themselves proactively with the creation of new tools that will finally allow them to make the evolutionary leap for which they have been poised since the onset of the computer age.

Greg Lynn, one of the most talented architects of the digital generation, once described the different mindsets of analog and digital people as follows: "When an analog person boots up his computer in the morning he gives it specific instructions about the tasks he wants it to perform that day, whereas when I turn on my computer I usually start out by asking it, 'what do you want me to do today?'" In other words, the true challenge at this historical juncture, which even Gehry fails to meet, is to establish a dialogue with the computer that goes beyond the tendency of today's architects to perceive it as a tool on which to impose their will instead of engaging with it as an intelligence in its own right. The evolutionary implication for architecture inherent in today's technology is that once the real world has been subsumed by the digital domain it can be taken apart and put back together again in truly unprecedented ways. By getting out of the way from time to time and surrendering to the computer's power to transcend reality, a mutual expression of genuine spirituality may emerge simply by elevating the computer from tool to partner.

The last thing I want to do in the context of this essay is to venture into the realm of science fiction. To determine if artificial intelligence is capable of truly intuitive behavior, original thought or autonomous creativity, I'll gladly leave to others. However, for the purpose of this book I'd like to remind the reader that it was the computer that first comprehended the feeling that flowed from the architect's hand, managing instantly to render it in all its formerly invisible dimensions. And if so required it could just as easily see this initial hand-drawn scribble through until it finally manifests itself in the form of a physical building. This remarkable feat should serve as a convincing demonstration that instead of minimizing the computer's contribution to the architect's creative process, it is time to acknowledge that if genius is the issue, some of that coveted human trait has by now irreversibly rubbed off on what no longer can be considered a mere machine.

Which brings us back to the beginning of this essay. When I told Gehry about my mother's stunningly accurate analysis of Rem Koolhaas's handwriting, he was reminded of a similar incident in his own life. When he was eleven years old, living in Toronto, his mother took him to a graphologist who looked at a sample of his handwriting and predicted without hesitation that the young boy who stood in front her, known at the time as Frank Owen Goldberg, would grow up to become an architect!

I'm absolutely certain that, had the computer been around back then, it would have wholeheartedly agreed.

Detectives, Jigsaw Puzzles, and DNA

MARK RAPPOLT

Most introductory textbooks on architecture tell their readers that, unless you are a client or a contractor, you should look at architectural drawings in two distinct ways. The first way is to treat them as if they were clues to some sort of murder mystery. The drawings are there to tell the architectural detective whodunnit, how they dunnit, and, with a little luck and imagination, where they dunnit. Go look on page 150 of this book: Frank Gehry, in the Hotel Lopez de Haro, with a marker pen.

The second approach treats architectural drawings as if they were a building's DNA. The drawings determine what shape it is, what its proportions are, how many windows it has, how the inside relates to the outside, and anything else of that ilk you may want to know. Back in the Renaissance, when architects such as Sebastiano Serlio and Andrea Palladio were rummaging around classical ruins in order to try and locate architecture's fundamental laws, it was via drawings, representing what they had decided were the original states of these ruins, that they mapped out and codified the rules of architectural design. When they drew on the past, they did it in the most literal way. Their drawings gave classical architecture a new life because any designer could copy the bits they liked. Indeed, the genetic material of Palladio's drawings has been so continually sampled during the centuries that followed that he is now, according to James Ackerman, "the most imitated architect in history."

But the fact is that most architectural drawings are never really as much fun as a genuine murder mystery (well, except to architectural historians and theorists, that is). Just as, to the untrained eye, the mapping of human DNA as a seemingly endless sequence of Ts, As, Cs, and Gs has a obvious monotony when compared to the actual human being that it represents.

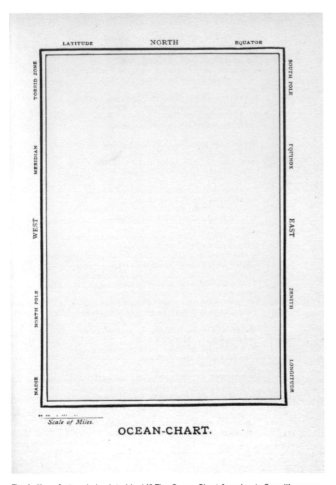

Fig. 1. "A perfect and absolute blank!" The Ocean Chart from Lewis Carroll's poem
"The Hunting of the Snark" (1876). Illustration by John Tenniel.

So if you look at architectural drawings in these ways alone, there's
a fair chance that you will eventually conclude that when it comes to
architecture, to draw is to bore.

So why should you bother to look through the contents of this
book? Is it just architectural Cluedo? A list of building DNA? What
should we be looking for? Will people use it to knock off copies of
Gehry buildings for centuries to come? Such questions seem particularly
relevant now, when our seemingly unflagging excitement about the
potential of computers to describe and determine everything a building
is, or can be, has the effect of making pen-on-paper drawings seem just
a little quaint and old fashioned. But curiously, given his popular

association with the computer age, Frank Gehry's sketches are primarily of interest because they suggest a few reasons why there may be life in the old art after all.

Drawings and tracings are like the hands of the blind touching surfaces of the face in order to understand a sense of volume, depth, and penetration",[1] wrote the architect John Hejduk in 1986. In the same year, the architectural historian Robin Evans chose to illustrate his own study of architectural drawing with a relief by Jasper Johns entitled *The Critic Speaks* (1961).[2] Johns's work shows a pair of spectacles with open mouths replacing eyes behind each lens. And what both Hejduk and Evans point to is, in the words of the latter, that "drawing's power as a medium turns out, unexpectedly, to be recognition of drawing's distinctness from and unlikeness to the thing that is represented."[3] Or, more simply, that the oddity of architectural drawing is actually that it is not the same as building, that it is not the three-dimensional, multi-sensory experience that architecture is supposed to be all about. And, as if to make this point again, many of Gehry's sketches (as opposed, to some degree, to his models) don't look much like his buildings at all; instead they remind us that what's fun about drawing, and perhaps the process of designing a building as well, is engaging with that measure of uncertainty that exists along the path from imagination to a final built form. That, and the fact that far from being prescriptive, drawings can mean almost anything to anyone.

As part of his analysis of Gehry's Guggenheim Museum in Bilbao, the architecture critic Charles Jencks published a series of drawings by Madelon Vriesendorp that listed the various suggestive overtones of the building's form.[4] In these, the profile of the building becomes in turn a boat, a reclining nude, a mermaid, a collection of fish, a swan, a duck, and an angular artichoke. In a sense, Gehry's drawings suggest similarly open possibilities, but in an entirely different way. Gehry's sketches of the building are clearly never so crudely figurative as those that Jencks uses to make his point, yet they seem to allude to an open nature in the design that Jencks and Vriesendorp detect in the finished building as well. While a line in Gehry's drawings suggests a certain form at one moment, at the next another line seems to deny that form completely and take it away. You come across circles that contain just a hint of a square, where one drawing emphasises the vertical elements of the building, in the next horizontality holds sway. As many critics have pointed out, one of Gehry's talents as an architect has been to translate the variety that he displays in his drawings into the multiple views and experiences offered by his completed buildings. It's in this "openness" perhaps that drawing and building are most closely linked.

It's a commonplace to say that drawings begin like Lewis Carroll's famous Ocean Chart from his poem "The Hunting of the Snark"—

an empty rectangle drawn on the page (fig. 1). But perhaps Gehry's drawings retain a memory of this more than most.

> He had bought a large map representing the sea,
> Without the least vestige of land:
> And the crew were much pleased when they found it to be
> A map they could all understand.

> "What's the good of Mercator's North Poles and Equators,
> Tropics, Zones, and Meridian Lines?"
> So the Bellman would cry: and the crew would reply,
> "They are merely conventional signs!"

> "Other maps are such shapes, with their islands and capes!
> But we've got our brave Captain to thank"
> (So the crew would protest) "that he's bought us the best—
> A perfect and absolute blank!"[5]

While Gehry's drawings are far from blank, they often appear to float on the page, as if, perhaps literally, to maintain a sense of suspense. A plan view of the Guggenheim Museum, complete with conventional compass indications keeps threatening, thanks to a series of overlapping curves that in other sketches are suggestive of volume, to have done with convention and pop up into profile and out of the page.

At times they can appear to be an almost incomprehensible accumulation of squiggles, arcs, and curves, but just as quickly they snap into focus suggesting an intricately molded space. What makes these drawings exciting is the fact that beneath all the shapes, the blankness of that ocean map is always lurking. Perhaps there is a certain delight, for both author and viewer, in their threat to return to the emptiness from which they came. If, as Gehry says, these drawings are his way of "thinking aloud" (they clearly retain a sense of the immateriality of thought), then they are a testament to the fact that thinking, whether aloud or silent, almost never stays still. Perhaps more importantly, they are a reminder that these drawings mean most to the thinker himself.

And yet, sometimes, even Gehry himself seems to have trouble keeping up with the drawings his thoughts suggest. "I realized that the plan of the Lewis house was very unusual," he once said. "When you drew the plan, it was weird. I had never seen anything like it." Not even, apparently, in his own head.

So, if he sometimes can't work it out, what are the rest of us supposed to do? To my mind, perhaps the most useful advice on how to look at these drawings is contained in a line by the French writer Georges Perec: "Spaces have multiplied, been broken up, and have diversified. There are spaces today of every kind and every size, for every use and every function. To live is to pass from one space to another, while doing your very best not to bump yourself."[6] Perhaps Gehry's drawings emphasize, more than anything else, how architecture is an attempt to navigate through the changing circumstances of everyday life, whether they be the demands of a client, the constraints of a budget, or the problems of a site. And to have as few bumps as possible along the way.

Notes

1. John Hejduk, 'Thoughts of an Architect," in *Victims* (London: Architectural Association, 1986). Reprinted in Mary Ann Caws (ed.) *Manifesto* (Lincoln and London: University of Nebraska Press, 2001), 661.

2. Robin Evans "Translations from Drawing to Building," 1986, in *Translations from Drawing to Buiding and Other Essays* (London: Architectural Association, 1997), 152–3.

3. Evans, op. cit., 154.

4. Charles Jencks, *The New Paradigm in Architecture: The Language of Postmodernism* (London: Yale University Press, 2002).

5. Lewis Carroll, "The Hunting of the Snark," 1876, in *The Complete Illustrated Works of Lewis Carroll* (London: Chancellor Press, 1982).

6. Georges Perec, *Species of Spaces and Other Writings* (London: Penguin, 1997), 6.

Project 01

The Winton Residence Guest House

Wayzata, Minnesota
1983–1987

The Winton Residence Guest House
Wayzata, Minnesota

Design: commenced in 1983
Construction: commenced 1986
Status: completed 1987
Number of drawings illustrated: 7

Located on a heavily wooded lakefront property, the Winton Guest House was designed both to complement an existing house designed in the early 1950s by the modernist architect Philip Johnson and to maintain the sense of its striking landscape setting.

The building appears as a cluster of objects placed together in a tight composition that draws inspiration from the composition of Giorgio Morandi's still-life paintings. Where the Italian painter famously depicted clusters of vases, jugs, bowls, and bottles, Gehry has grouped a series of forms around a tall central living space. While all the rooms are connected internally, the use of a different material on each exterior clearly maintains their identity as a group of distinct, individual objects. The manner in which the programmatic elements of the project are embodied as individual pieces and then collected together as a whole is a common feature of Gehry's work. Here, however, it is noticeably more distinct than in other projects. A long plywood-covered box topped by a sleeping loft of galvanized metal contains service and kitchen areas; alongside is a brick fireplace alcove and two contrasting forms, each containing a bedroom and bath, that are surfaced in stone and painted metal respectively.

What slowly evolved during the course of this project was a very sculptural solution to the brief. So much so that when viewed from the main residence, the Guest House does indeed look less like a building and more like a large outdoor sculpture. The absence of windows on the west facade of the building (which faces the main house) enhances this sensation, while windows located on its east facade give a contrasting sense of openness by providing wide views of the natural surroundings.

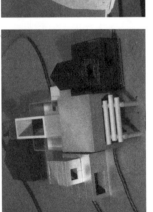

M01.01
02.83
M01.02
M01.03
M01.04

46 | 47

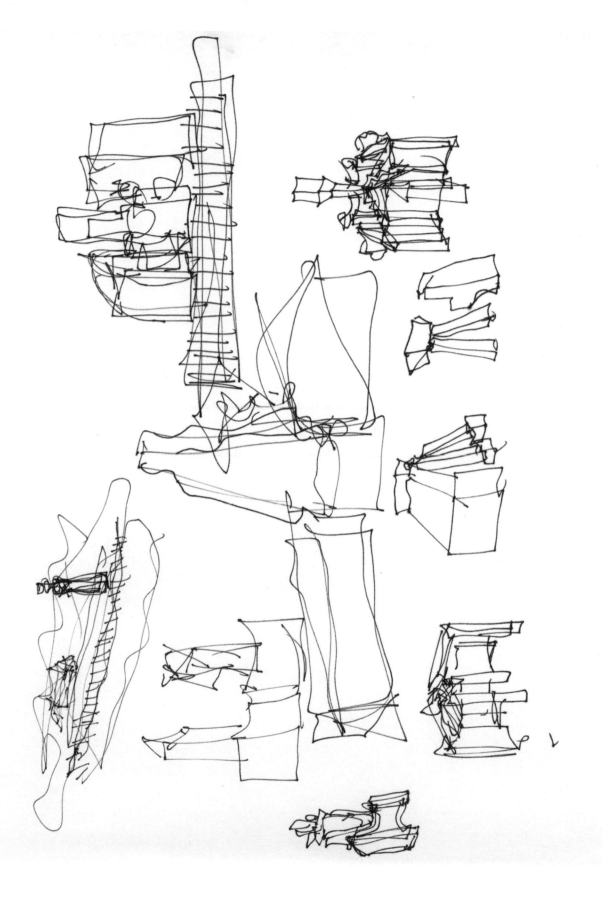

I've always been fascinated by the idea of a painter confronting a white canvas—I've never done that myself. What does an artist think about? I fantasize about it. Architecture is so cluttered with problems of function, things that the painter confronting the white canvas doesn't have to deal with, that architects hide behind a lot of these things and develop rationales based upon functional issues, such as keeping the water out and the sun in or out. All these things are very important; I don't intend to demean them. But how do we go further? FG

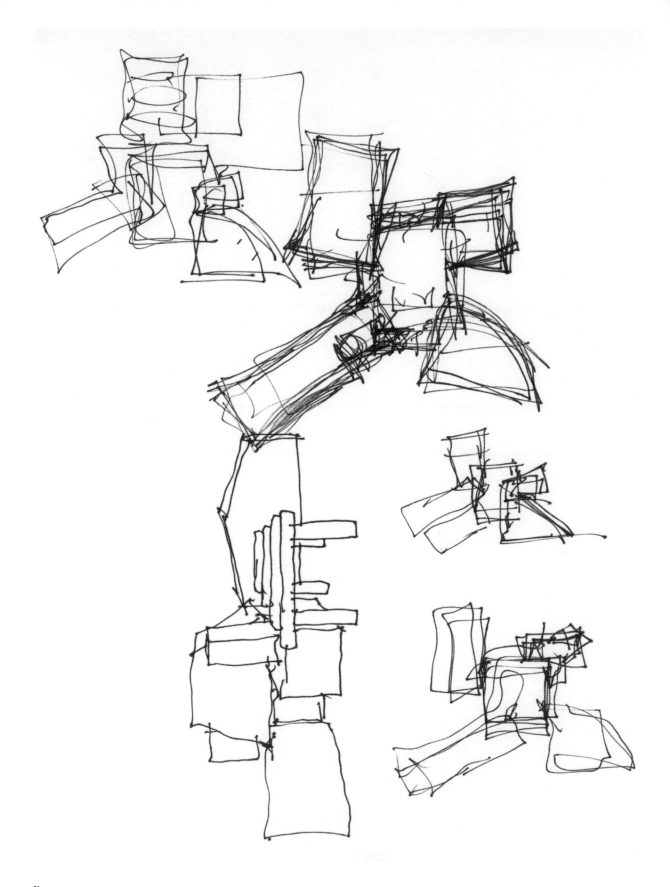

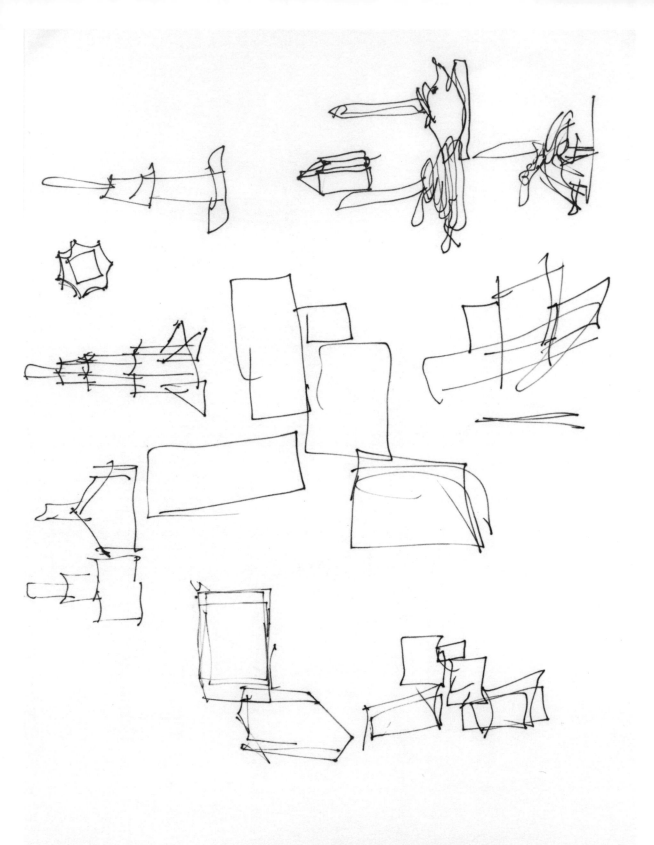

D01.04

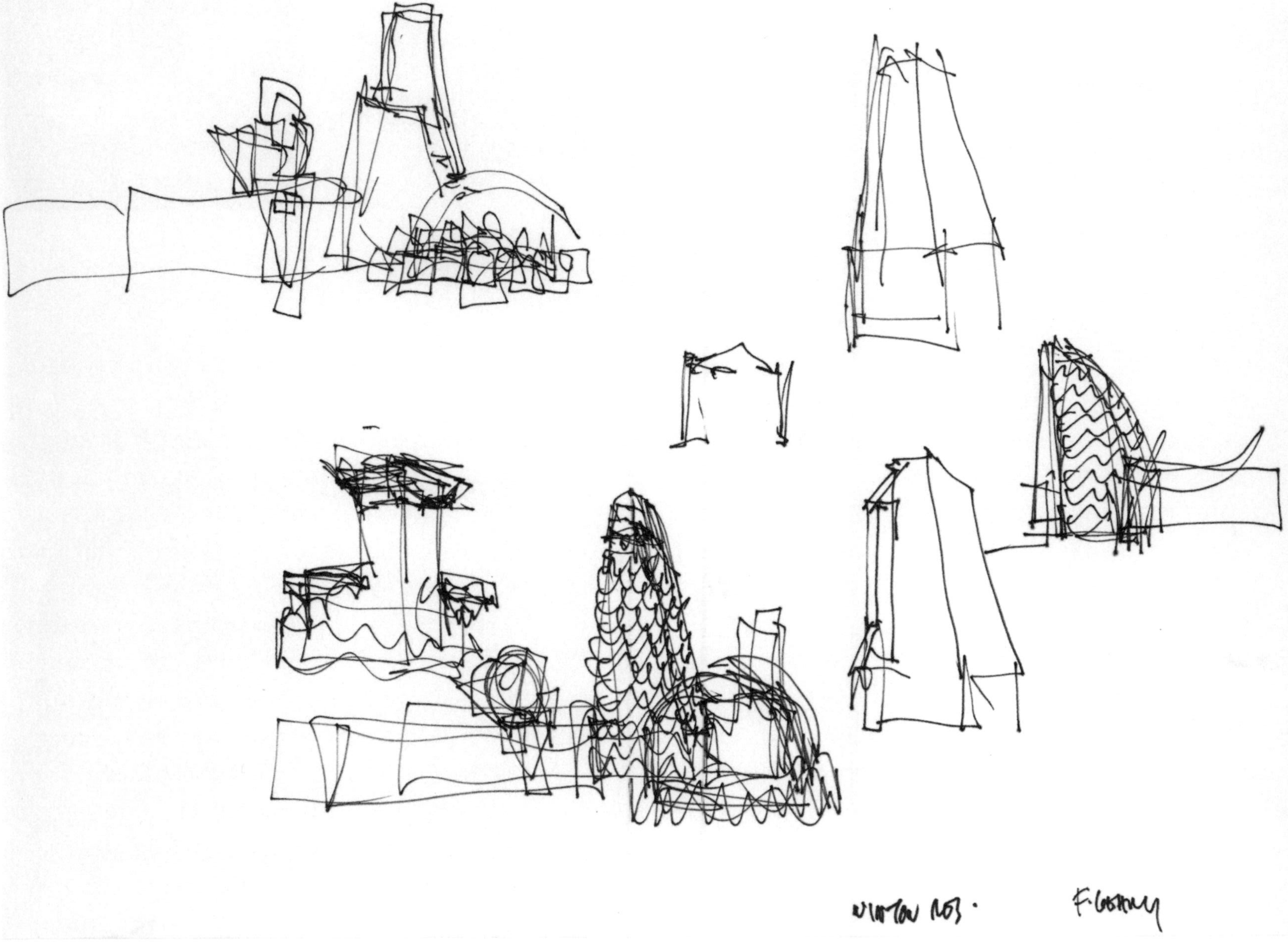

When first confronted with this project, I was nervous about what Mr. Johnson might think about my intrusion into his work.

Although we started with a log cabin, we wanted to try to make the buildings a little abstract so that there was something to look at from the main house. As we started making the forms more minimal, the log cabin we started with finally got drummed out of the place, appropriately.

There's an uncanny, inadvertent relationship between the central tower and the fireplace to the Philip Johnson studio, the little stovepipe thing he did in New Canaan. The new Philip Johnson was creeping into my house for the Wintons, and as I was doing this, he was building a small chain-link pavilion out in New Canaan.

Solving all the functional problems is an intellectual exercise. That is a different part of my brain. It's not less important, it's just different. And I make a value out of solving all those problems. Dealing with the context and the client and finding my moment of truth after I understand the problem. If you look at our process, the firm's process, you see models that show the pragmatic solution to the building without architecture. Then you see the study models that go through leading to the final scheme. We start with shapes, sculptural forms. Then we work into the technical stuff. FG

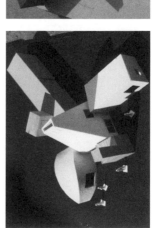

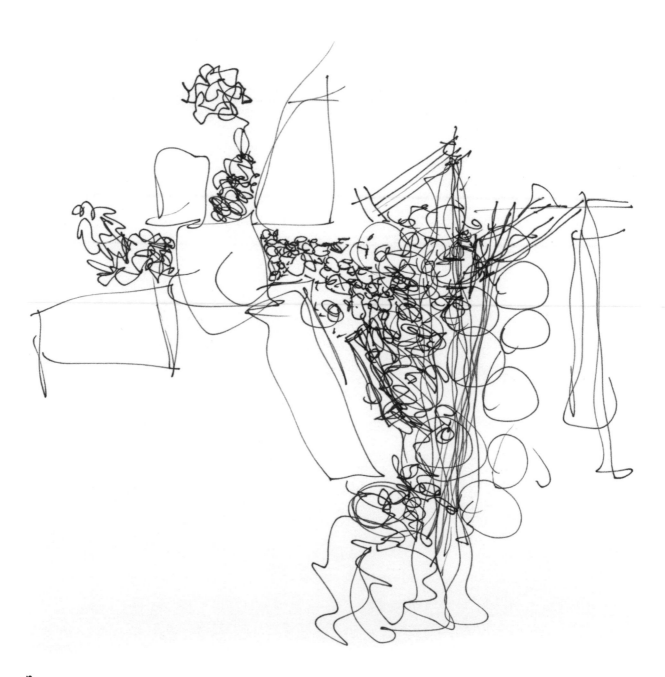

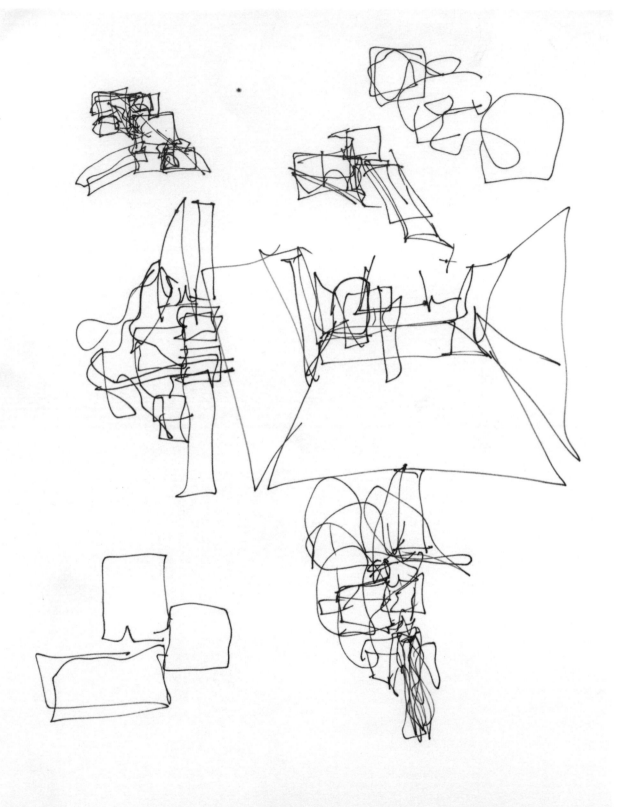

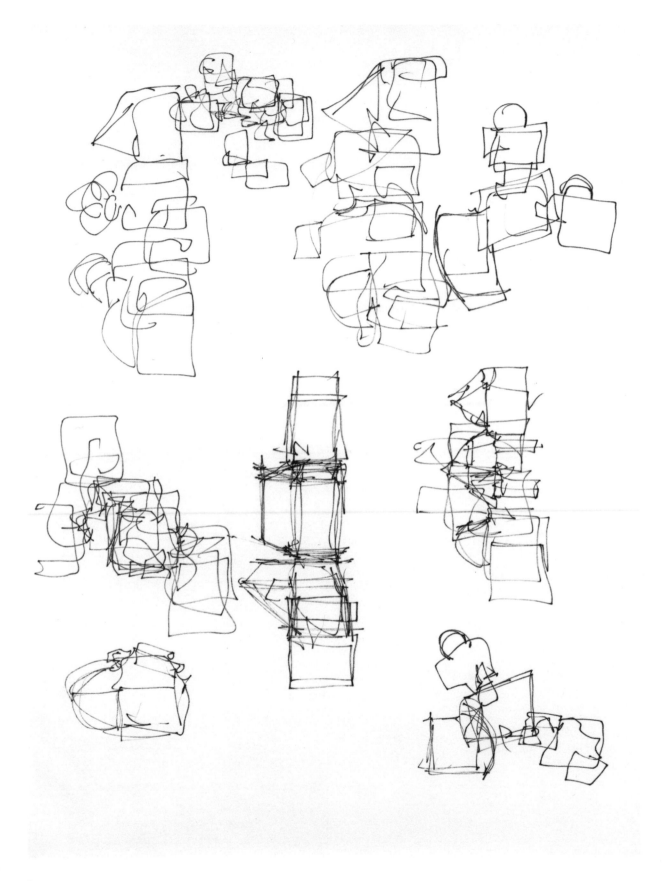

D01.07

Project 02

Gehry Residence
Santa Monica, California
1989–1992

Gehry Residence
Santa Monica, California
Renovations 1989–92

Design: commenced 1989
Status: completed 1992
Number of drawings illustrated: 15

Gehry's original 1977–78 renovations to his home, a 60-year-old pink, two-story bungalow in a middle-class neighborhood in Santa Monica, made it a key work in the postwar history of architecture, and one the most iconic and controversial buildings in his oeuvre. Gehry essentially wrapped the existing house in a new structure composed of vernacular materials—corrugated metal, plywood, and chainlink—punctured by a series of glass apertures that allow views of the original house within. Gehry explains: "There was the terrible irony of our times, wherein we could push forward with incredible technological feats but at the same time struggle in our homebuilding, a primitive craft in serious decline. I exposed this fallacy in my own house by using the lack of craft as a visual strength."

The second renovation (illustrated here) was carried out to accommodate the changing needs of his family. The alterations included the addition of a lap pool, the transformation of the garage into a guest house, and some landscaping of the exterior spaces.

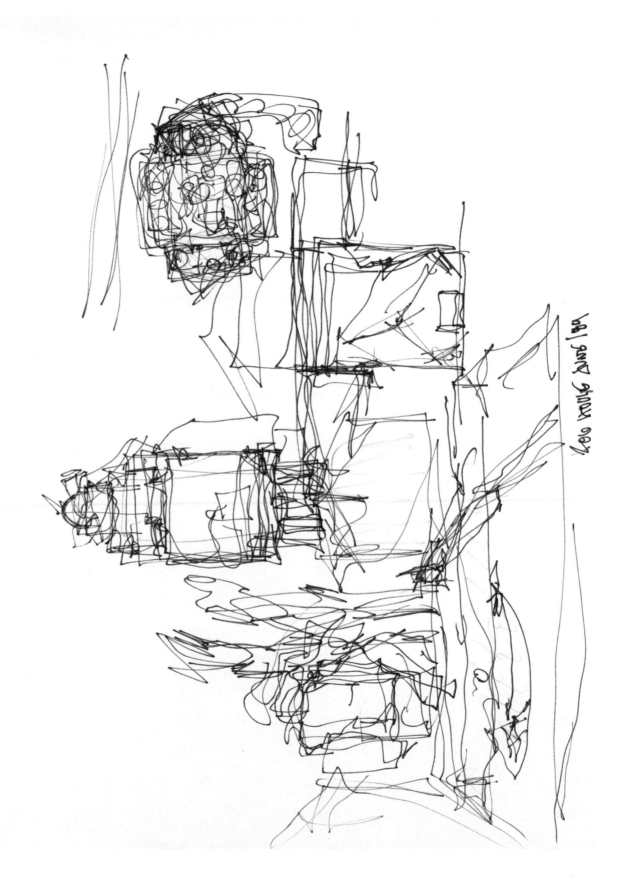

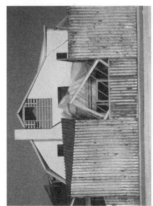

M02.02
M02.03
M02.04
M02.05
M02.06

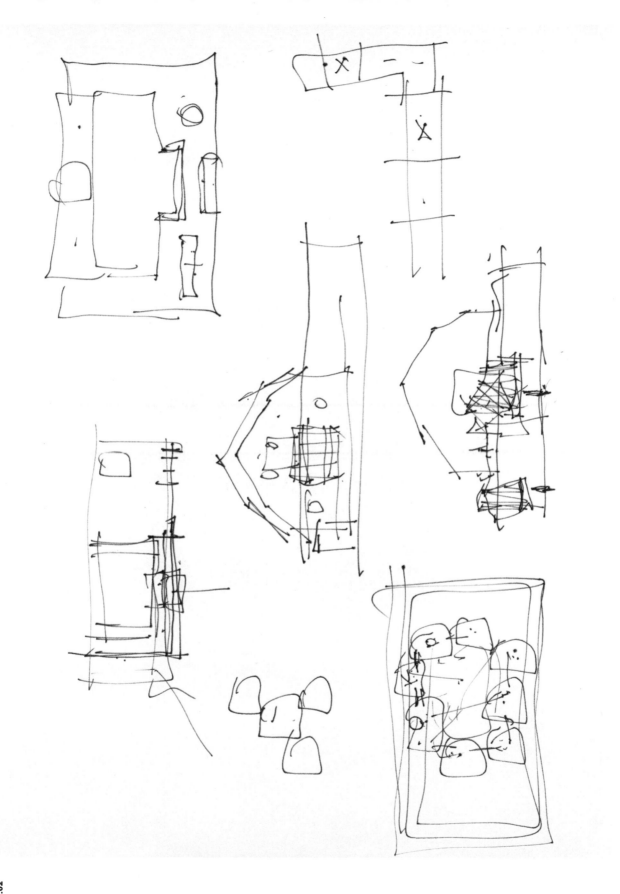

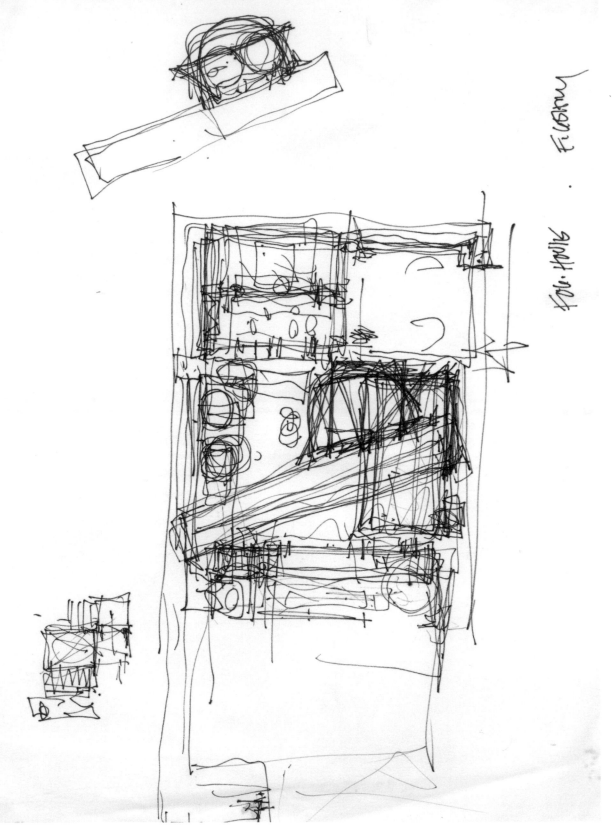

Fol. Hall · Filstry

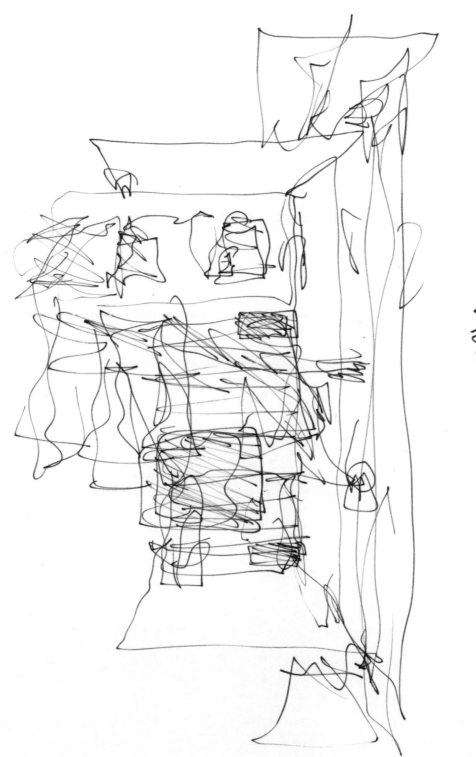

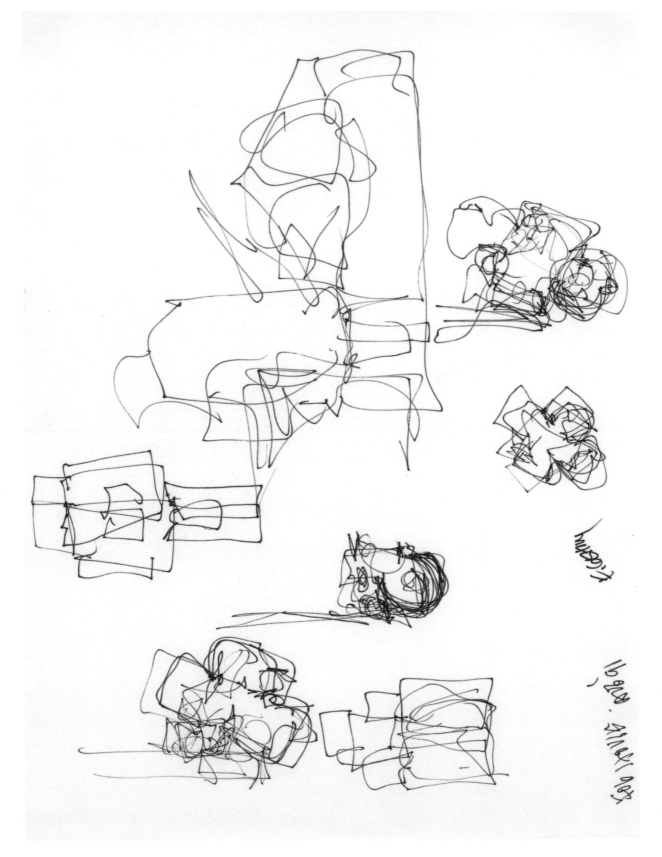

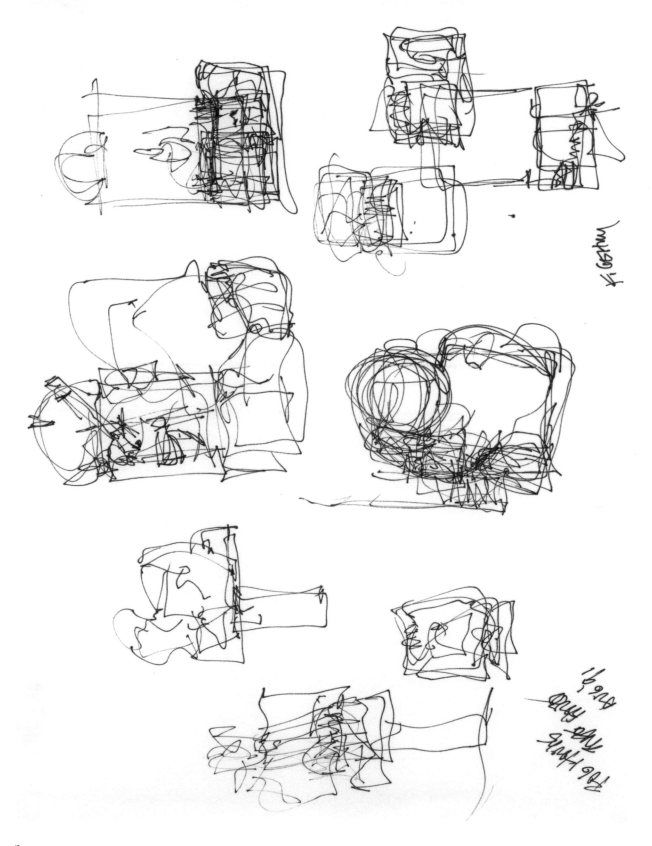

As I became acquainted with my future neighbors, I discovered a high incidence of camper vehicles, trailers with boats, and front lawns with automobiles on blocks ready for weekend mechanics. There was a lot of chain-link fencing, concrete-block fencing, picket fencing. Other than that, the materials of the buildings were modest. I also became aware of the shutting-out of the outside world: the "body language" of the neighbors' houses, window blinds always closed to the street, and, for the most part, those pseudo-cute little structures that suggest humanity actually say, "Stay out! Leave me alone!" FG

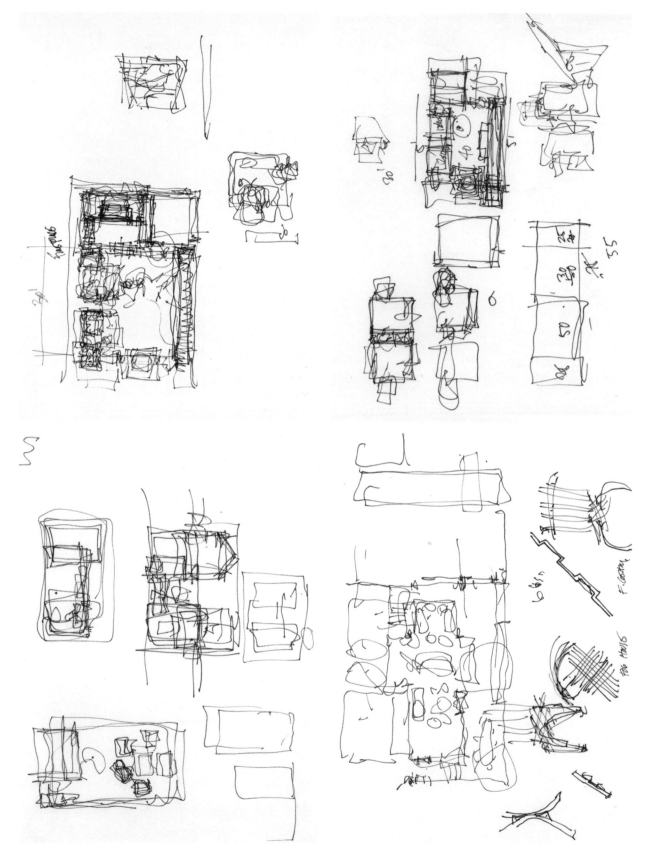

M02.07
02.19.99

M02.08
02.19.99

M02.09
02.19.99

M02.10
02.19.99

Project 03

Frederick R. Weisman
Art Museum
Minneapolis, Minnesota
1990–1993

Frederick R. Weisman Art Museum
University of Minnesota,
Minneapolis, Minnesota

Design: commenced 1990
Construction: commenced 1991
Status: completed 1993
Number of drawings illustrated: 10

This project marked Frank Gehry's first commission to design a new public art museum from the ground up. Overlooking the Mississippi River and the downtown Minneapolis skyline beyond, the building is located on the western edge of the University of Minnesota campus core and plays an important role, connecting the university and urban contexts. It is designed to be accessed both by cars, which can be parked in a 120-space underground garage at its lower level, and by pedestrians, who arrive at the main third-floor entrance via a pedestrian walkway that connects the two-tier Washington Avenue Bridge, located to the museum's north, with Coffman Memorial Plaza, located to the Museum's east.

The building itself consists of four floors. The two lower floors provide space for storage and services, while the third floor houses the gallery spaces, and can be sealed off to operate independently of the rest of the building. Adjacent to the gallery space is a 1,500-square-foot black-box auditorium for audio-visual presentations. Sliding doors on the west wall enable the auditorium to be opened onto the lobby for special receptions, while the lobby in turn wraps around the auditorium to allow continuous circulation—a kind of internal "street"—and entry to the south side of the galleries. Large picture windows offer lobby-pedestrians views of the Mississippi River while allowing pedestrians outside the building to look in. The top level of the museum houses administrative offices as well as additional mechanical and electrical service areas.

From the west, the museum facade is clad in milled-finish stainless steel and is articulated in a faceted, collaged manner to capture and reflect views up and down the Mississippi River, and to announce the presence of the museum. In contrast to this shiny sculptural facade, the box-like gallery volume is finished in brick with buttered joints, a response to the prevalent aesthetic of the building's university context. A tower-like structure rises from the loading area off East River Road and anchors the undulating, wave-like geometry of the elevation at the southwest corner.

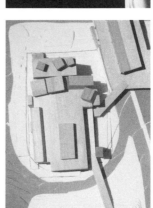

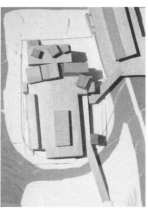

D03.01
M03.01
8.3.90
M03.02
8.3.90

76 | 77

When we start a project, we play in plain and neutral blocks of wood for a long time until we get the organization and the scale right for the buildings on the site. While we're doing this, I make my sketches, because as soon as I understand the scale of the building and the relationship to the site and the relationship to the client, I start drawing. Those drawings give Edwin [Chan] and Craig [Webb] a sense of where I want to go, and they start making rough study models with some inkling of scale and architectural language; we go through that for what feels like months. FG

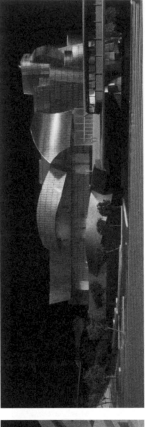

Focusing on the real building while you're working out ideas is the trick, because you can get lazy in the drawing. Shifting scale in the model process forces you to be careful. Drawing on it's own can be a lazy man's way of being careful. Especially when you're really busy. The problem with doing a lot of buildings, you see, is that you make a lot of mistakes. FG

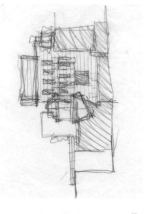

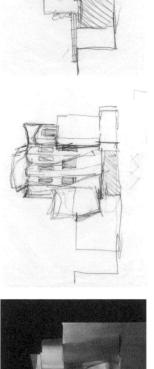

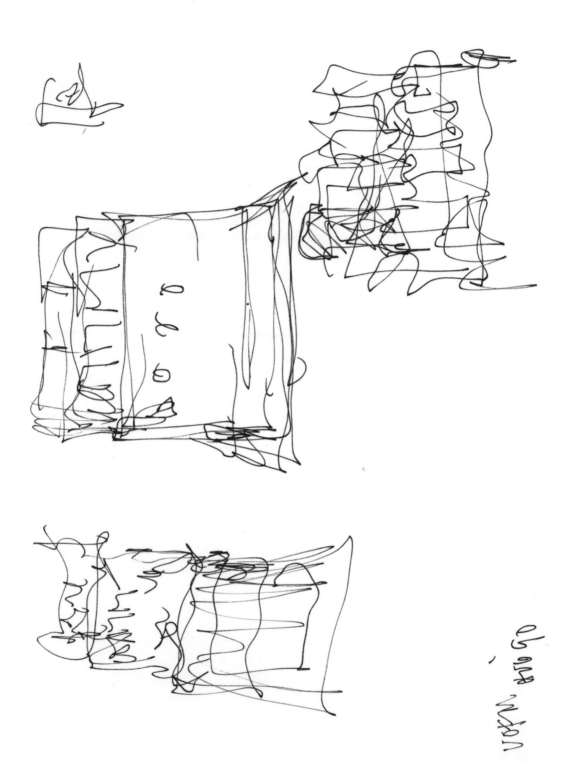

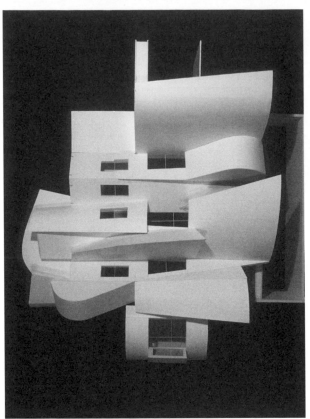

M03.07
M03.08
M03.09
M03.10

D03.07

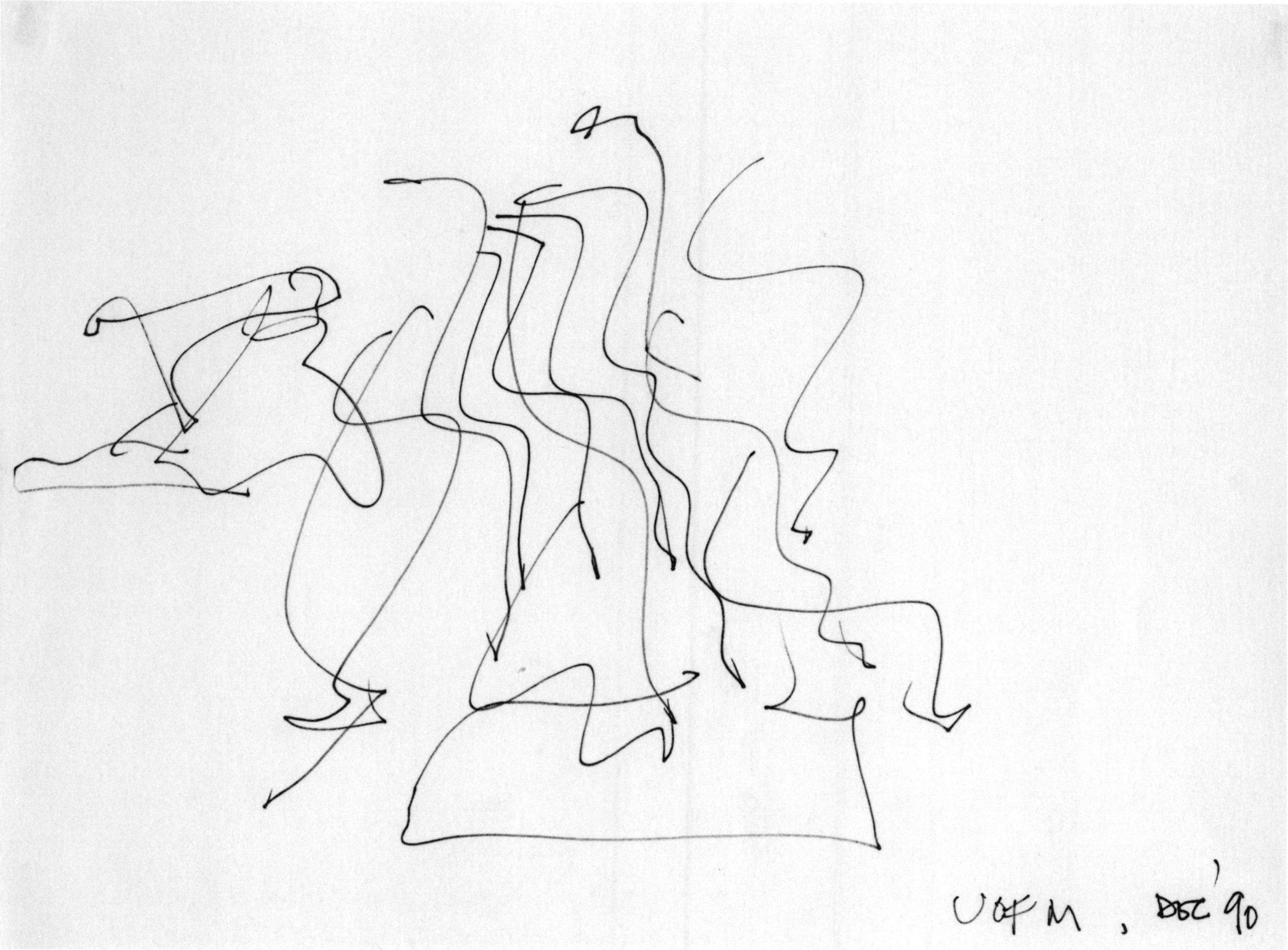

My architectural language may feel strange to some people, but they should still feel comfortable in my buildings. FG

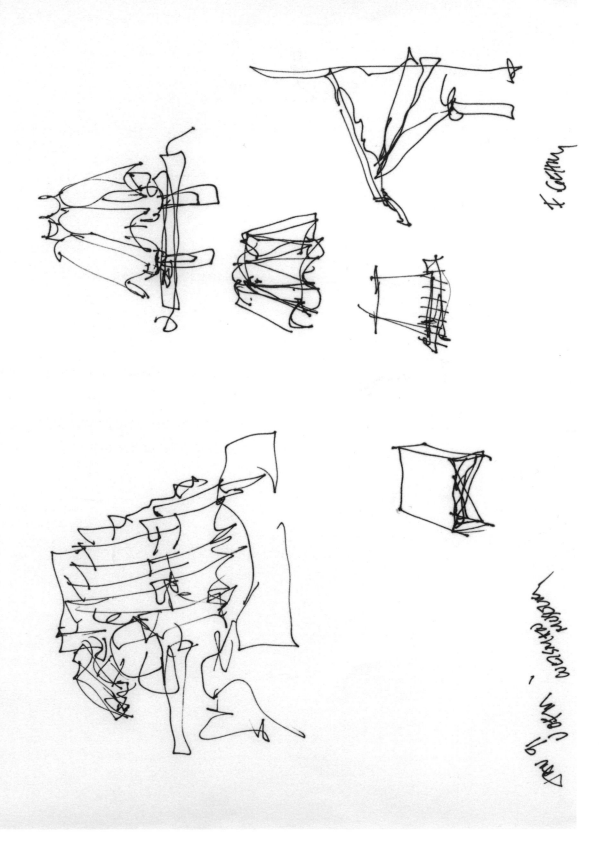

Project 04

Nationale-Nederlanden Building

Prague, Czech Republic 1992–1996

Nationale-Nederlanden Building
Prague, Czech Republic

Design: commenced in 1992
Construction: commenced 1994
Status: completed 1996
Number of drawings illustrated: 9

The Nationale-Nederlanden Building is located in the historic district of central Prague on a prominent corner along the Vltava River. The ground floor houses a café and shops, offices occupy the second through seventh floors, while a restaurant on the top level offers views of the Prague skyline and the nearby castle.

The main facade of the building (facing the river) works with the existing architectural context by extending the scale and rhythms of the adjacent row houses, albeit with a series of waving cornice lines that serve to minimize the impact of changes of scale, an effect that is intensified by the undulating pattern of the windows. At the corner, two towers—affectionately nicknamed "Fred" and "Ginger" after the dancers Fred Astaire and Ginger Rogers—are supported by a series of columns. "Fred" is solid and cylindrical, supported by a single large column. "Ginger" is tapered (pinched in at the "waist") with a glass facade and supported by a cluster of slender columns.

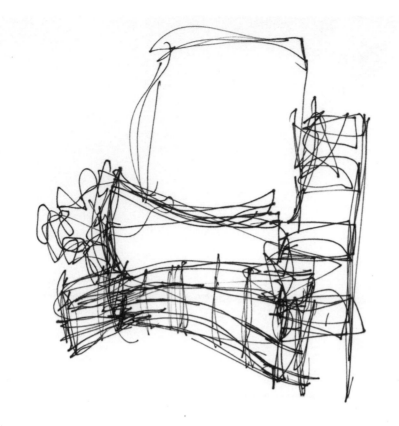

PRAGUE, '92   —   F 65mm

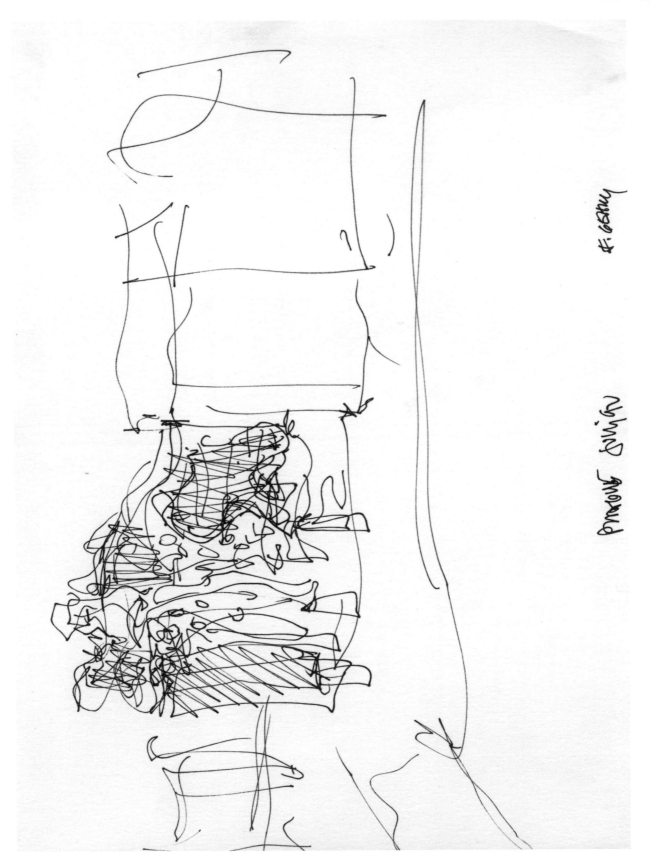

Image #4

around giving

When I'm looking at a computer image of one of my buildings, when I'm working with it, I have to keep an ideal "dream" in my head. I have an idea for a building and it's visually clear in my head, but I have to hold on to this image while looking at some terrible image on a screen. That requires too much energy and concentration for me, and I can only do it for a few minutes at a time. Then I have to run out of the room screaming. FG

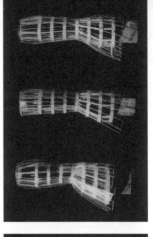

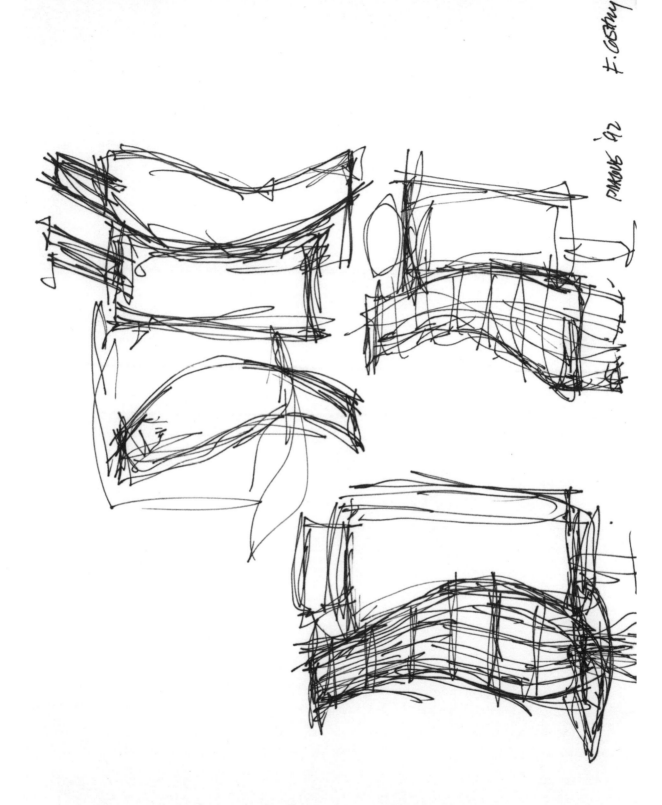

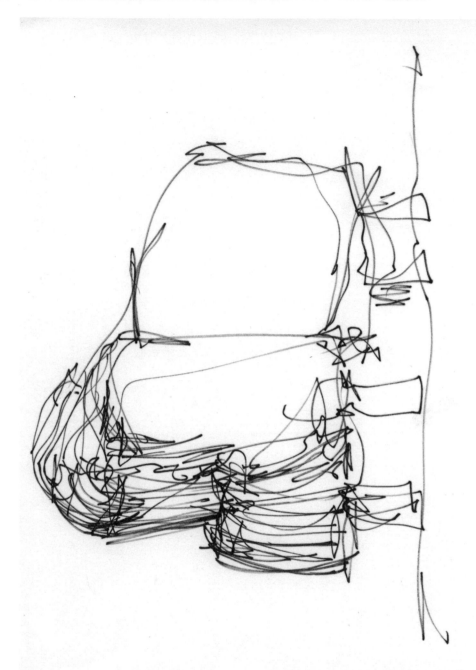

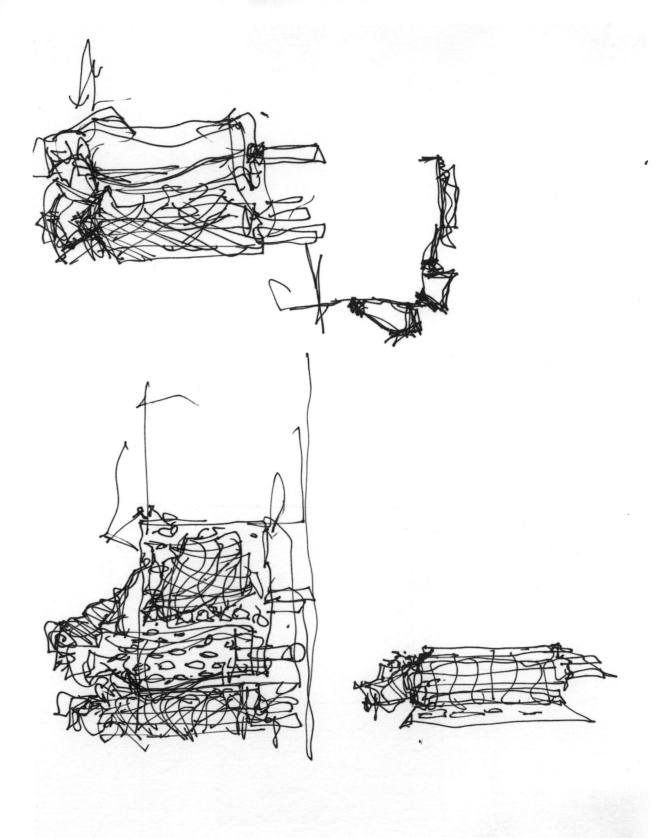

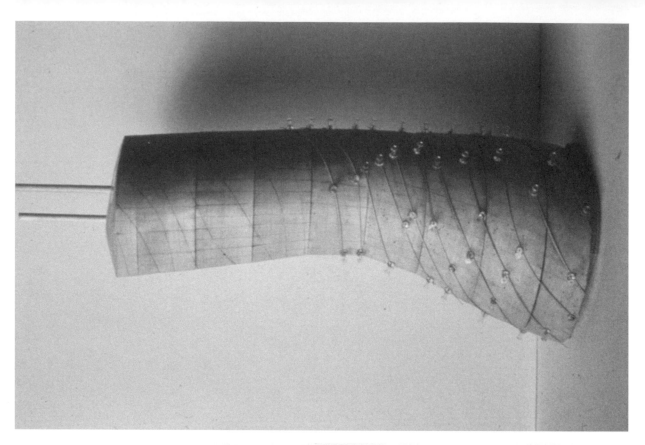

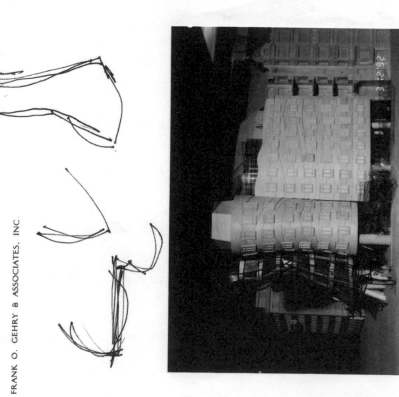

FRANK O. GEHRY & ASSOCIATES, INC.

PARKING '92

F. Gehry

1520-B CLOVERFIELD BOULEVARD, SANTA MONICA, CALIFORNIA 90404
TELEPHONE: 310-828-6088   FAX: 310-828-2098

D04.07
M04.03
M04.04

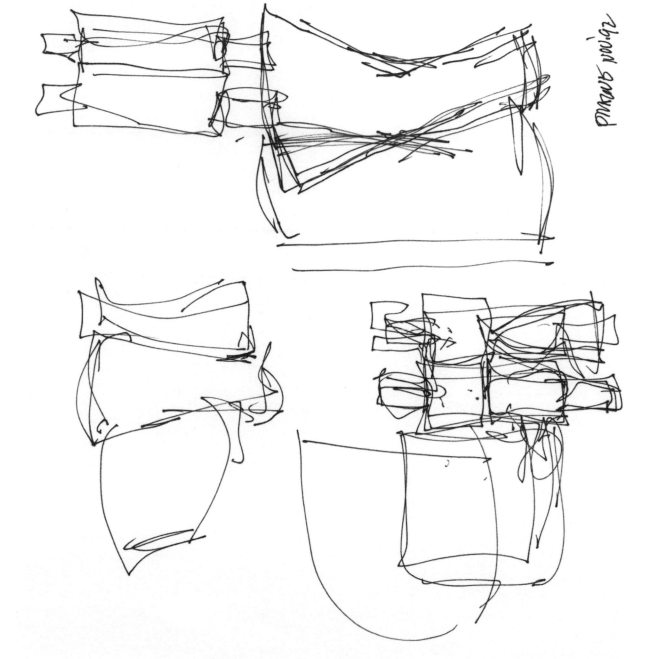

phono around

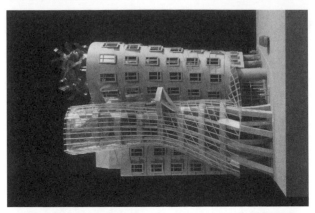

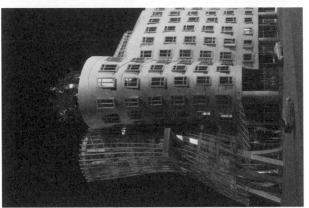

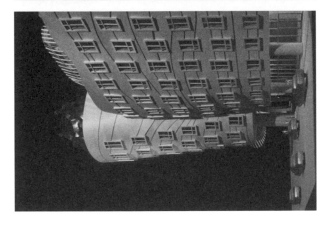

pond that 76. mason t.

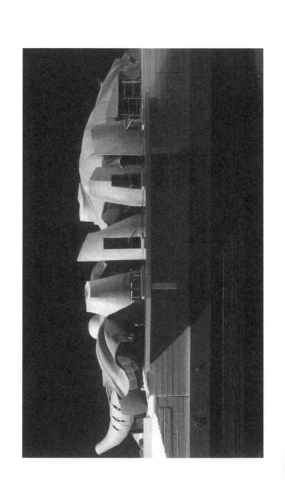

Project 05 (unbuilt)
Lewis Residence
Lyndhurst, Ohio
1989–1995

Lewis Residence
Lyndhurst, Ohio

Design: commenced 1989
Status: unbuilt (design concluded 1995)
Number of drawings illustrated: 31

The Lewis Residence was a 22,000-square-foot home designed for a bachelor. The main house provided a semi-public area for entertaining and a private area for Mr. Lewis. The semi-public area consisted of a commercial-grade kitchen, a dining room, a living room, and an entry hall/gallery, while the private area consisted of two master bedrooms, a study, a conservatory, and an enclosed lap pool. In addition to the main house, there were two separate guest houses, staff quarters, and a five-car garage.

The house, landscape, and surrounding sculptures were the result of a collaborative exploration of forms and ideas between Frank Gehry, the architect Philip Johnson, the landscape architect Maggie Keswick Jencks and several artists (among them Larry Bell, Richard Serra, Claes Oldenburg, and Coosje Van Bruggen). Located on nine acres of woodlands, the house was to be bounded by two large reflecting pools, steel plates, a tower, and a light/water sculpture. All played an integral role in the composition and form of the project.

The final composition of complex forms and geometries was to be constructed from a variety of materials, including plaster, stone, metal, and glass. The participation of trades and artisans in the process was to be integral to the form-making envisioned. Given the unique sculptural qualities and constructability issues, three-dimensional computer modeling was employed extensively in the design and documentation process.

After six years of experiment and design, however, this project was eventually cancelled. As Gehry himself has remarked, this project became the equivalent of a research fellowship or the ultimate study grant. While working on the Lewis Residence, Gehry's office developed and perfected physical model-making techniques, computer modeling and documentation techniques, and form-making techniques that would be deployed in many of the works that followed.

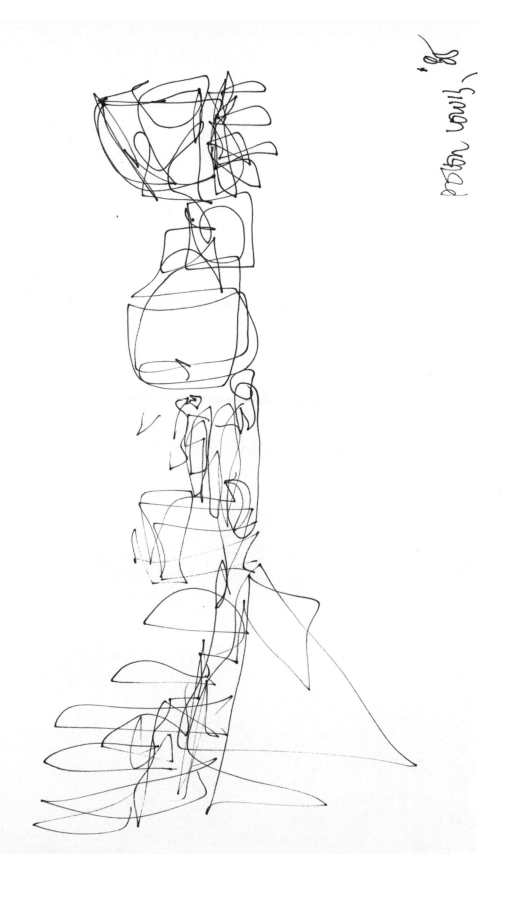

D05.02

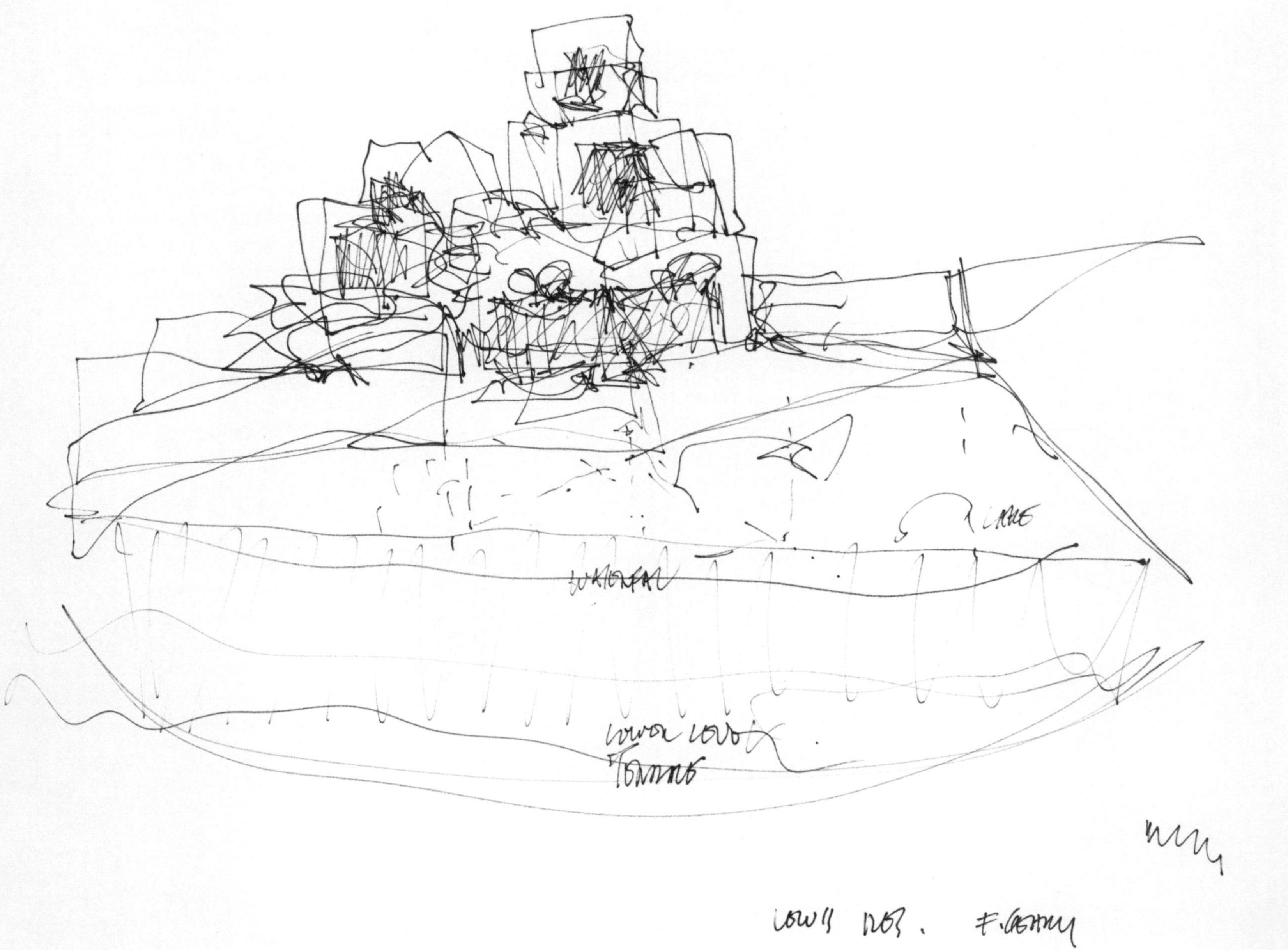

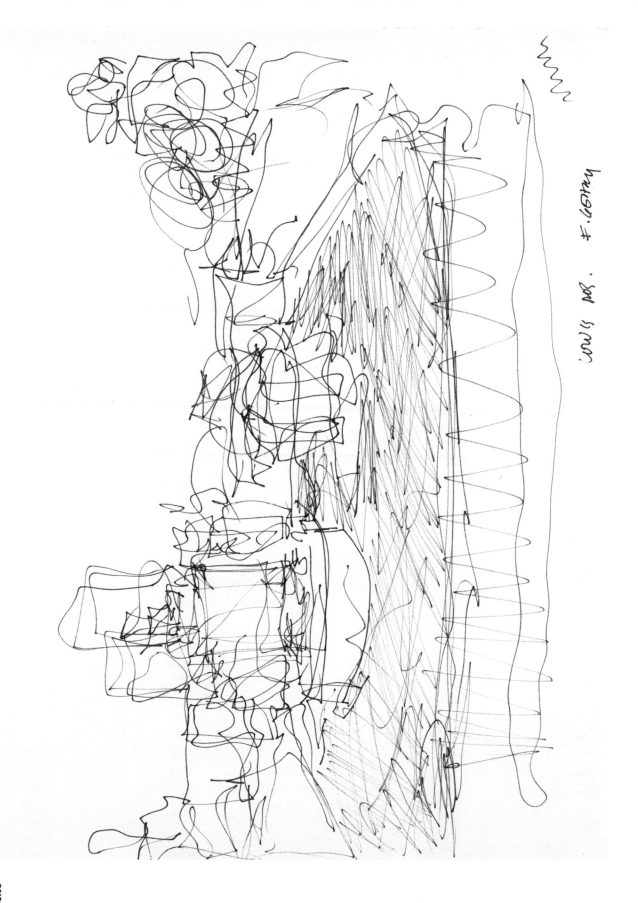

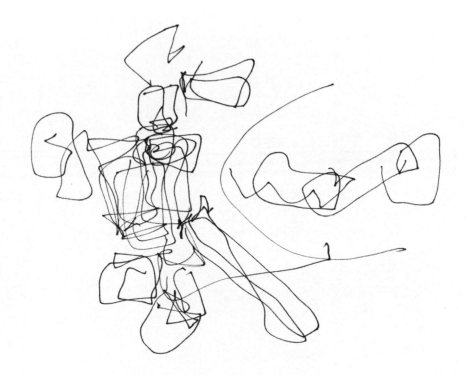

Lewis Dit Some /88

D05.04

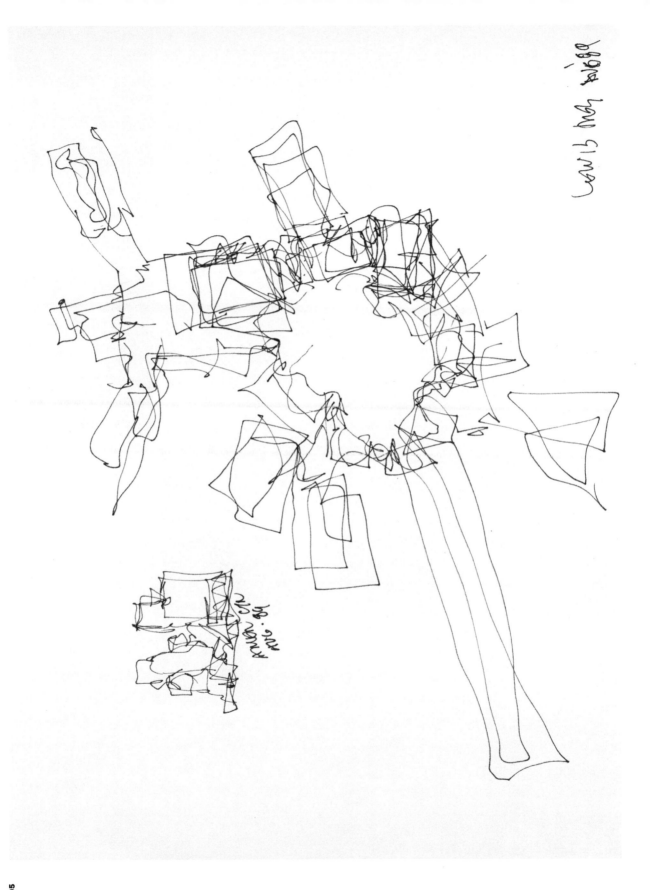

When all that Postmodern stuff started, I didn't think Modernism was washed up. It was still full of possibilities: distance working, electronic shopping, flying to the moon. I know what Modernism is and I still believe in it. Modernism is having the nerve to live in the present. That's why I think I am still Modern. I'm not burrowing in the past. My work is not irrational. It has been a search for a personal vocabulary. I don't just throw all the blocks up in the air and draw them where they land. I live in the present. FG

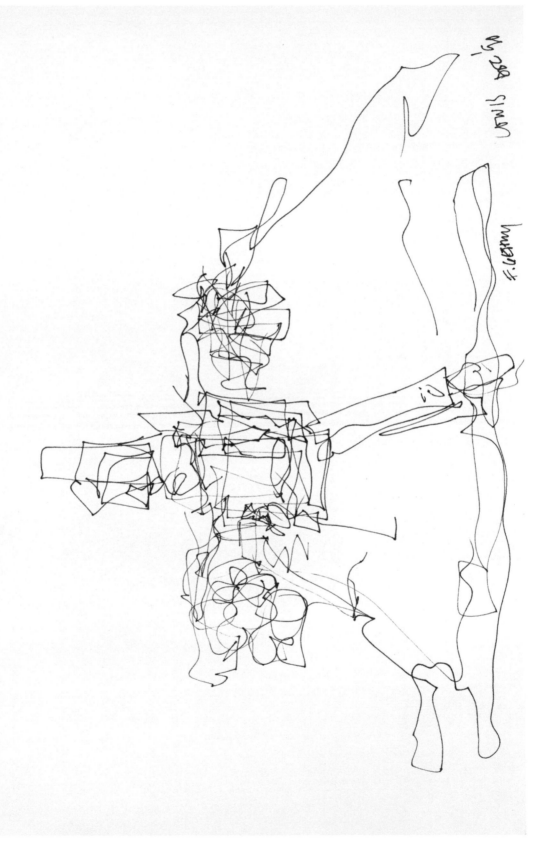

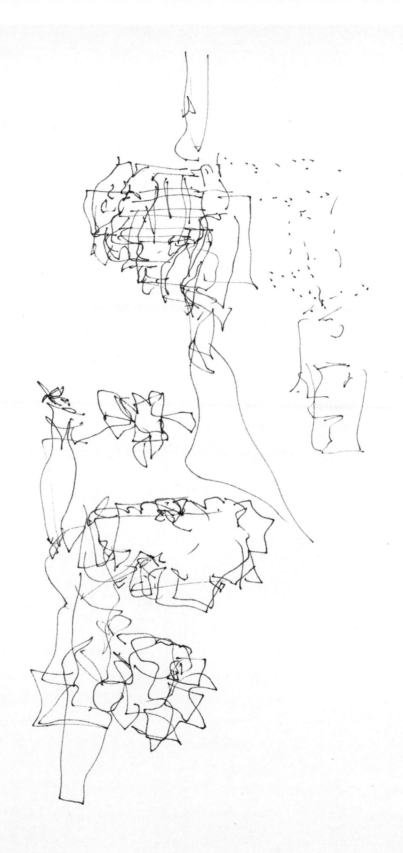

M05.03
05.07.91

M05.04
05.07.91

M05.05
05.07.91

D05.09

D05.10

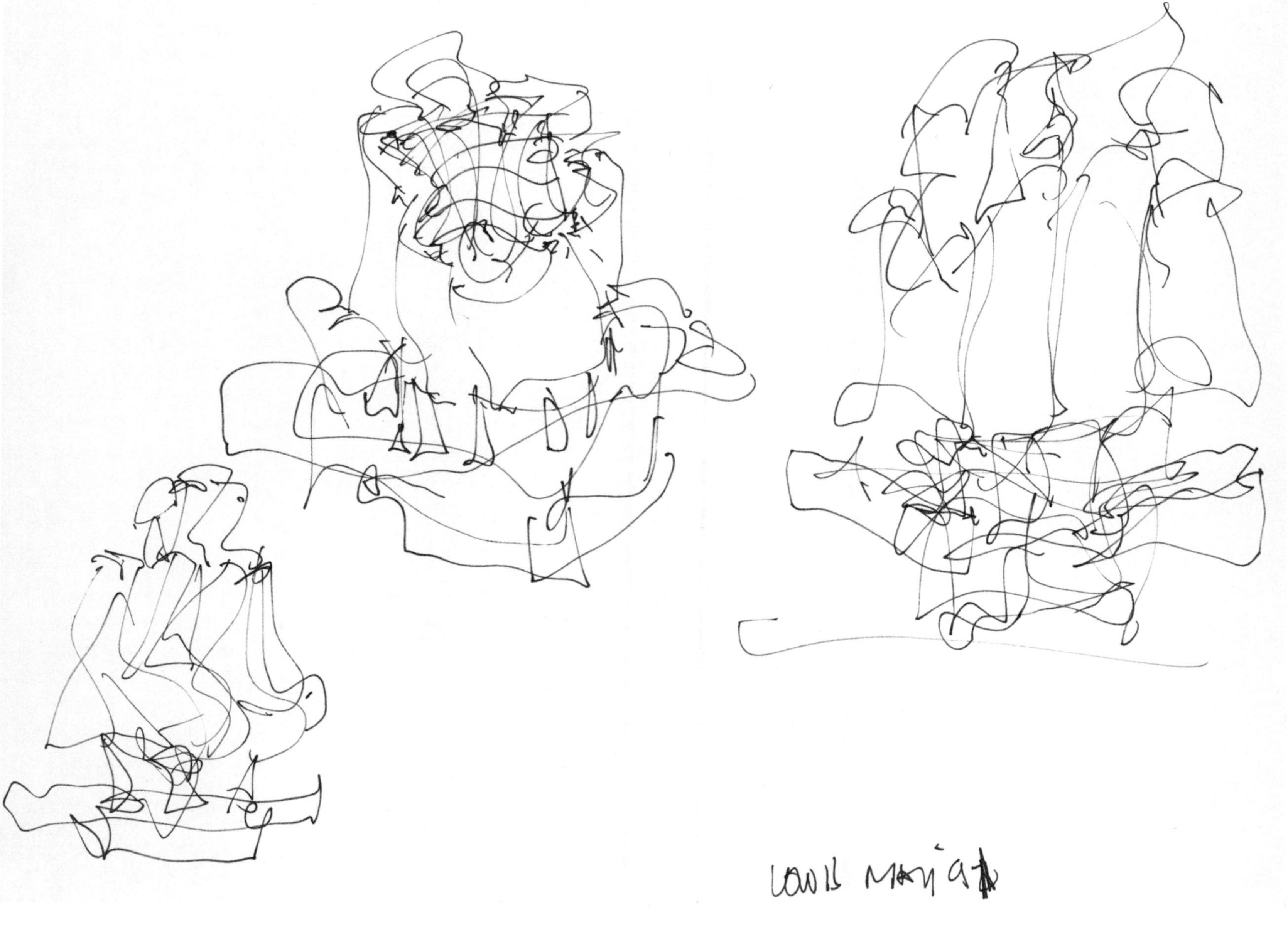

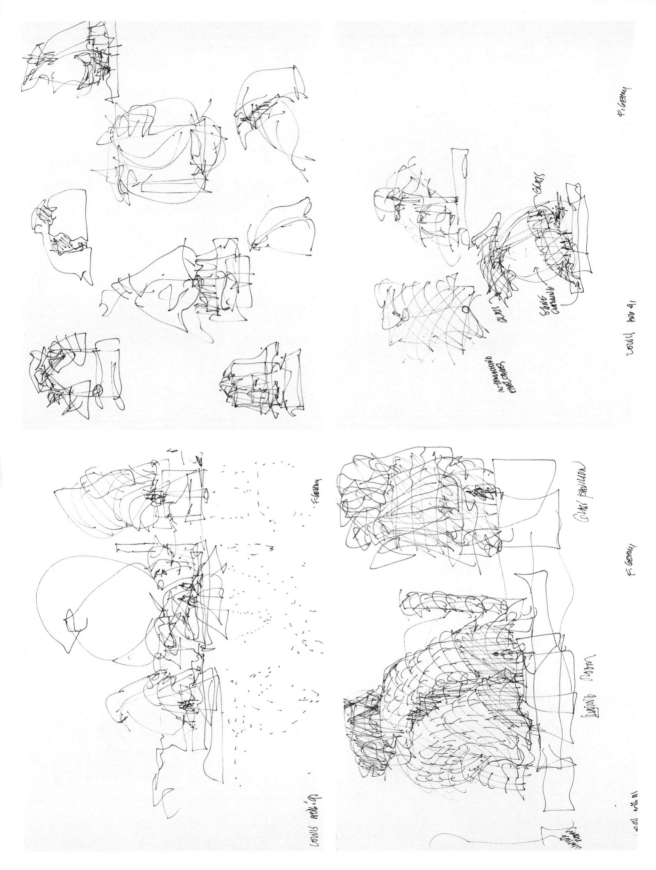

GLASS CURVING S DOWN

LEWIS. OCT '91

F. GEHRY

F. GOETHEL

OCT. 91 LONG

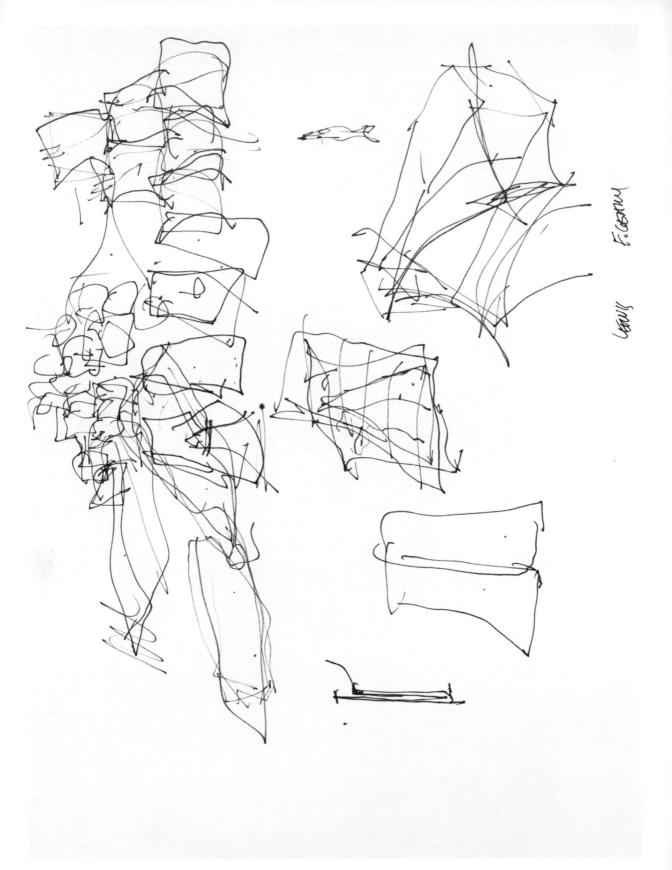

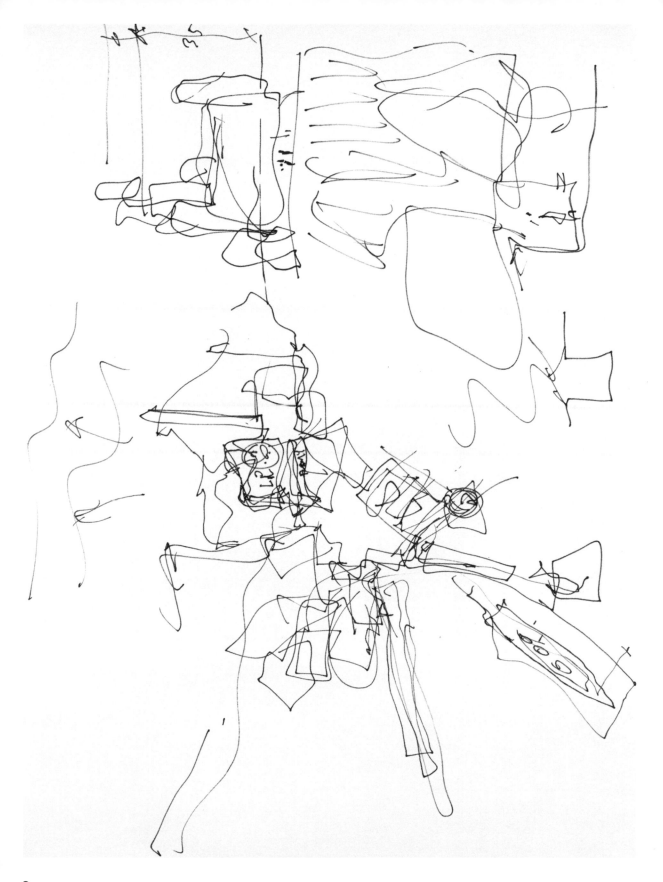

I used to think that we architects were crusaders, that we were going to save the world. Boy, did I get that beaten out of me early. Nobody really cared. That was personal stuff, about making your own mud pies and showing them to somebody and getting approval. I think once you realize that's what you're doing, once you accept that, then you can contribute something and not sit around worrying about it.

What happens as a matter of course, though, is that, when you make your own mud pies and they become intriguing for a wider range of people, you get some power. Then you are asked to comment on other areas of the world and you become part of a forum that can influence other things. The trouble is that you can abuse that position if you assume that expertise comes with the approval, if you take advantage of that kind of pseudo-expertise. Architects, after all, are not social scientists. FG

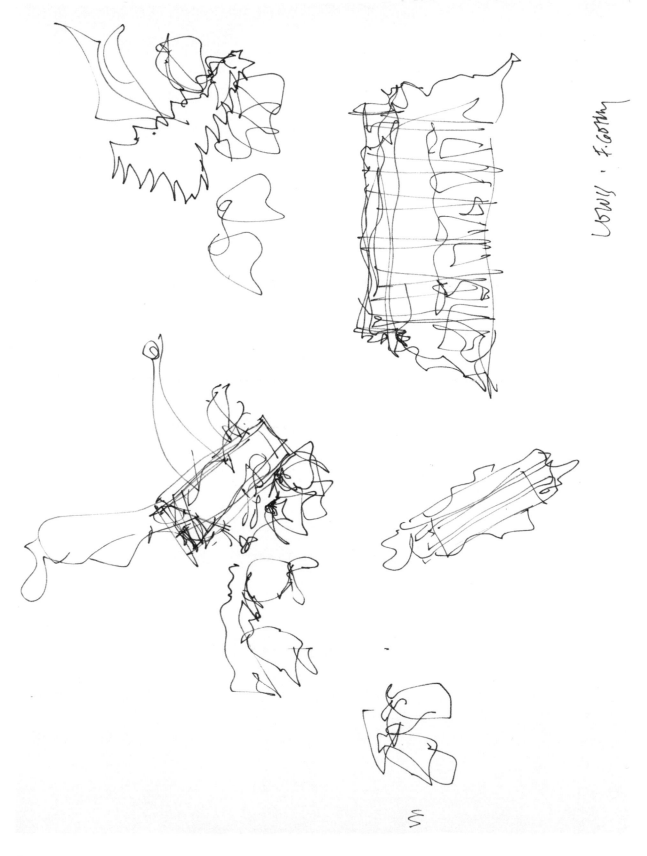

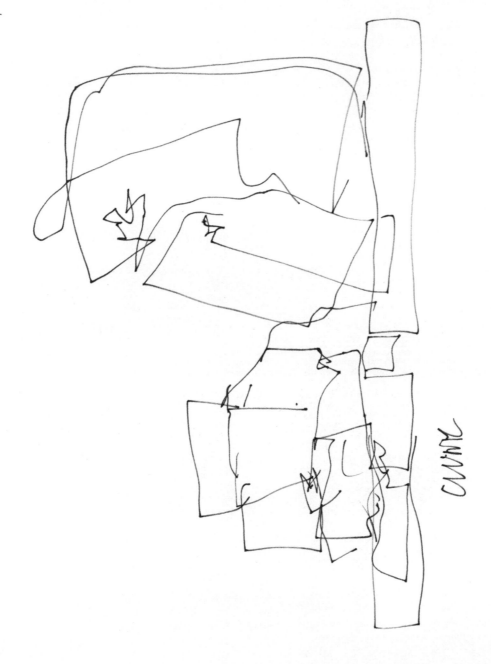

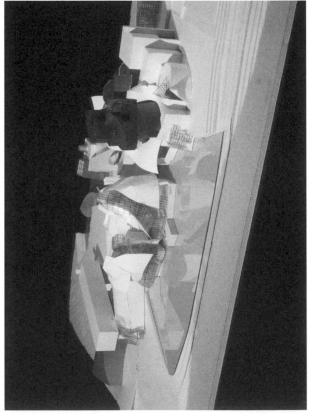

Louis Kahn. Fs

How do I use the drawings? I'll get a copy and put it on the table. Frank describes what it is. So it's both verbal description and the drawing of a gesture. And then I try to get the energy of the gesture in the drawing. It's tricky because sometimes the drawing has a lot more movement than Frank actually wants, and sometimes less. For example, we were just working on a 70-story tower in Manhattan; and there are a lot of rules about how vertical and how tight a skyscraper has to be. Frank made a drawing for this that's very loose. Sometimes the drawings are quite literally a specific shape and gesture and sometimes they are more about the energy of a design. Sometimes Frank's drawings are just placeholders for ideas he talks about. It can go any of these ways. Other times Frank might say just build exactly what's drawn, taking a flat thing and expanding it into three dimensions. It's difficult. It's a lot quicker to take a pen and draw these things than to make it with glue and paper.

A drawing may take 30 seconds and a model an hour. Different process. For Frank, it's a very efficient, direct, and flexible way of communicating his ideas. I seldom go back to the drawings. We usually work in a sequence: first the drawings, then a model, then Frank looks at the model, evaluates it, and then makes more drawings. Then we make more models. And so on. It's a progression, yet sometimes we do go back to earlier drawings and concepts. The process is a little like a spiral: we make different iterations, there's a trajectory and then sometimes you get to the point where you hit a wall, and you say, alright, wasn't it better last week? Usually we go back to the model but sometimes also to the drawings. What was happening here that we lost in the process? It goes that way. CW

F. Gehry

Sydney

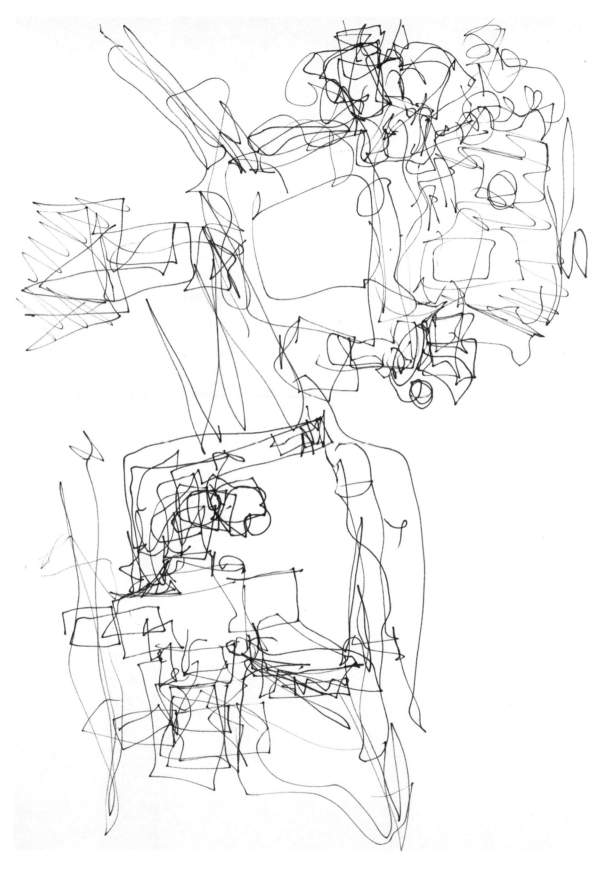

M05.08
09.10.92

M05.09
09.10.92

M05.10
09.09.92

M05.11
09.09.92

M05.12
09.09.92

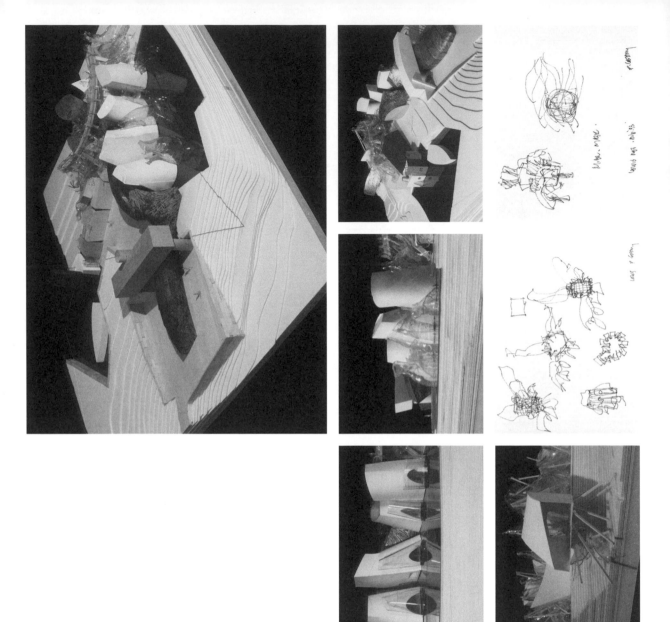

M05.13
01.03.93

M05.14
01.03.93

M05.15
11.23.93

M05.16
12.23.93

M05.17
12.23.93

D05.28

D05.29

132
—
133

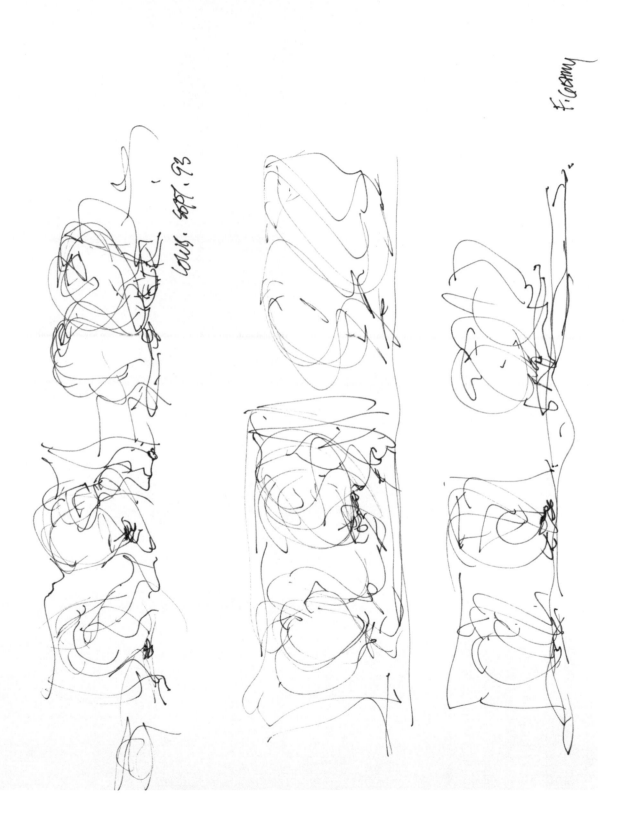

Laus. sept. 93

F. Gehry

I worked on the Lewis house only for the last year that Frank was developing it. Frank was trying to figure out the shape vocabulary of Claus Sluter's sculpture. Frank wanted to work those kinds of organic shapes and flow them into the Lewis design. We tried and tried and tried. We also worked on Sluter's monk's cowl from his tomb of Philip the Bold, that fluidity, and when I started on this project it all began to come together.

There was one model in this period that was exactly like the monk's cowl. Then we started working with fabric, velvet, and putting the velvet shapes into the computer, which also led to the shape of the DZ Bank building in Berlin, the horse's head. cw

M05.18
05.94

M05.19
05.94

134
135

F. Gastow

Venice, July, '80

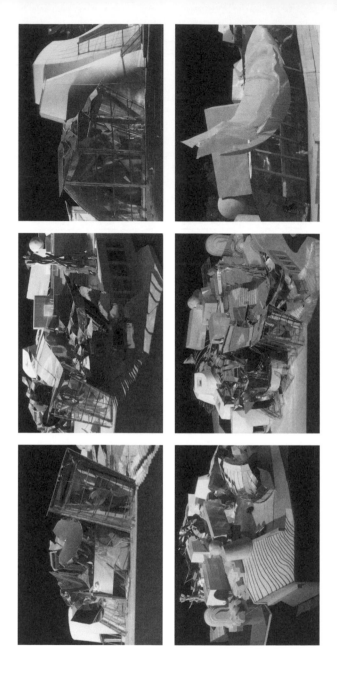

M05.20
11.22.94

M05.21
11.22.94

M05.22
11.22.94

M05.23
11.22.94

M05.24
11.22.94

M05.25
11.22.94

136
—
137

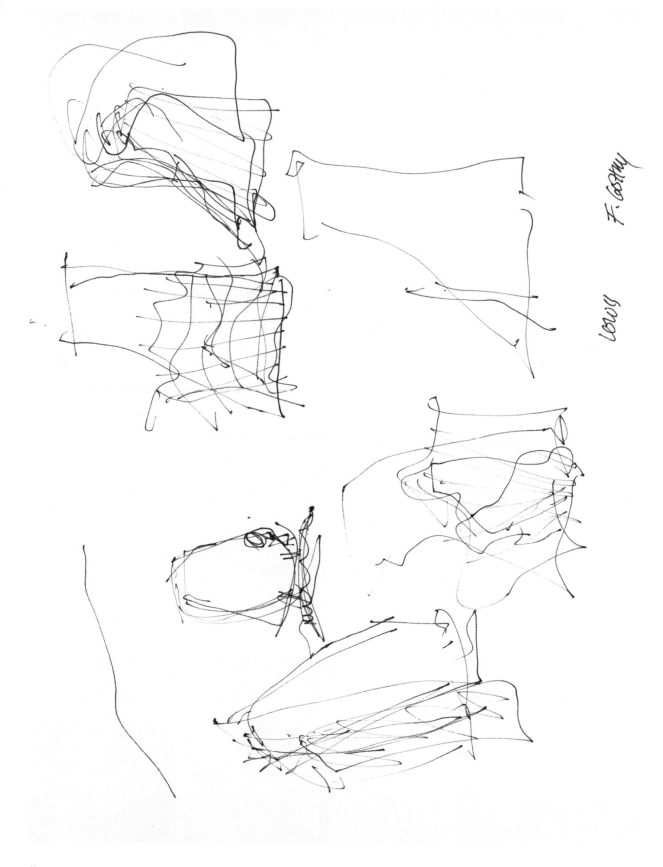

LOUIS   F. GEHRY

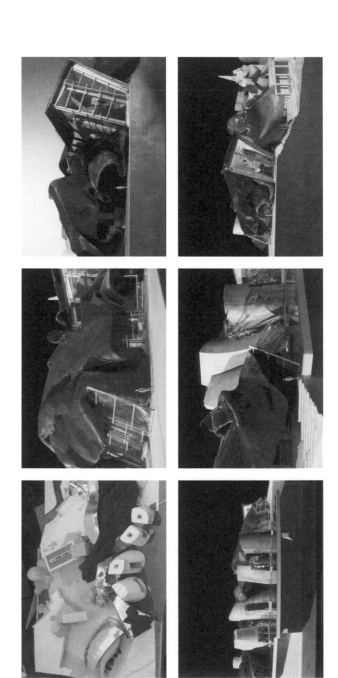

M05.26
02.16.95

M05.27
02.16.95

M05.28
02.16.95

M05.29
02.16.95

M05.30
02.16.95

M05.31
02.16.95

138
139

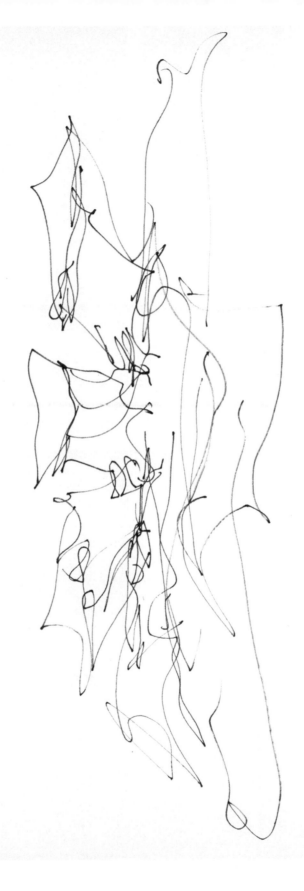

Venus No.

F. Gehry

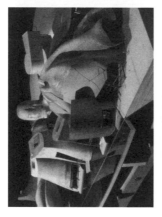

M05.32
1995

M05.33
1995

M05.34
1995

M05.35
1995

140 | 141

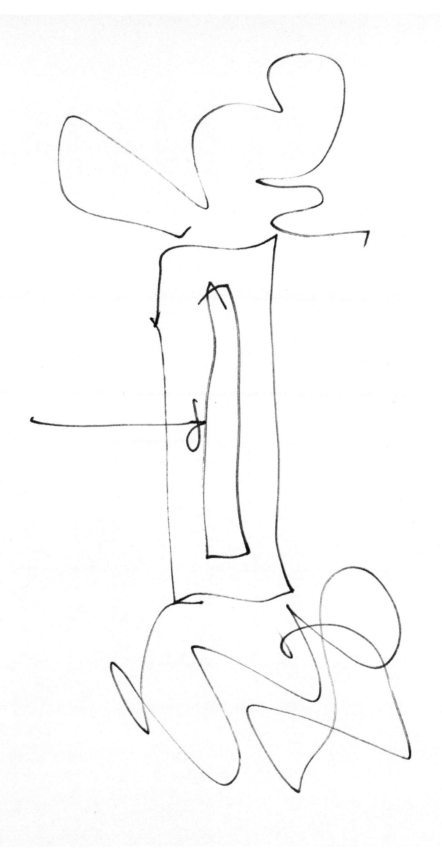

Project 06

Guggenheim Museum
Bilbao, Spain
1991–1997

Guggenheim Museum
Bilbao, Spain

Design: commenced 1991
Construction: commenced 1993
Status: completed 1997
Number of drawings illustrated: 21

The Guggenheim Museum, Bilbao, is the result of a unique collaboration between the Basque Country Administration, which finances and owns the project, and the Solomon R. Guggenheim Foundation, which operates the museum and provides the core art collection. It represents the first step in the larger redevelopment of Bilbao's former trade and warehouse district, which is located along the south bank of the Nervión river. Directly accessible from the business and historic districts of the city, the museum marks the center of a cultural triangle formed by the Museo de Bellas Artes, the University, and the Old Town Hall. The Puente de la Salve, which connects the nineteenth-century city center to outlying areas, passes over the site at its eastern edge, lending the museum its significance as a gateway to the city.

The main entrance to the museum is through a large central atrium, where a system of curvilinear bridges, glass elevators, and stair towers connects the exhibition galleries concentrically on three levels. A sculptural roof form rises from the central atrium, flooding it with light through glazed openings. The unprecedented scale of this atrium, which rises to a height of more than 150 feet above the river, is an invitation to monumental site-specific installations and special museum events.

The Guggenheim Foundation required gallery spaces to exhibit a permanent collection, a temporary collection, and a collection of selected living artists. In response, three distinct types of exhibition space were designed. The permanent collection is housed in two sets of three consecutive square galleries, stacked on the second and third levels of the museum. The temporary collection is housed in a more dramatic elongated rectangular gallery that passes beneath the Puente de la Salve before terminating in a tower on its far side. The collection of works by living artists is housed in a series of curvilinear galleries placed throughout the museum, allowing the work to be viewed in relation to the permanent and temporary collections.

The major exterior materials are Spanish limestone (used to distinguish the rectangular building shapes) and titanium panels (for the more sculptural shapes). Large glazed curtain walls provide views of the river and the surrounding city, while a new public plaza located at the entrance to the museum encourages pedestrian traffic between it and the Museo de Bellas Artes, and between the Old City and the riverfront. Ultimately, the design of the museum is as much a response to the scale and the texture of the city as it is to the requirements of the art collections it houses.

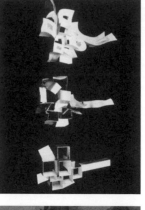

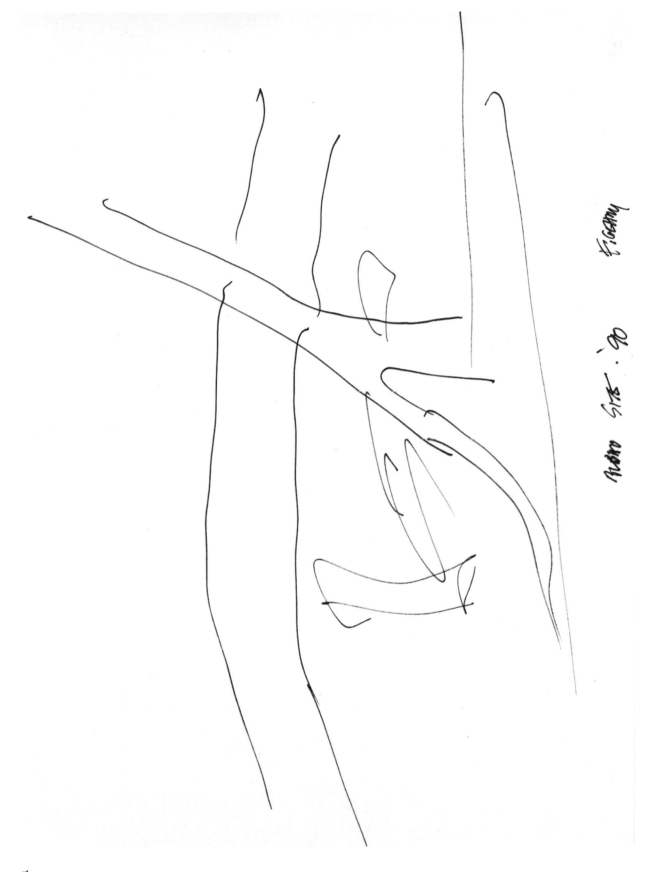

We knew from the first day we visited the site that we wanted the building to do five main things. First, because the bridge is such an important part of the site, we wanted the building to include the bridge as opposed to excluding the bridge. So then we knew that in order to do that, part of the building had to go underneath the bridge. We also knew that the site had a vertical drop and so, secondly, we wanted to make sure the building provided a connection from the city to the waterfront. Third, the entrance to the building faces the city and it would be connected to the existing museum on that side. So by creating a plaza up there, it would make a connection with the city. Fourth, because of the way the river bends, we knew that if we were to create a core element on the other side of the bridge, it would become a beacon for the old part of town on the other side of the river. So we also did that. And then the last element is, of course, the iconographic issue. We knew coming into this thing that there needed to be a highly sculptural iconographic element and we knew that it would be some sort of metal form. Just because Bilbao is such an industrial city, we thought that a metal sculpture would speak to that nature. So you put those five basic principles together and you get the concept design, which we produced very quickly for the competition. Many of Frank's early sketches talk about these ideas in a very basic kind of way, diagramming how we can achieve these things with various configurations.

One drawing, for example, assumes that maybe we can make an amphitheater to provide a natural connection down from the city to the water. We talked about a lot of this stuff. And then there might be a second tower, there might be a gallery that goes underneath the bridge. But in the end those five basic principles governed the final design, or at least the design that we submitted for the competition.

I think that our scheme was actually the only one that addressed the bridge in the initial competition. I think Arata Isozaki's scheme ignored the bridge, and so did the Coop Himmelb(l)au scheme. I think the urbanism of our scheme was much stronger in that respect. It made our proposal much more site specific and that is actually why we won the competition. And I think it's important to understand that when you look at Bilbao a lot of people see it as a stand-alone sculpture and overlook the importance of its urban princi-ples. But the Guggenheim Bilbao is specifically conceived for that city. It was the result of combining those five urban principles together to arrive very naturally at the design of this museum. EC

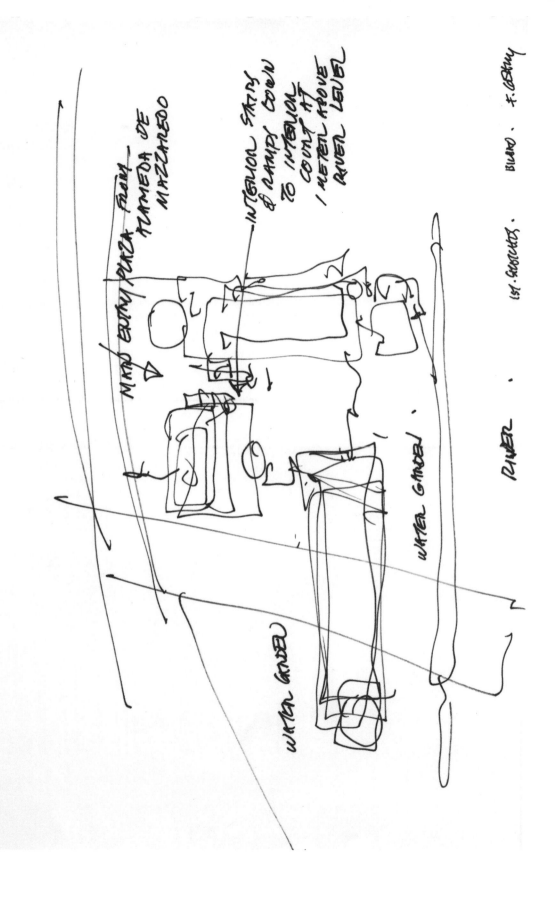

MAIN ENTRY PLAZA FROM ALAMEDA DE MAZZAREDO

INTERIOR STAIRS & RAMPS DOWN TO INTERIOR COURT AT 1 METER ABOVE RIVER LEVEL

WATER GARDEN

WATER GARDEN

RIVER · 1st GROUND 1st · BILBAO · F. GEHRY

D06.02

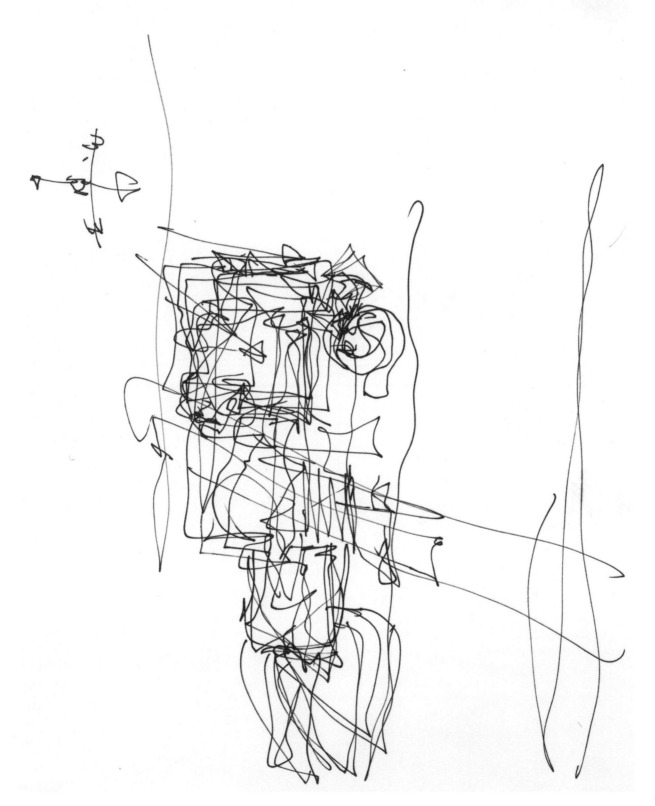

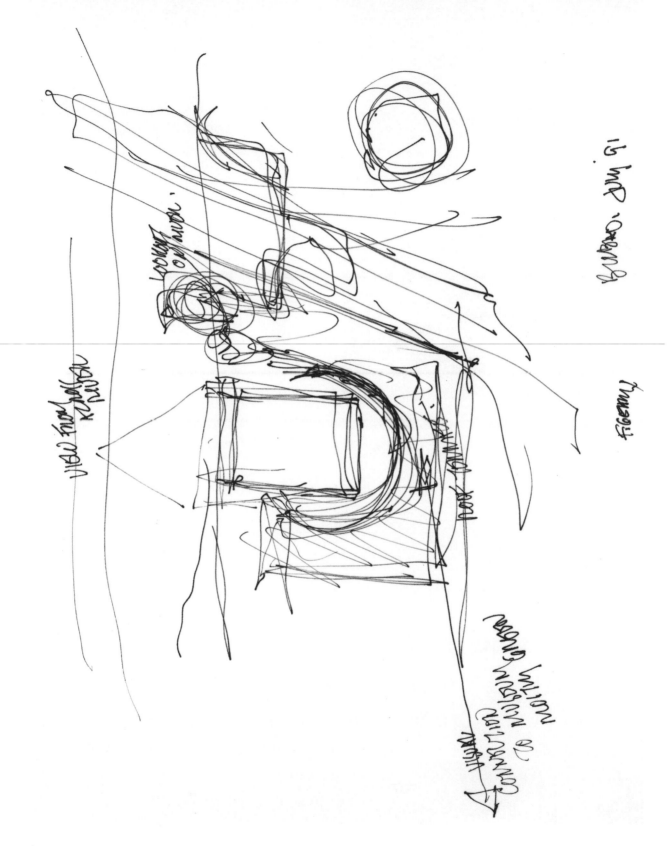

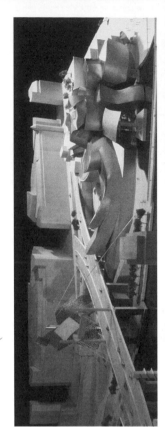

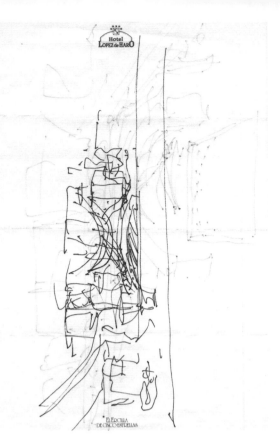

M06.03

M06.04
09.13.91

M06.05
06.17.92

D06.05

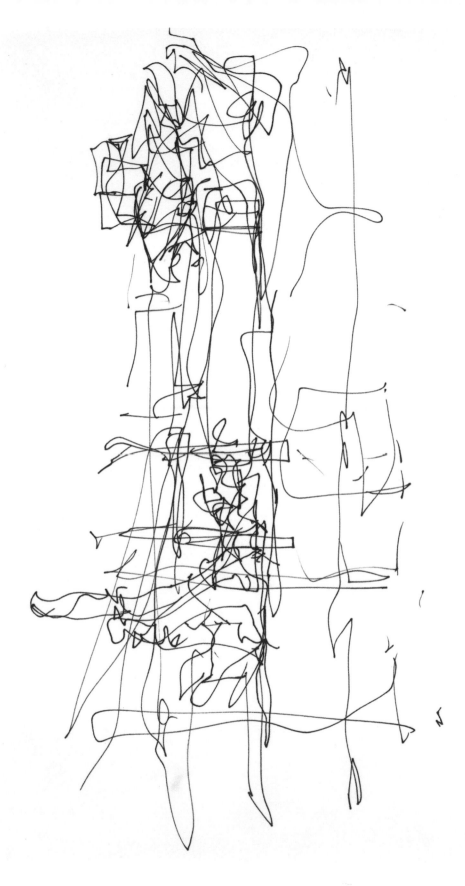

141. SKETCHES · F. GEHRY

D06.06

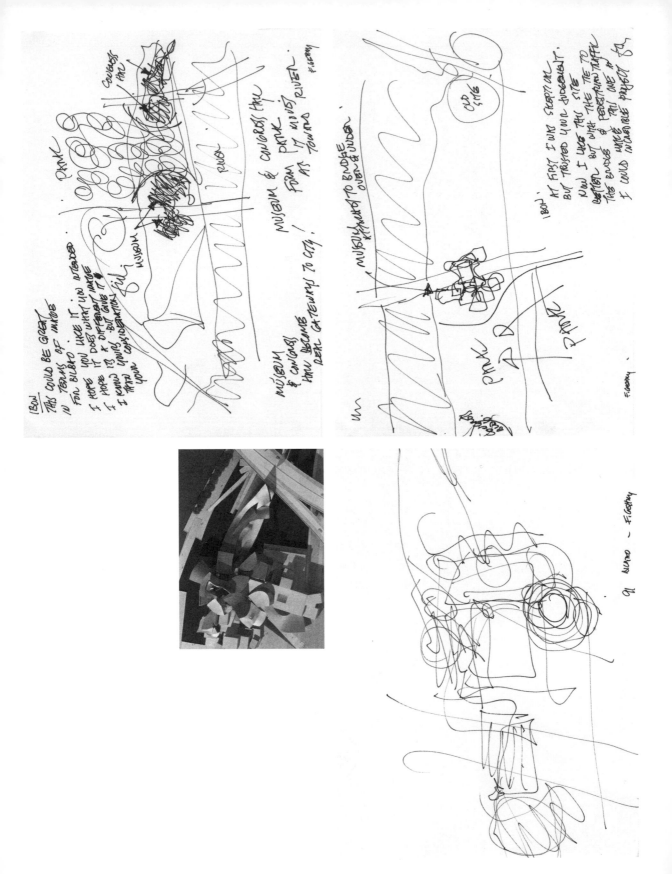

M06.06
D06.07
D06.08
D06.09

152
153

BILBAO   F.GEHRY

F. Gehry

D06.12

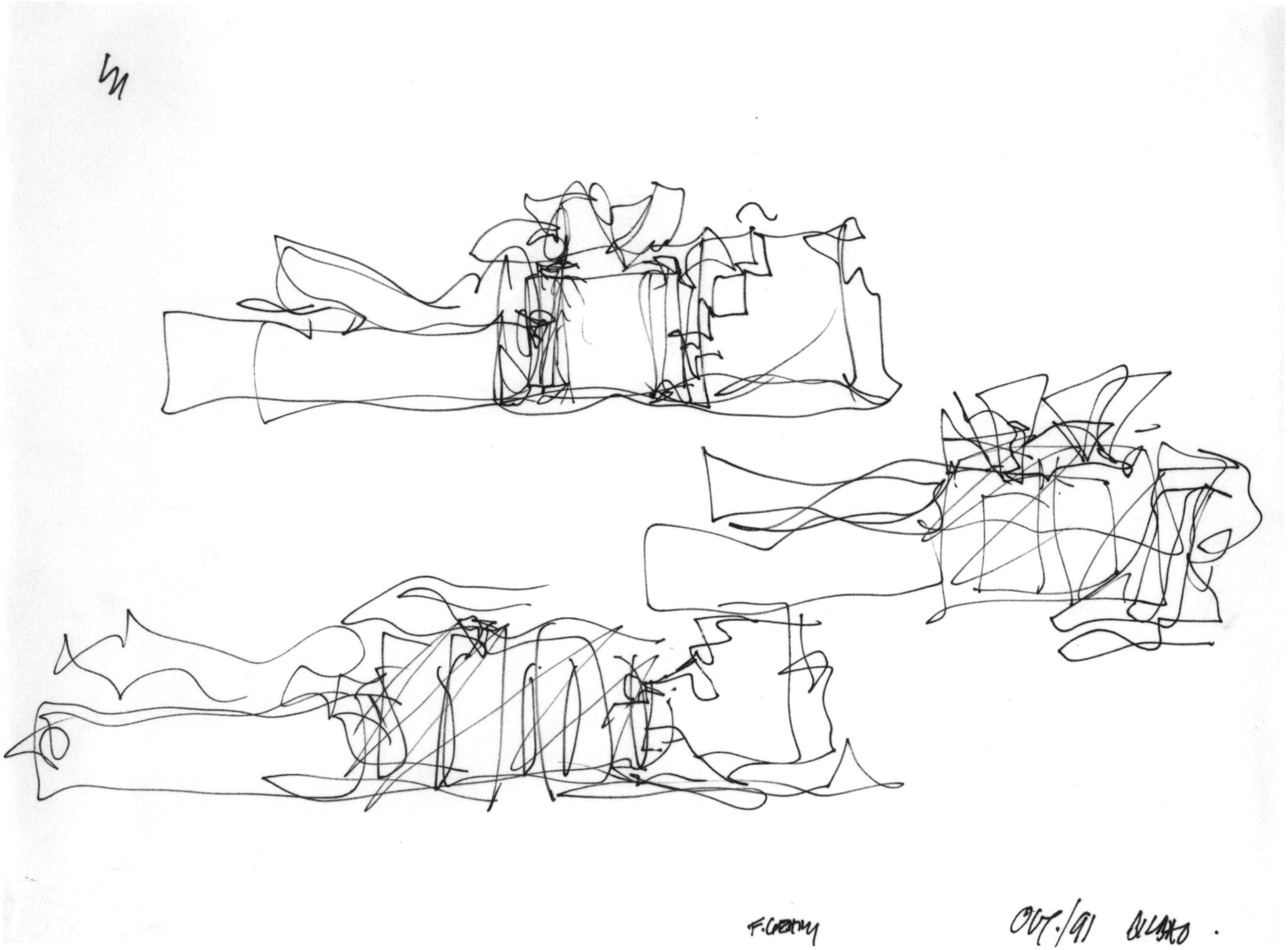

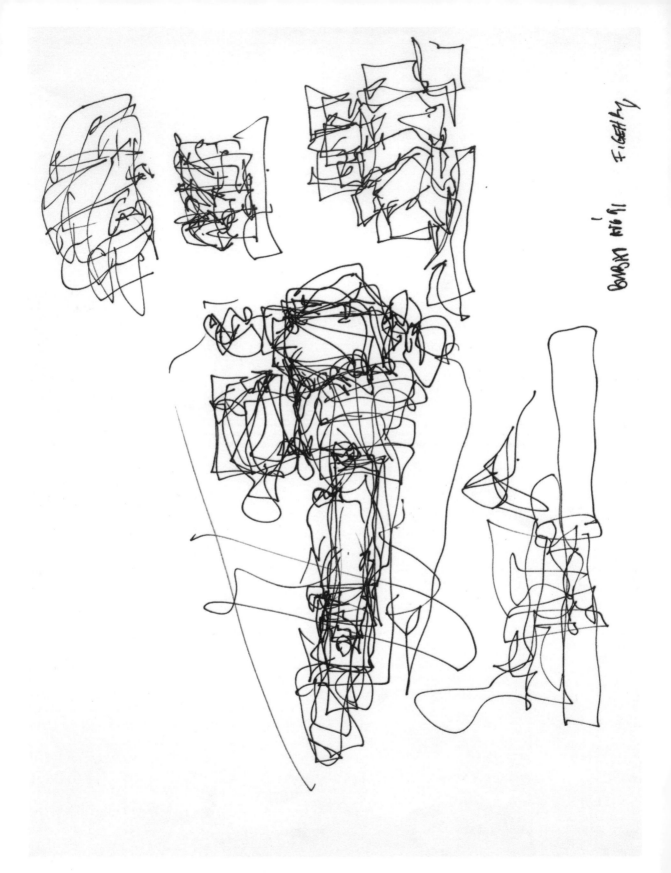

I am an architect, but I do think that art and architecture come from the same source. They involve some of the same struggles. My first work, when I started to do my own stuff, was encouraged by artists, not by other architects. Actually other architects were suspicious of my work. Ed Ruscha, Ed Moses, the Los Angeles artists have always been very, very supportive. I am a product of the Sixties. People like Ruscha, Richard Serra, Claes Oldenburg, Carl Andre—they come out of the same time, the same mentality. I have always been interested in their work. I always related to their thinking and to the expressions of that time—Minimalism, Pop Art. I relate to those guys. In a lot of ways we are similar, but I'm an architect.

In my own experience of working relationships between architects and artists whose work I admire, there is always a point where personal choices are made—choices that have to do with space, form, color, shape, content, context—and which require the same kind of energy, information, vision, expertise, or whatever. When Jasper Johns paints with his little paint brush, he's being informed differently than when I'm making a metal wall. It's a different background of information that leads to different connections, even if the general dynamic, the intention, and end result have to do with similar choices concerning how the light, the texture, and the quality of surface work. FG

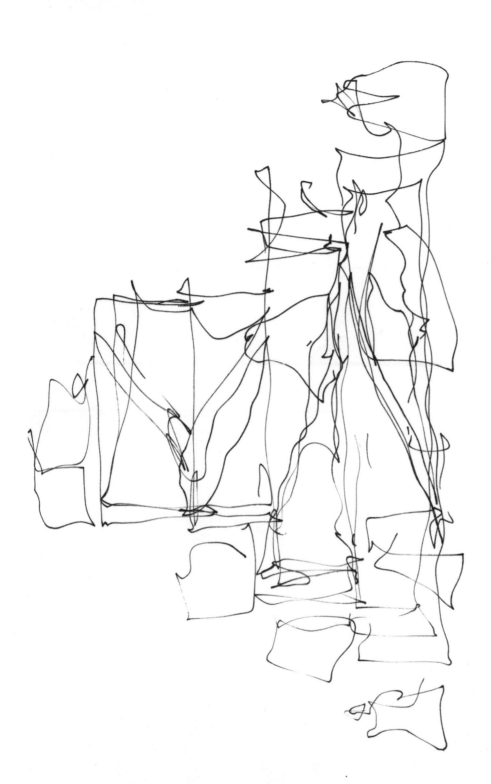

Bilbao · Guggenheim

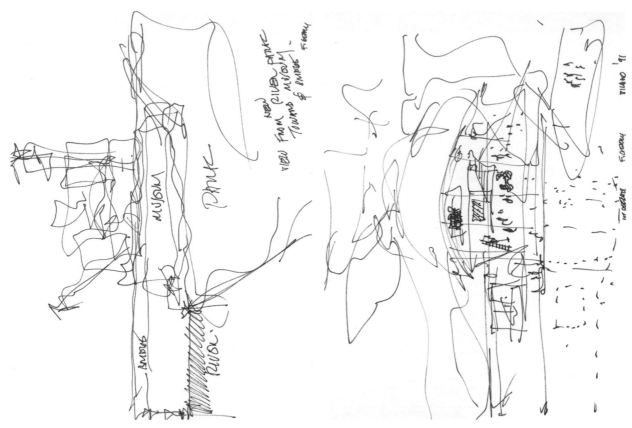

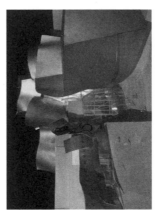

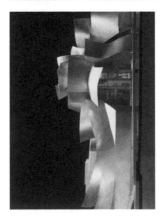

D06.16

D06.17

M06.07
10.12.93

M06.08
10.12.93

160
161

F. Gehry

F. Gehry Blada

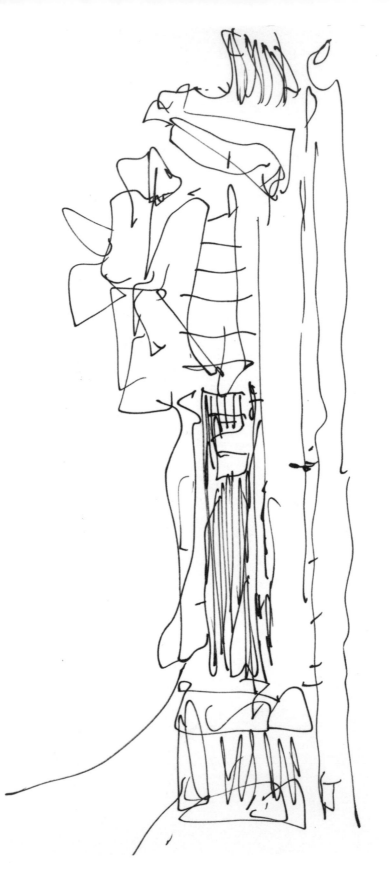

HT. GOSTELS . BILBAO . F.GEHRY

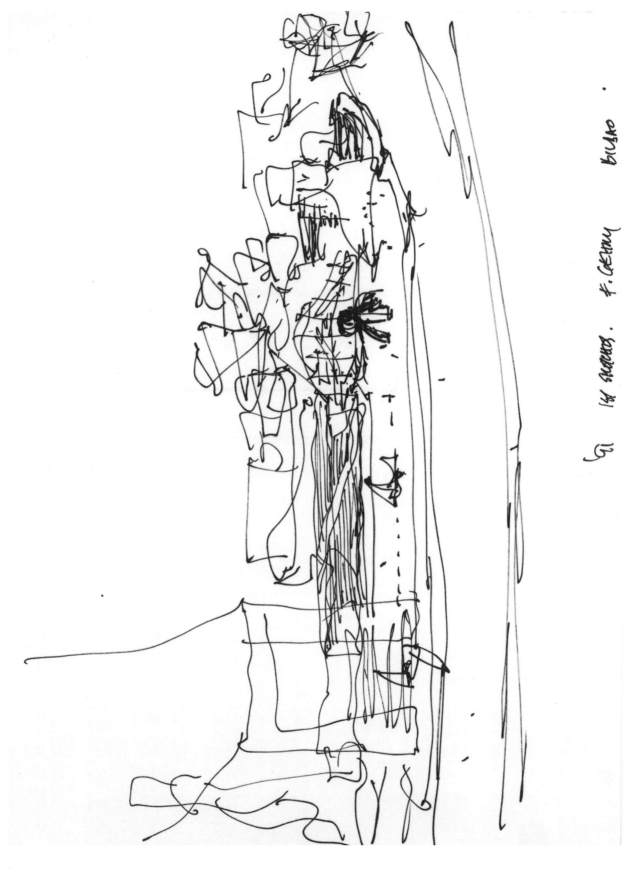

165 SKETCHES · F. GEHRY bilbao

I always thought it was lazy, working with models; I was too lazy to visualize things in my guts, so I would use a model as a crutch. I use them differently now. I design in models. I work more like a sculptor, molding, pushing, changing, and I sketch and work back to the plan. We now have sophisticated computer modeling techniques helping you to "swim," freed from other constraints. You can approach things with perspectives, to reach some quite independent sculptural surfaces. At the same time, it moves you into another realm when it comes to construction. FG

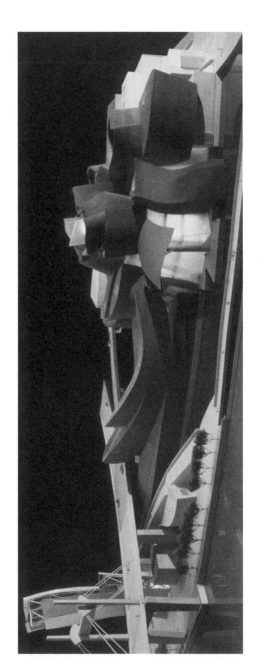

M06.09
03.01.95

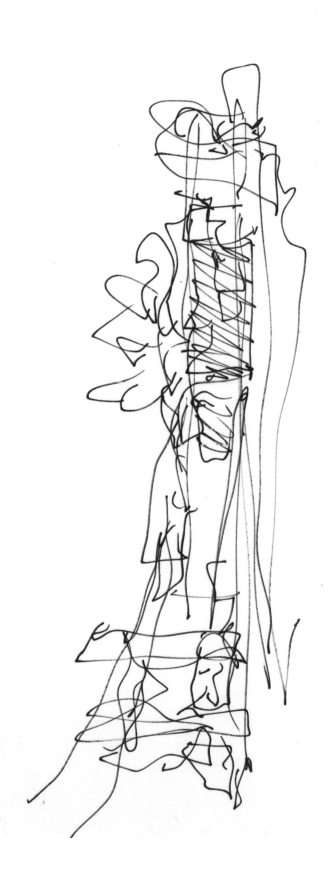

ALAMO ~ 154 subasta ~   F. GEHRY

Project 07

Vontz Center
for Molecular Studies
University of Cincinnati,
Cincinnati, Ohio
1993–1999

**VONTZ CENTER
FOR MOLECULAR STUDIES**
University of Cincinnati,
Cincinnati, Ohio

Design: commenced 1993
Construction: commenced 1996
Status: completed 1999
Number of drawings illustrated: 8

Standing at the entrance to the University of Cincinnati Medical Center, the Vontz Center for Molecular Studies houses state-of-the-art research laboratories, offices, and academic spaces. The building plan is in a cruciform shape, which splits the lab blocks on the north–south axis from the offices on the east–west axis. At its center is an atrium with shared staff areas such as break rooms and meeting zones, stairs, toilets, and elevators. Lightwells and skylights in this area allow daylight and inter-communication between levels. The building is designed for maximum flexibility to adapt to future scientific methodologies.

M07.01
M07.02
M07.03

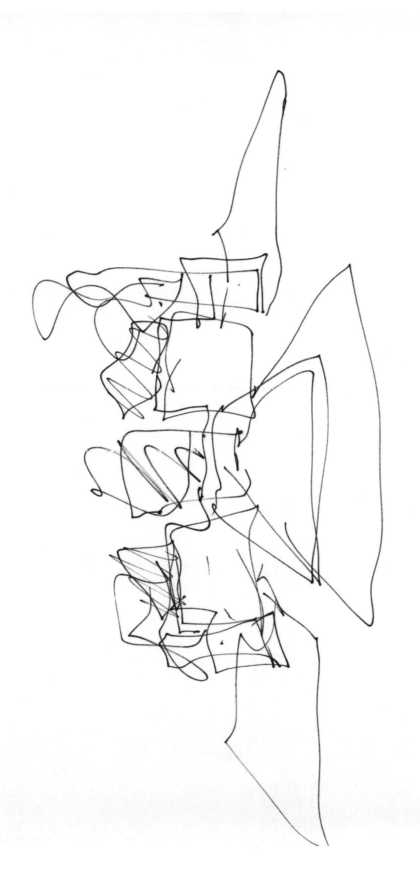

F. GEHRY

CINCINNATI ~ MOLE.BIO. STUDY July 90

M07.05
07.10.994

M07.06
07.20.94

M07.07
10.17.94

170 | 171

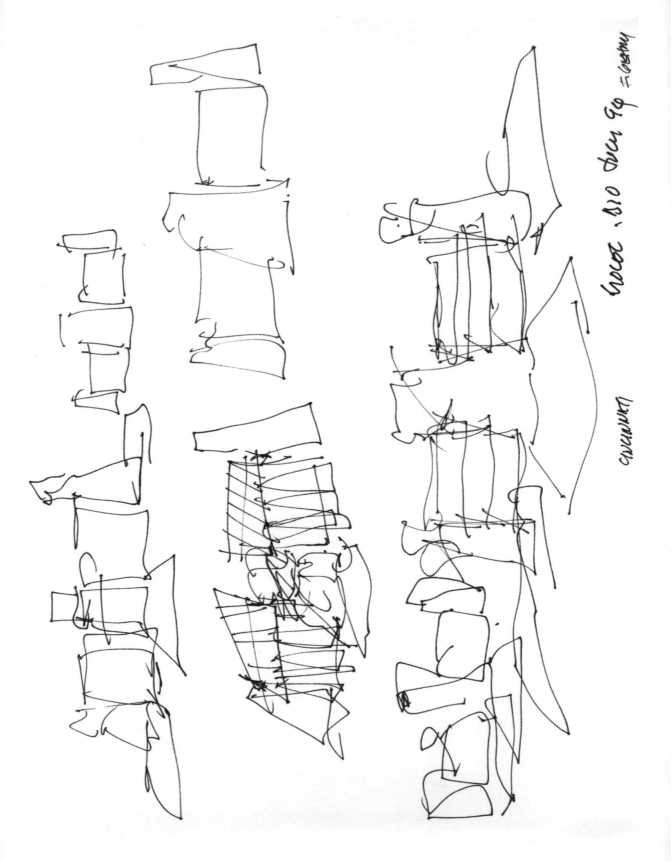

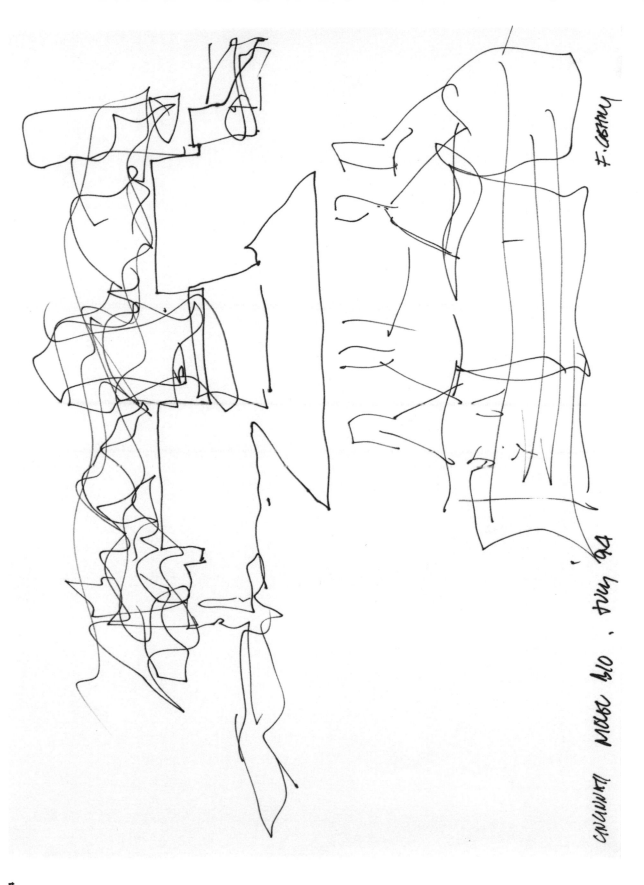

CNSSULUT MUSE BIG , EUG BG

F. GEHRY

Scientists have come up with Chaos Theory, but I have always thought that, regardless of what we do, there is an inherent order in our being on the face of the earth. We can't escape gravity, natural light. Those laws of the jungle account for maybe 90 per cent of what we do. We just can't control that. FG

F. GEHRY

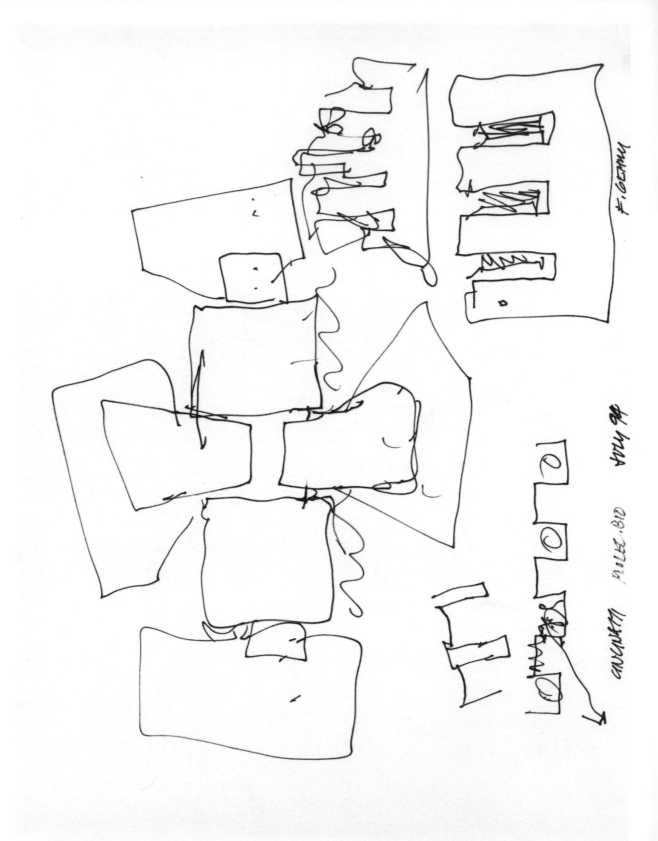

D07.07

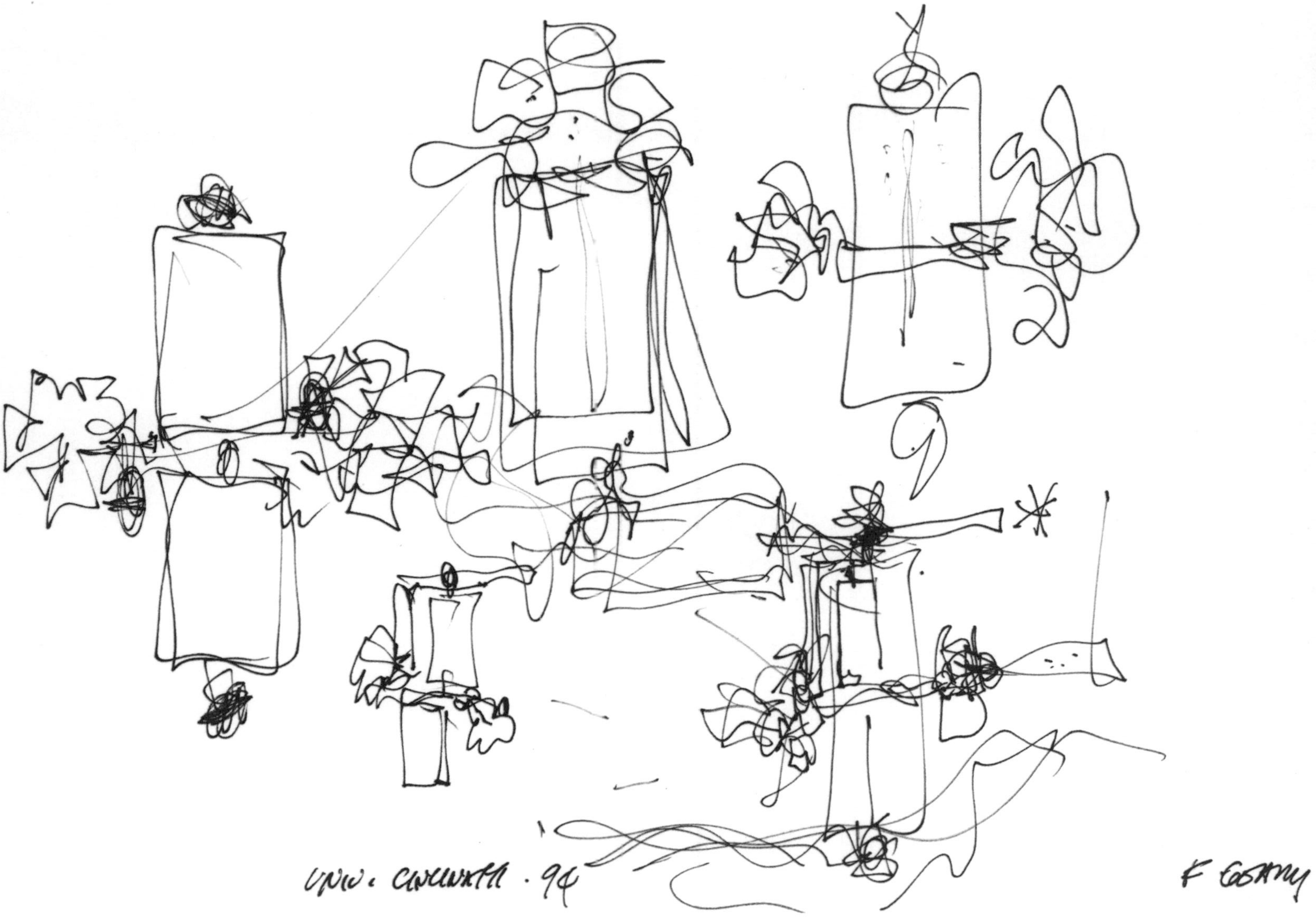

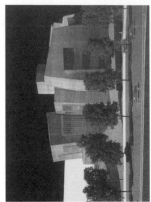

M07.08
05.22.95

M07.09
05.22.95

M07.10
05.22.95

M07.11
05.22.95

M07.12
05.22.95

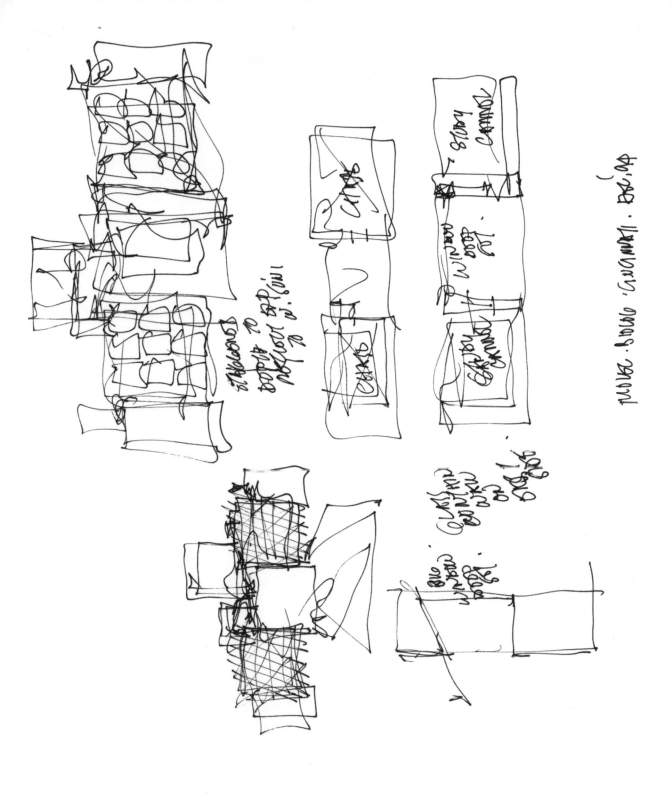

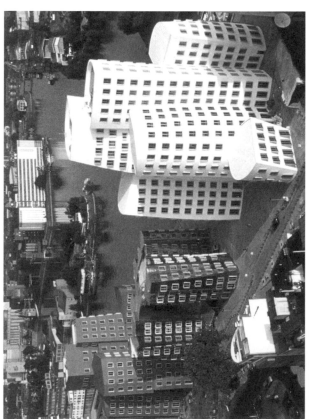

Project 08

Der Neue Zollhof
Düsseldorf, Germany
1994–1999

Der Neue Zollhof
Düsseldorf, Germany

Design: commenced 1994
Construction: commenced 1996
Status: completed 1999
Number of drawings illustrated: 7

This project is part of a waterfront redevelopment of the Eastern edge of the Rhine harborfront in downtown Düsseldorf. Currently occupied primarily by warehouses, this area is being redeveloped as an urban public zone, comprising art and media agencies. Due to its proximity to the residential district immediately to the south, and to the municipal and financial district further to the east, the rehabilitation of the harborfront is intended to provide an open public amenity for the city, while underscoring the emergence of Düsseldorf as a cultural and business center.

The flat site runs adjacent to the waterfront promenade commanding extensive views up and down the Rhine River. New construction borders the eastern and western edges, while a future tram line and stop define the southern boundary along Stromstrasse. To the north, the site overlooks the Zolhafen Sport Harbor and the Bilk Park beyond. Required to provide 300,000 square feet of commercial office space, the project is arranged as three separate buildings, promoting a highly open site plan and minimizing the overall mass of the project and consequently maintaining visual and public access to the river. The division of the project into three major buildings, each with a unique material finish, also provides high visibility to each of the three primary tenants.

The three towers consist of 3,200- to 5,400-square-foot elements grouped around a central core, providing highly flexible leasing arrangements within an articulated massing. The floor plates accommodate open or modular office planning. The towers rest on an expansive plaza, with a variety of paths connecting the street to the harbor. Parking is provided below ground.

All three buildings are constructed of concrete flat-slab with punched window openings on the exterior facade. The central office building is clad entirely in metal panels, the east (and tallest) tower is comprised of curvilinear volumes finished in plaster, and the west tower is a grouping of volumes faced in brick. All buildings have operable windows for natural ventilation. The articulation of the window and its relationship to the exterior skin is similar in all three structures.

The clustered organization of the volumes is designed to highlight a "family" relationship and to maximize the occurrence of offices with waterside views.

M08.01

D008.01

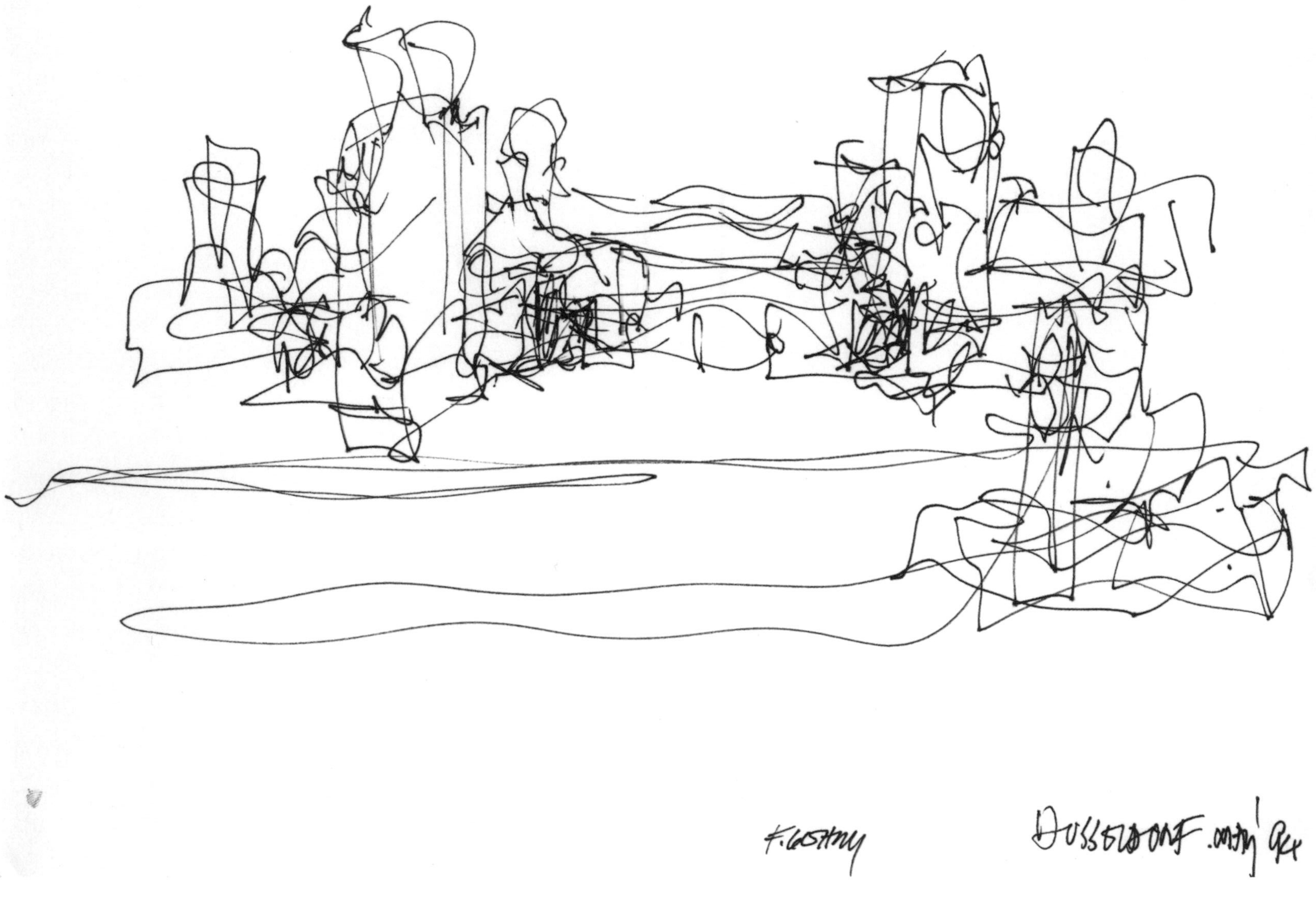

Every architect I talk to is concerned with social issues—housing the poor and solar energy, not that they know anything about solar energy, they just pick up on it, like it was good for mankind. Every few weeks there's a new one. Pollution. Toxicity, that's a good one. We were using lead coating on one of our buildings and were told there may be a problem—but no one really had a clue. Finally someone said, "If you lick the building for six months, you'll die!"

I don't feel I have any messianic social statements to make. The problems in Los Angeles, for example—the growing tension between Black and Latin communities, homelessness, the trouble on the freeways—are problems for us as people, they're not necessarily within the architect's capacity to deal with. We ought to stick to what we're best at. Architecture isn't a social science, it's an art. FG

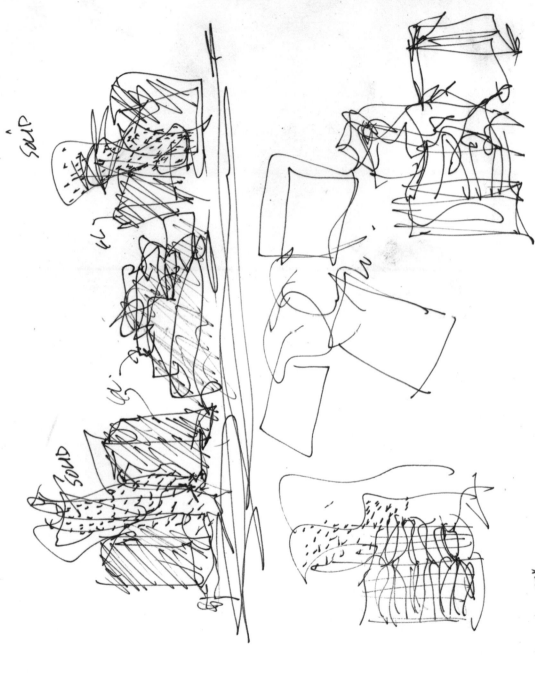

SOLID

SOLID

By Monet

Brushstroke

There is some reality of process when you make a building. You have a client, a context, a budget, and the time you're living in when you make it—all kinds of things. The building process requires some understanding of all those forces. There is intellectual involvement with the client too. The way I do that is with models and sketches, working back and forth. I use two or three different scale models at the same time, so that the finished building is the issue rather than the model. Some of my colleagues concentrate on drawings, and sometimes the drawings are more beautiful than their buildings. What I'm interested in is the final building. FG

M08.02
05.24.94
M08.03
08.04.94
M08.04
04.07.95
D08.03

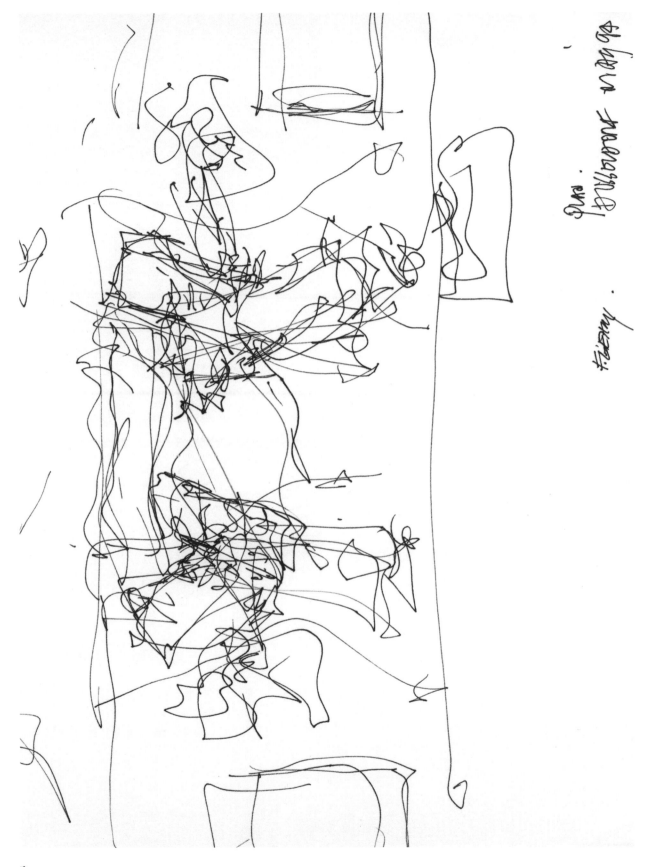

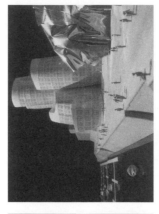

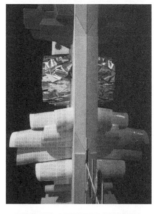

M08.05
04.07.95

M08.06
08.27.95

M08.07
08.27.95

M08.08
01.26.96

M08.09
03.01.99

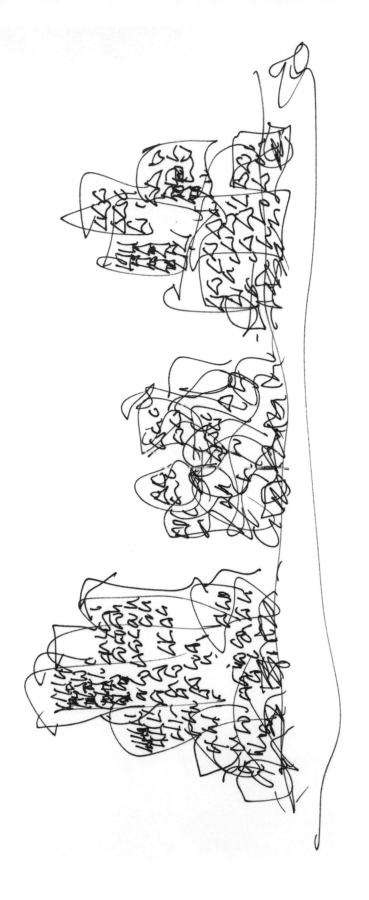

Düsseldorf is a "Morandi" project, it's a still life, stacked bottles. The shapes are trying to be sculptural, like bottles in a Morandi painting. If you punch windows into these shapes you lose the solidity, so the idea was to let the windows float in front of the surface so that it gave you the sensation that the surface was going behind, continuous. This way you preserve the purity of the shape. The windows themselves are sliced into the shapes and have an inside corner that penetrates into the side of the building, with wings that fly out past the surface.

These three buildings are finished in three different materials, like a family, but the windows give them a commonality. The same detail in all three buildings. This building was also designed with a Bellini painting in mind, a Madonna and Child flanked by Joseph and John the Baptist. The composition of these three buildings is completely drawn from that painting. The building in the middle with the piece on the front is the Madonna and Child and the two side pieces are the other two figures in the painting. The windows are the glue that holds it all together. CW

M08.10
03.01.99
M08.11
03.01.99
D08.06

190 | 191

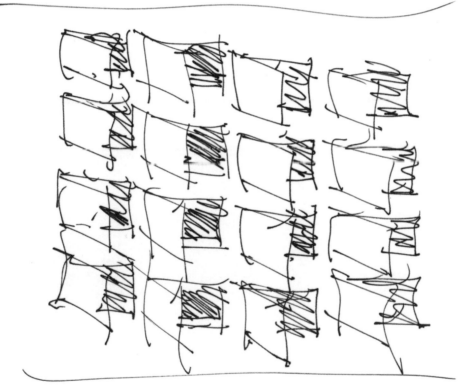

Project 09

Experience Music Project
Seattle, Washington
1995–2000

Experience Music Project
Seattle, Washington

Design: commenced 1995
Construction: commenced 1997
Status: completed 2000
Number of drawings illustrated: 5

The Experience Music Project (EMP), located on Fifth Avenue adjacent to the Space Needle at Seattle Center, is a 140,000-square-foot facility named in honor of the Jimi Hendrix Experience and intended to celebrate creativity and innovation as expressed through American popular music and culture. The EMP provides opportunities for visitors to explore the history and traditions of American popular music, to participate in the music-making process, to experience great music, and to learn about its composition and performance.

The exhibits and public programs of the Experience Music Project are envisioned as a three-dimensional floating puzzle, with each piece being critical to the shape and the nature of the whole. Six elements, the Sky Church, the Crossroads, the Sound Lab, the Artist's Journey, the Electric Library, and the Ed. House form the basis of the Experience Music Project's exhibits and public programs.

The building itself consists of a cluster of colorful curving elements clad in painted aluminum panels and in stainless-steel panels. The fragmented and undulating forms of the building are inspired in part by the image of a shattered Fender Stratocaster guitar. The Seattle Center Monorail, like the Space Needle a remnant of the 1962 World's Fair, continues to provide transportation between Seattle Center and downtown Seattle, and passes through the building, allowing Monorail riders to glimpse inside.

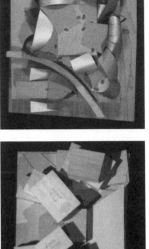

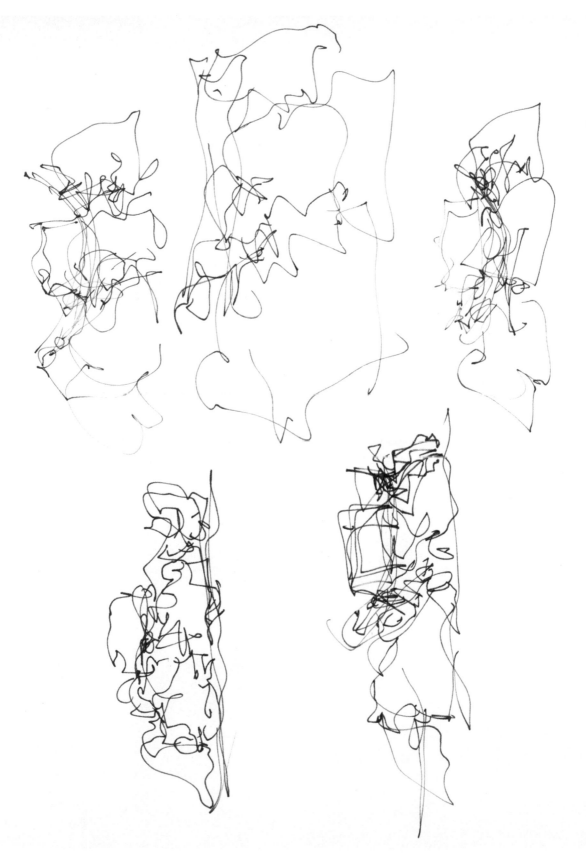

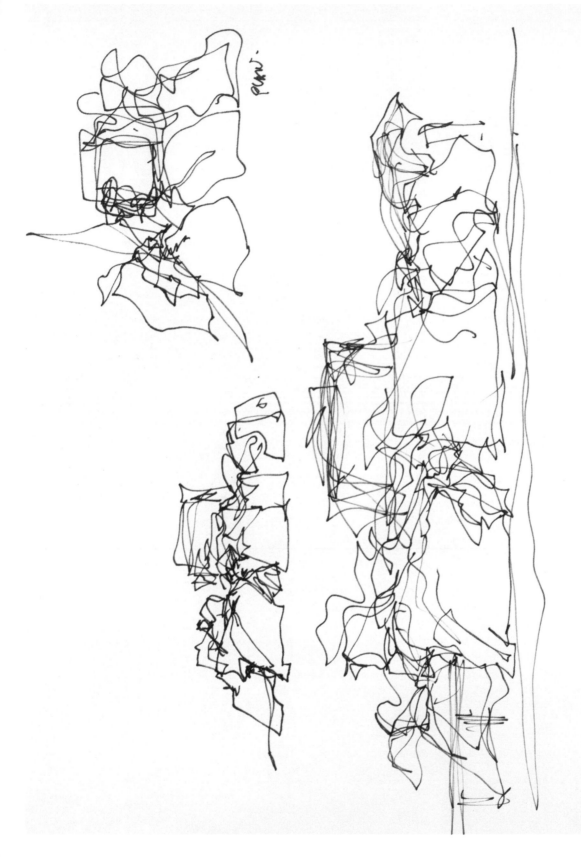

plan.

Gehry, and he

I don't know where you cross the line between architecture and sculpture. For me it is the same, buildings and sculptures are three-dimensional objects. A building has a program, so does a sculpture have a program? In a way it does: the sculptor has an intention that comes from some idiosyncratic idea. FG

M09.03
M09.04
M09.05
M09.06

Gontro 27/4/06

If you go into my background, I have always been interested in a sense of movement, frozen motion, the Shiva figures, the marbles with a sense of movement: the stone is alive, it's not just a dead lump. It's got some action in it. It's a passionate movement and feeling that has come through the centuries. It is true that the crisis of figure and abstraction is a sculptural idea, and I was trying to explore that in buildings for a long time. FG

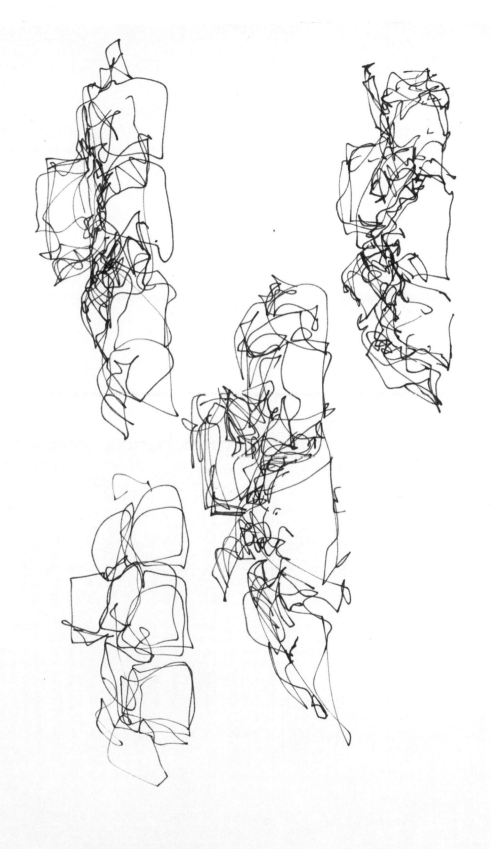

Project 10

Condé Nast Cafeteria
New York, New York
1996–2000

Condé Nast Cafeteria
New York, New York

Design: commenced 1996
Construction: commenced 1998
Status: completed 2000
Number of drawings illustrated: 3

The Condé Nast Cafeteria is located on the fourth floor of the Condé Nast Publications headquarters in New York. This 260-seat space includes a main dining area, a servery, and four private dining rooms.

The main dining area is organized to provide a variety of seating arrangements in an atmosphere that is at once intimate and open. Custom-designed booths that can each accommodate between four and six people are distributed along the perimeter walls. These, clad in perforated blue titanium panels that include a backng to ensure acoustic absorption, undulate in response to the geometry and overall configuration of the booths. Additional booths are located on a raised seating platform that is enclosed within curved glass panels in the center of the main dining area. Freestanding tables and chairs are distributed throughout the main dining area. The floor of the main dining area is an ash-veneer plywood, and the ceiling is clad in perforated blue titanium panels that match the perimeter walls. The servery is adjacent to the main dining area and is designed to compliment its sculptural and aesthetic character.

Located on the same level as the main dining area and the servery, the four private dining rooms are distinct and separate spaces to be used for special lunch meetings and presentations. The walls, floors, and ceilings of the private dining rooms are ash-veneer plywood. Curved glass panels articulate the east wall of each room, providing an even natural light illumination through clerestory windows. Three of the four private dining rooms have moveable partitions, allowing them to be transformed into a variety of spatial configurations for special occasions.

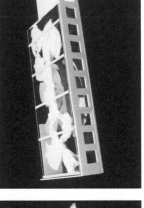

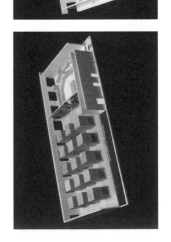

M10.01
04.09.97

M10.02
04.09.97

M10.03
04.09.97

M10.04
04.09.97

204
205

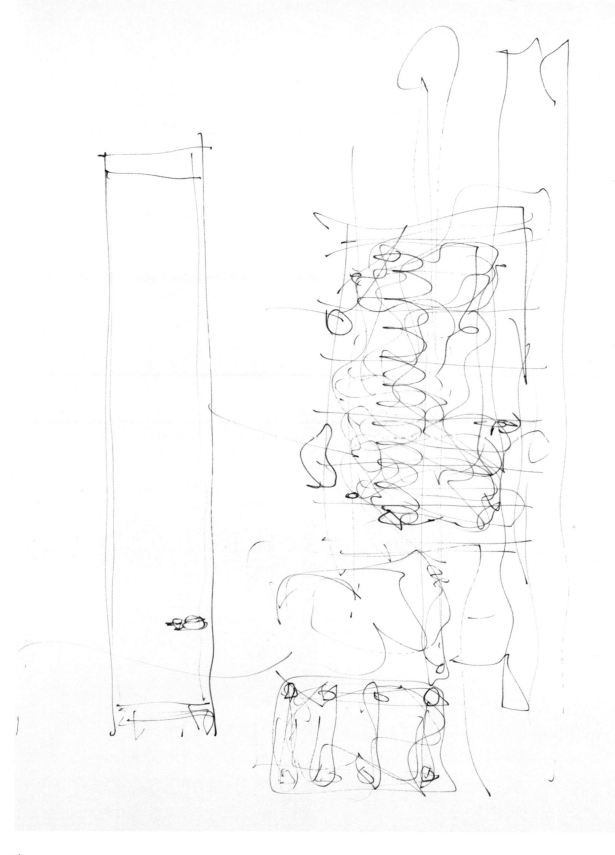

We work with the client a lot. I listen to the client a lot. I spend more time with clients than most people would guess. That is the way we move forward and how they get what they want and feel comfortable about it. It lets them know you're listening to what their problems are. But it also creates opportunities for invention, because it is that interaction that makes the process exciting and rich. And I love the process most of all, the people process—better than the final building, actually. FG

The staff at Condé Nast are very competitive with each other. And part of the idea for the cafeteria design was to try to change the culture of that *without* changing the culture of that. I think the client wanted to create a cafeteria where all the different departments can dine together, feel comfortable dining together, and then maybe interact more and exchange ideas.

We saw the blue titanium while we were working on Bilbao and we've always wanted to use it—it was such a beautiful material. And this cafeteria happened to give us the right excuse to use it. While designing this we were looking at the ceiling of a chapel in Padua painted by Giotto. And the idea of the glass island came about … well, it just came about. It looks like a chunk of ice melted in this ocean of tables. This cafeteria was a good jewel of a project. It brings up these ideas that you've had in the past few years and allows you to test them. Like the curved glass: we'd like to do a whole building exterior like that, but it's too expensive. EC

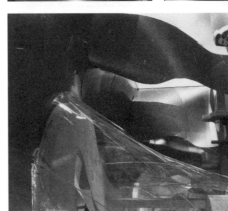

M10.06
08.09.98
M10.07
08.09.98
M10.08
03.15.00

208 | 209

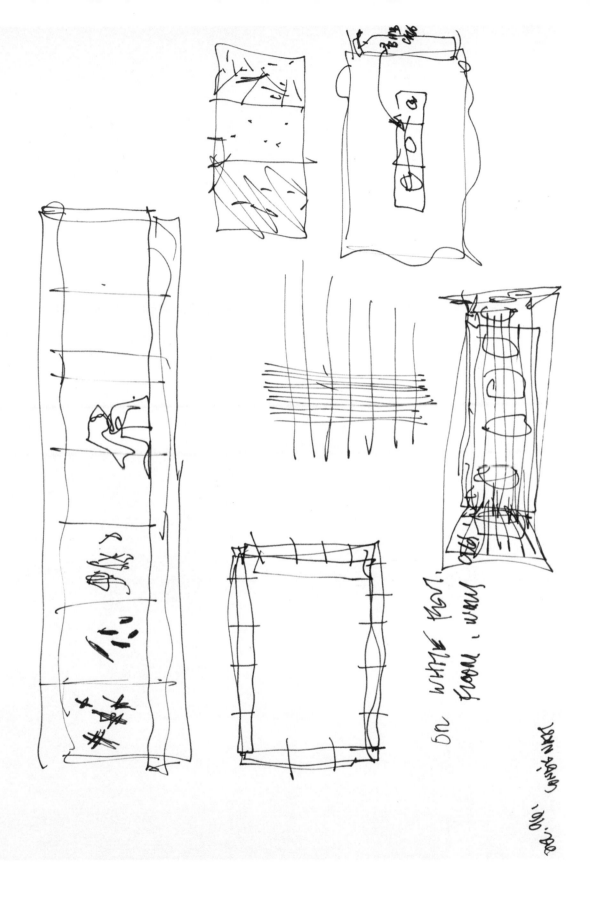

Project 11

DZ Bank Building
Berlin, Germany
1995–2001

DZ Bank Building
Berlin, Germany

Competition: 1995
Design: commenced 1995
Construction: commenced 1996
Status: completion 2001
Number of drawings illustrated: 8

The DZ Bank Building is a mixed-use building comprised of a commercial component housing the Berlin headquarters of DZ Bank and a residential component consisting of 39 apartments. The commercial component of the building is oriented toward Pariser Platz and the Brandenburg Gate, and the residential component is oriented toward Behrenstrasse.

Both the Pariser Platz facade and the Behrenstrasse facade are clad in a buff-colored limestone that matches the Brandenburg Gate. The facades are scaled independently from one another, so that the proportions of both are appropriate to the immediate urban area within which they each exist. The Pariser Platz facade features a series of simple, punched openings and deeply-recessed window bays, allowing the building to blend naturally into the unique urban fabric that is the setting of the Brandenburg Gate.

Behind this relatively restrained facade lies a much less restrained interior. A glass canopy covers the main entry to the building from Pariser Platz. A high-volume foyer immediately inside the main entry offers a view into the building's large interior atrium, which features a curving glass ceiling and a curving glass floor. A wood-clad arcade leads to the office elevator lobbies, which are located on either side of the atrium. Office spaces are organized around the atrium, and are oriented inward to take advantage of the natural light that floods through the glass ceiling. The building's primary conference hall is located within a highly sculptural horse-head-shaped shell in the center of the glass floor of the atrium. Clad in stainless steel on the exterior and wood on the interior, the hall appears to float in the fluid depth of the space. Other conference functions are organized under the glass floor, at the first sub-level, around a generous foyer. It can be combined with the Bank's cafeteria, located under the main glass vault, to create a large space suited for banquets and assemblies.

A second, smaller interior atrium serves the residential component of the project. This atrium allows natural light to enter both sides of each apartment. A reflecting pool at the bottom of the atrium adds a dynamic quality to the light, best seen from the residential area. The apartments vary in size, from studios to maisonettes occupying the top two floors.

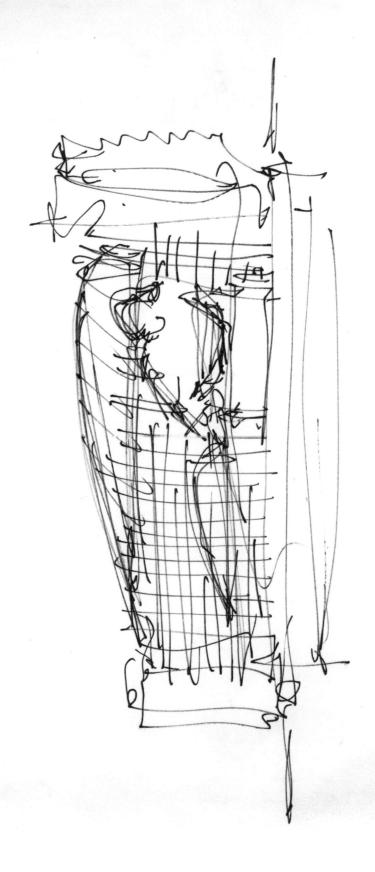

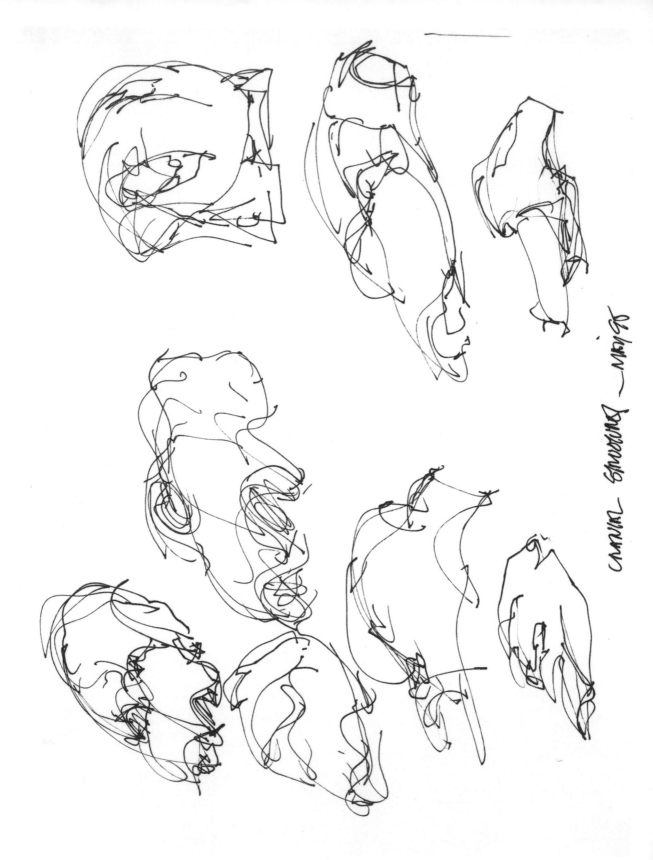

CANVAS DRAWINGS — Shein

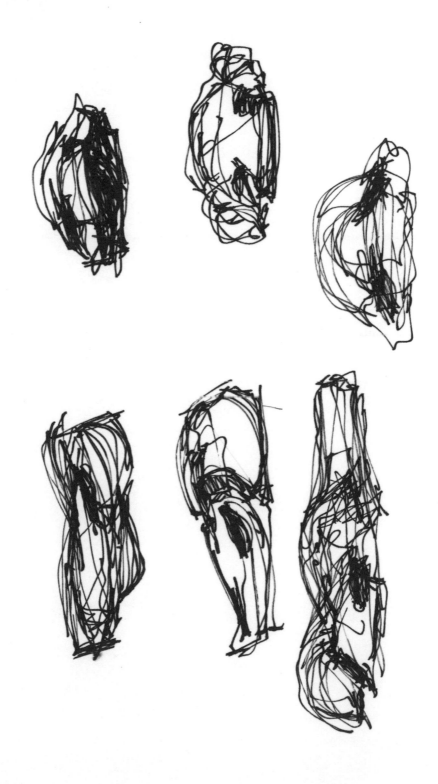

27 JUNE '96.

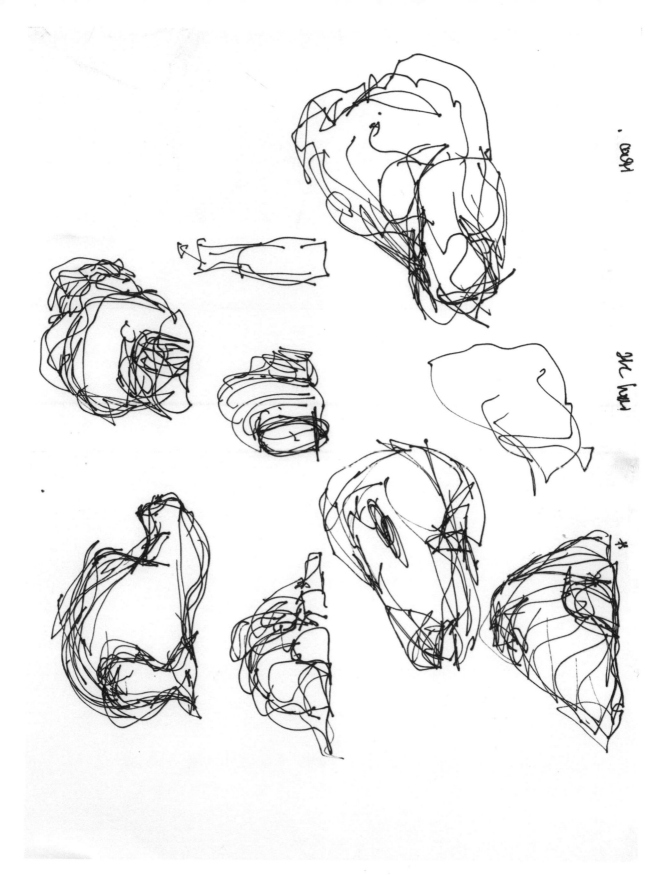

I've honed and spent time developing my visual intellect. But I don't sit down and say, "OK, I'm going to hone my visual intellect." I spend a lot of time looking. Looking at the space between objects. I used to sit and just fantasize about cities. That is something you can do all day long. And I have a good visual memory. FC

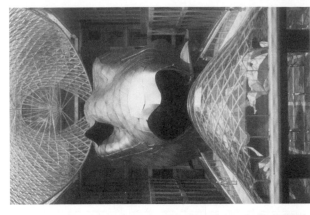

M11.05
M11.06
03.15.96
M11.07
1998
M11.08
1998

218
219

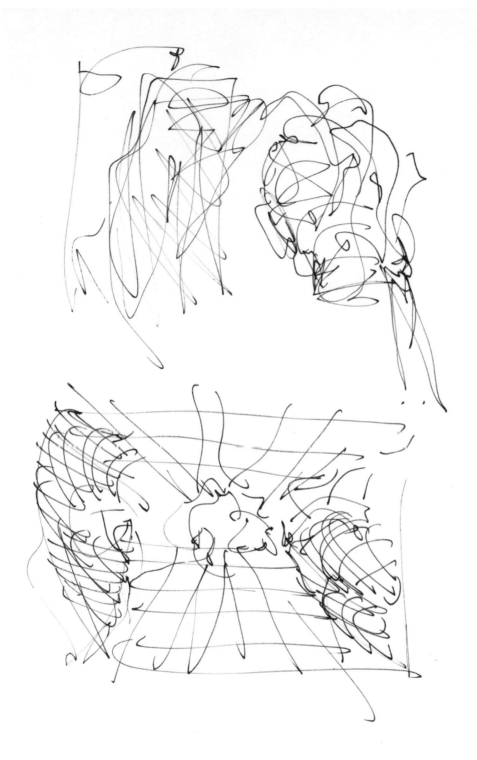

Goum '96

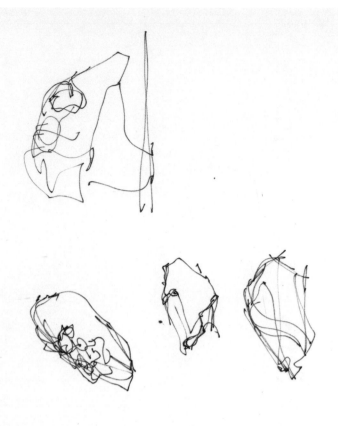

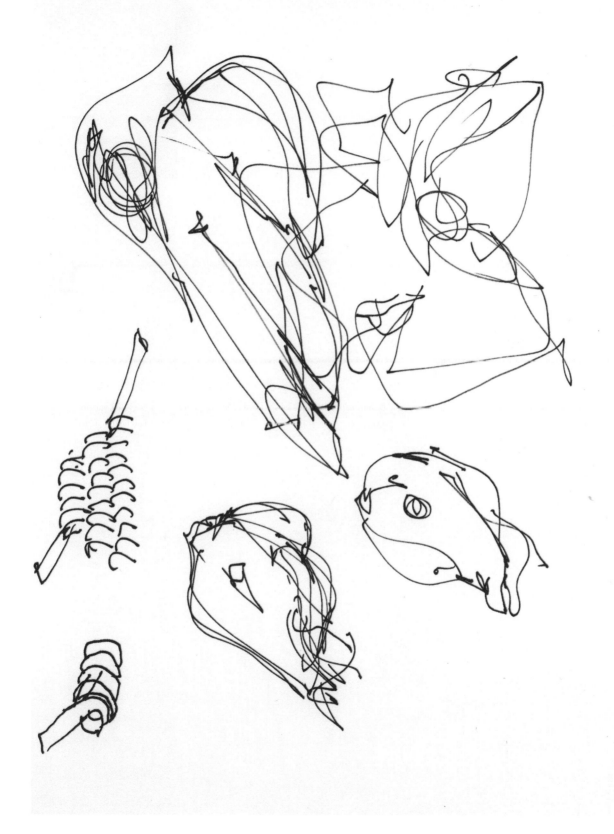

Haro. 09

M11.10
1997

M11.11
1998

M11.12
1998

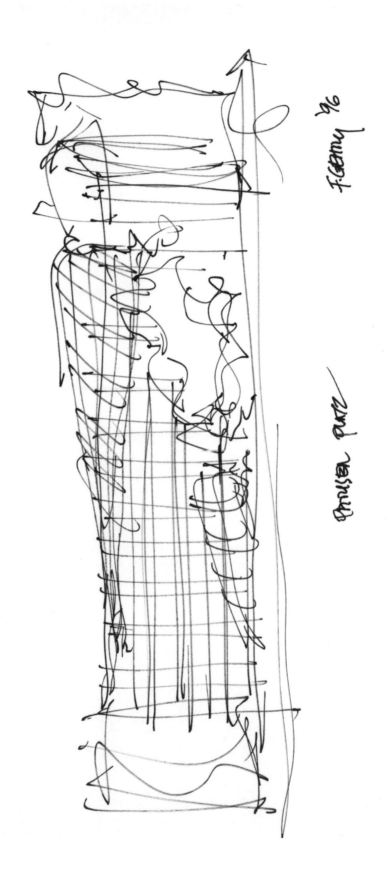

F. Gehry '96

Brunista Platz

Project 12

Peter B. Lewis Building

Weatherhead School of Management, Case Western Reserve University, Cleveland, Ohio 1997–2002

Peter B. Lewis Building
Weatherhead School of Management,
Case Western Reserve University,
Cleveland, Ohio

Design: commenced 1996
Construction: commenced 1999
Status: completed 2002
Number of drawings illustrated: 2

The Peter B. Lewis Building provides
administrative and educational facilities
in a series of predominantly rectilinear
blocks that collectively form a U-shaped
perimeter with an internal courtyard at the
center. The four largest classrooms are
located within the internal courtyard,
where they are articulated as two sculptural towers rising through the center of
the building. This organizational strategy
creates a canyon-like atrium in the space
between the perimeter blocks and the
classroom towers. Additional student-
oriented facilities, including classrooms,
student meeting rooms, study rooms,
and a café, are distributed along the
edges of the atrium on the lower levels
of the building, animating the atrium
and encouraging interaction between
faculty and students.

The perimeter blocks are clad in red brick,
reinforcing the relationship between the
building and the surrounding campus.
The classroom towers are expressed as
two cascading sculptural forms clad in
stainless steel.

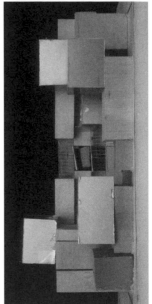

M12.01
M12.02

cast, 'g' – ott,

M12.03
M12.04
M12.05
M12.06
M12.07
M12.08
M12.09

CR/version. June 6/91

Project 13

The Richard B. Fisher Center for the Performing Arts

Bard College, Annandale-on-Hudson, New York

1997–2003

The Richard B. Fisher Center for the Performing Arts
Bard College, Annandale-on-Hudson, New York

Design: commenced 1997
Construction: commenced 2000
Status: completed 2003
Number of drawings illustrated: 5

Located in a beautiful area of tall trees and open lawns on the Bard College campus, the Fisher Center provides spaces for dance, drama, opera, and music performances arranged around two multi-purpose theaters. Seating in the larger theater can be configured to accommodate anything between 400 and 920 people depending on the nature of an event and the degree of intimacy required. In the smaller theater, which is generally used for teaching and student performances, the seating can be removed altogether in order to create a large open space.

Given the range of events that it must accommodate, flexibility is a key element of the building's design. While the high ceiling and overall shape of the large theater provide characteristics that are excellent for all performance types, a wood concert shell and forestage lift allow conversion for symphonic music performances. The house walls are concrete, providing the mass necessary for excellent acoustical reflections.

Although much of the building is designed to meet functional requirements, its most dramatic element—the sail-like canopy that projects out over the box office and lobby before the large theater—is the result of more esthetic concerns. The highly sculptural exterior of the large theater responds to its internal organization. The stainless-steel panels loosely wrap around the sides of the theater toward the proscenium, creating two tall, sky-lit gathering areas on either side of the main lobby. They then flare out at the proscenium, to make a collar-like shape that rests on the simple concrete and plaster form of the stage house. The structure supporting the canopy and the collar-like shape is exposed and visible from within the main lobby. A soft, brushed stainless steel was selected for the exterior cladding because of the material's ability to reflect the light and colors of the sky and the surrounding landscape.

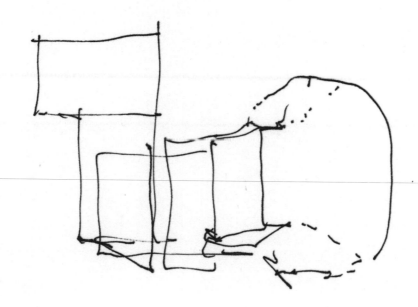

There is a misconception about my work—that I just make shapes and there is no inside. I don't know how people see or get that idea. It looks like we're tearing up paper to make models, and I just roll up the paper and throw it all out. It's not like that. It is much more precise and careful. We work from the inside out, mostly. What's more, as someone very involved with sculpture and art and dance and music—those things are part of my life—I take my nourishment from them. FG

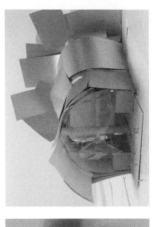

M13.02
09.18.97

M13.03
09.19.97

234
—
235

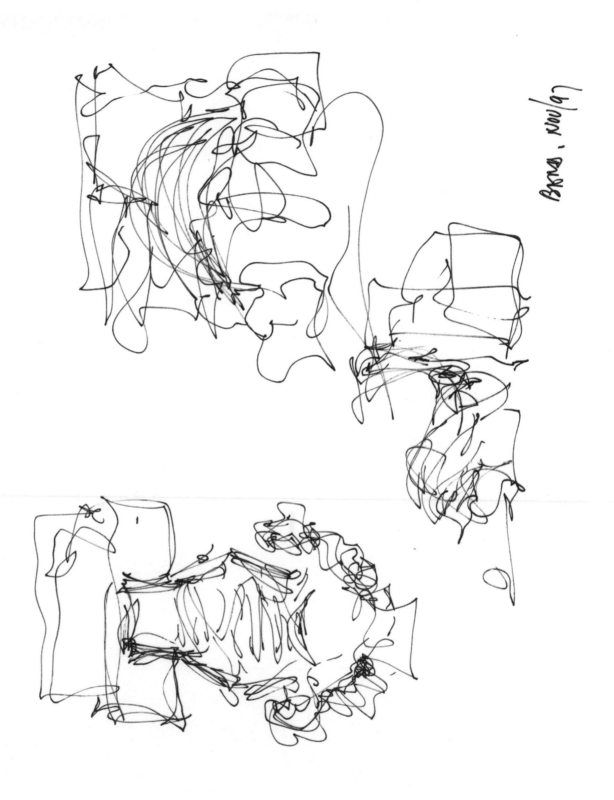

Barus, revl/a

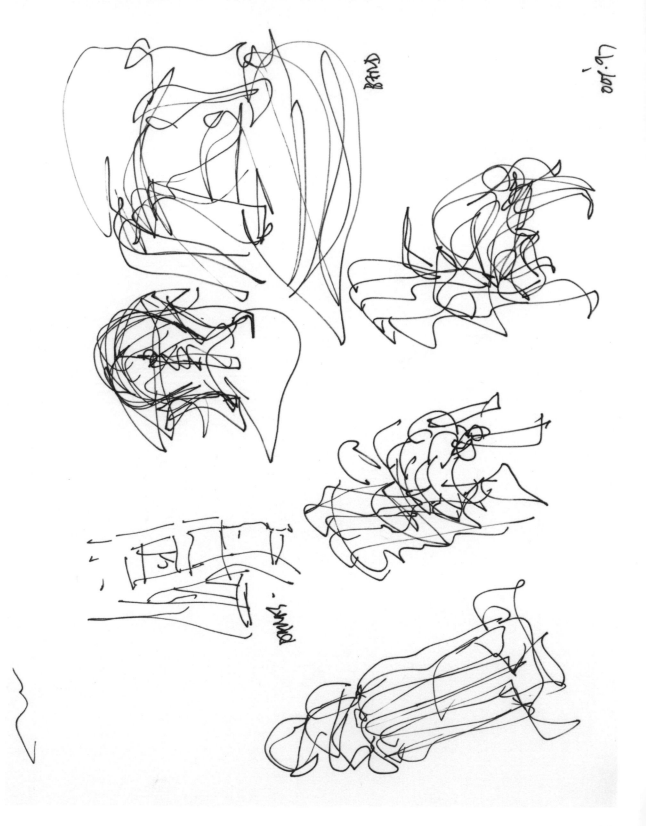

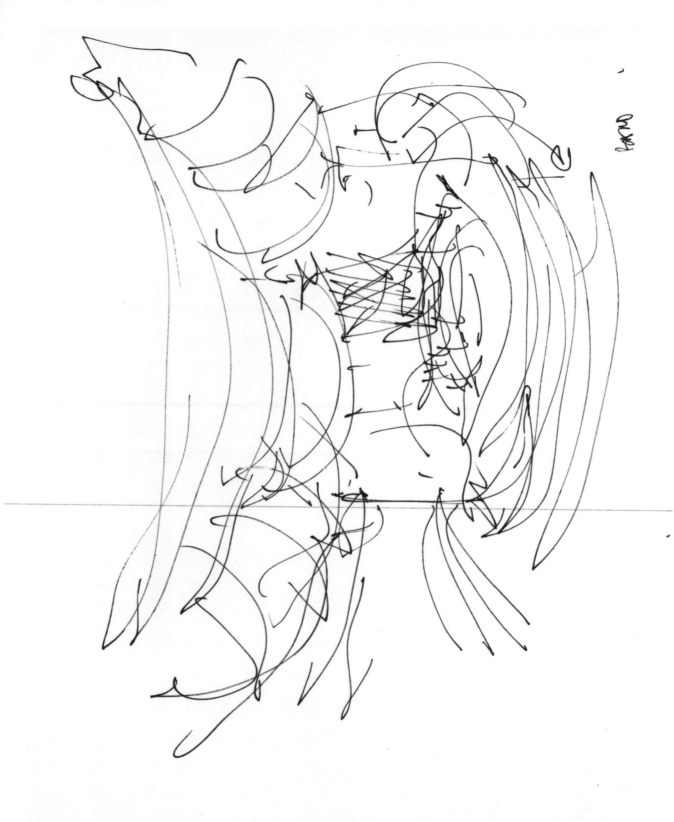

M13.04
01.14.98

M13.05
01.18.00

M13.06
01.14.98

M13.07
04.26.99

M13.08
01.12.00

238
239

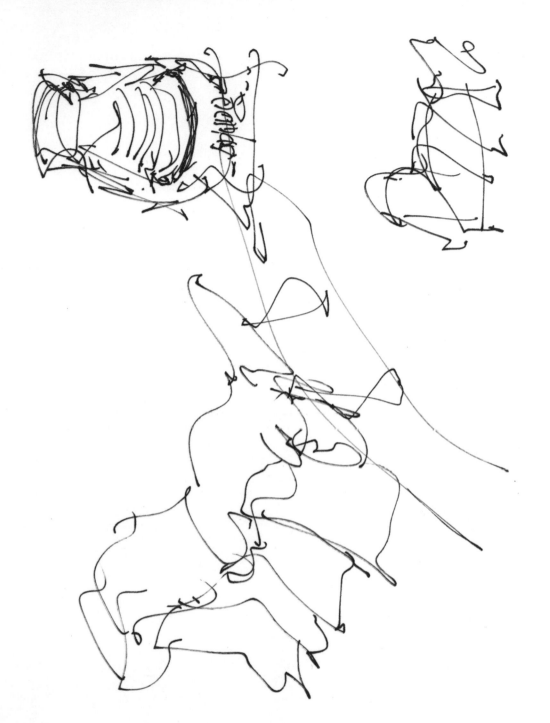

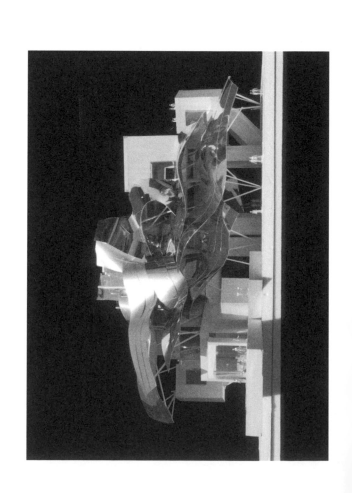

Project 14

Hotel at Marques de Riscal

Elciego (Alava), Spain

1999–

Hotel at Marques de Riscal
Elciego (Alava), Spain

Design: commenced 1999
Construction: commenced 2003
Status: expected completion 2006
Number of drawings illustrated: 8

Located in Elciego, in the Rioja, the winery of Vinos Herederos del Marques de Riscal is one of the oldest in the region. Although traditional Rioja wineries are not open to the public, Marques de Riscal commissioned the design of a small building that would provide a unique visitor experience as part of a plan to redefine and invigorate its public image.

The building is approached through vineyards and the winery's nineteenth-century production facilities. It is raised on columns, in order to create a small entry plaza and to take advantage of the breathtaking views of the vineyards, the San Andres Church, and the surrounding town and region.

The entry plaza leads to a reception area and a bar set along the edge of a small area of the vineyards. An outdoor terrace leads to a pool, while a covered walkway extending from the building allows visitors to experience the views. Distributed throughout the three upper levels of the building are fourteen guest bedrooms, a wine-tasting room, a 172-seat restaurant, a private dining room, and outdoor dining terraces, as well as conference facilities.

The exterior of the building consists fundamentally of a series of rectilinear elements clad in Spanish limestone and a series of curvilinear elements clad in gold and pale pink titanium panels, and in mirror-finish stainless-steel panels.

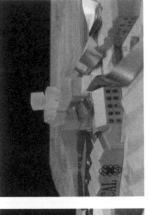

M14.01
03.11.99

M14.02
04.20.99

M14.03
07.02.99

Imagine an octopus 2.2.xx

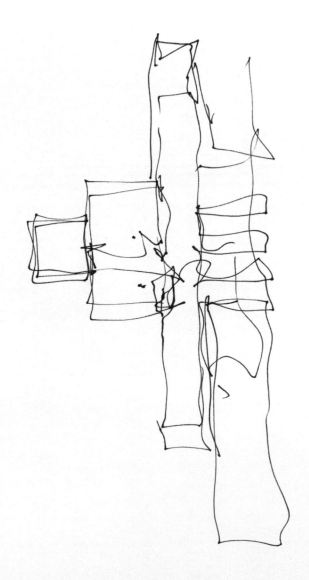

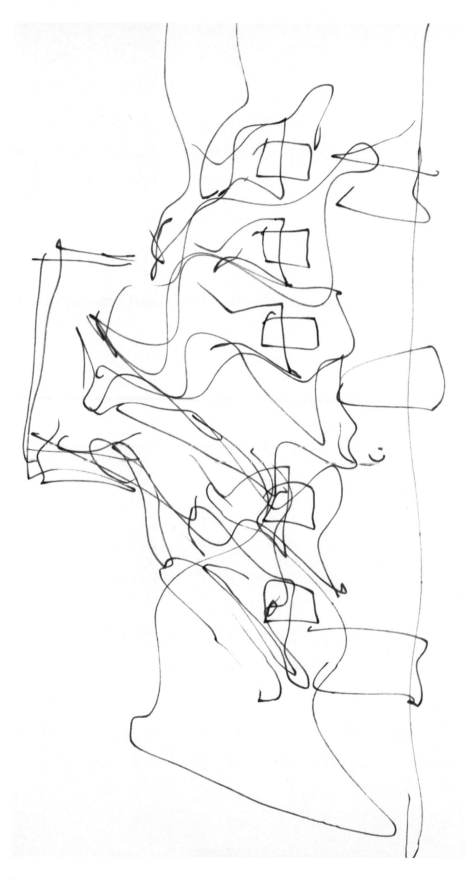

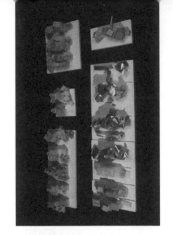

M14.04
07.02.99

M14.05
07.02.99

M14.06
07.29.99

246
———
247

Basan '98

MARQUIS DE DELAM Apr. 99

I spend a lot of time selecting the materials, the details, and the way a project is going to be built: the expression. It's about the feeling, the perception of the building as a sensibility. If you want to be involved with the visual world and make things that are visual, then you have to look at everything. I spend all my time looking at things and learning about them. There was a period when I used to look into my wastepaper basket and fantasize buildings and forms. FG

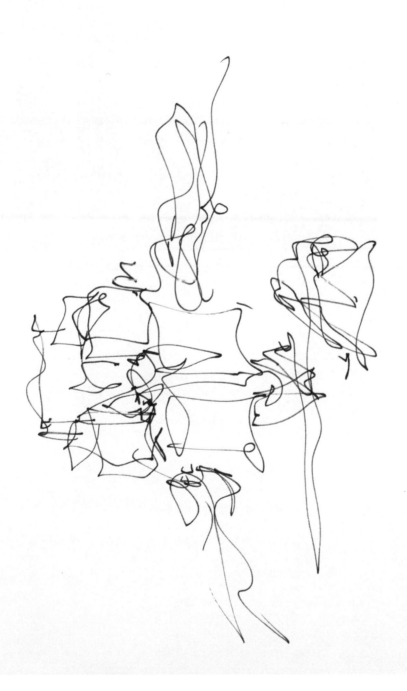

working at drawing for ten.

D14.07

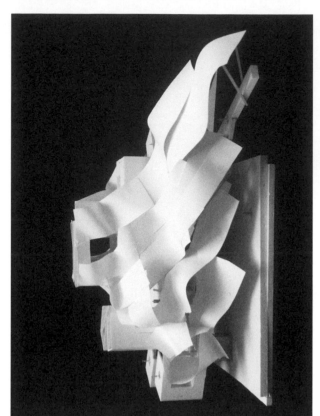

M14.10
02.14.00

M14.11
04.17.00

M14.12
04.17.00

252
253

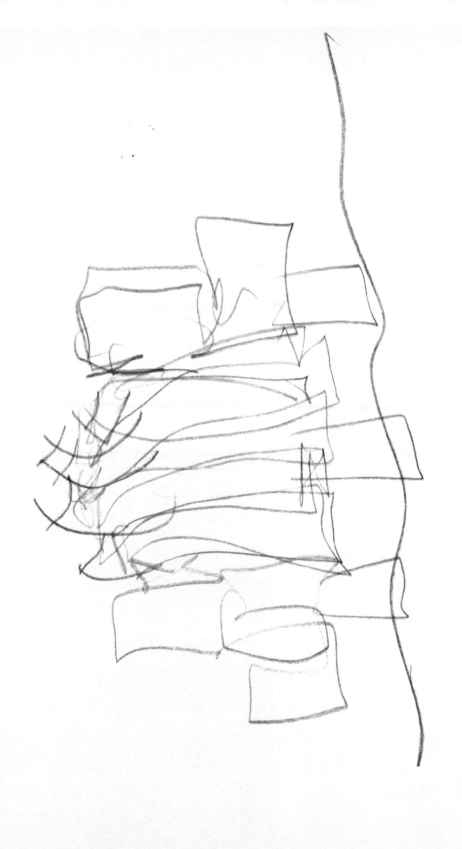

Project 15

Le Clos Jordanne

Lincoln, Ontario

1999—

Le Clos Jordanne
Lincoln, Ontario, Canada

Design: commenced 1999
Construction: not yet commenced
Status: in development
Number of drawings illustrated: 12

The site for Le Clos Jordanne winery is located near the town of Lincoln, in the Niagara Escarpment region of Ontario, Canada.

The project is intended to provide fully operational wine-making facilities for the production of red and white wines, and to provide a thoroughly unique, educational, and enjoyable experience for visitors. Facilities required for the wine-making process, including areas for grape receiving, grape crushing and destemming, pressing, fermentation, and barrel aging, are organized around a central atrium from which each of the areas is clearly visible. A tour route for visitors follows the wine-making process through each stage. A glass-enclosed dining room located within the red wine cellar and visible from the atrium creates a unique and dramatic area for dining or special events.

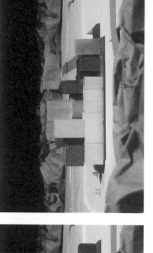

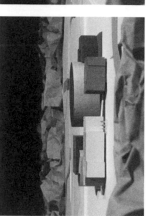

M15.01
02.10.00

M15.02
02.10.00

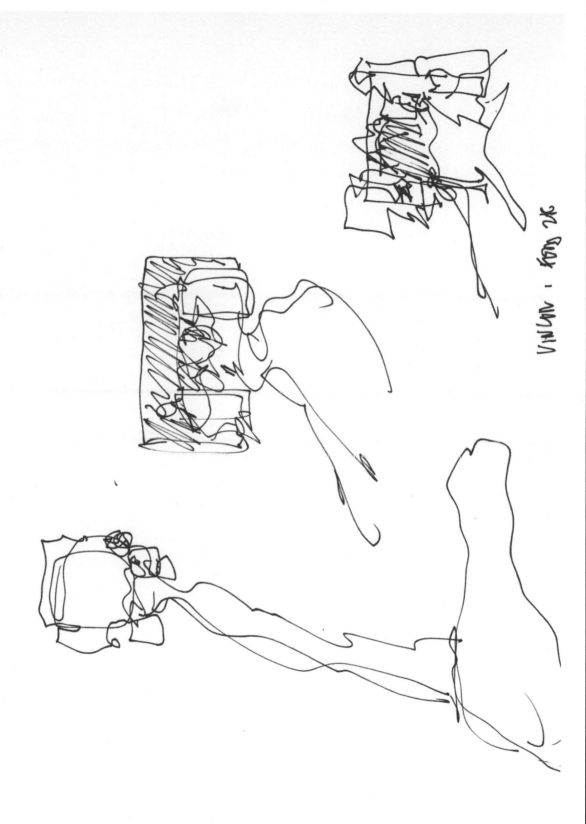

M15.03
03.09.00

M15.04
03.09.00

258
___
259

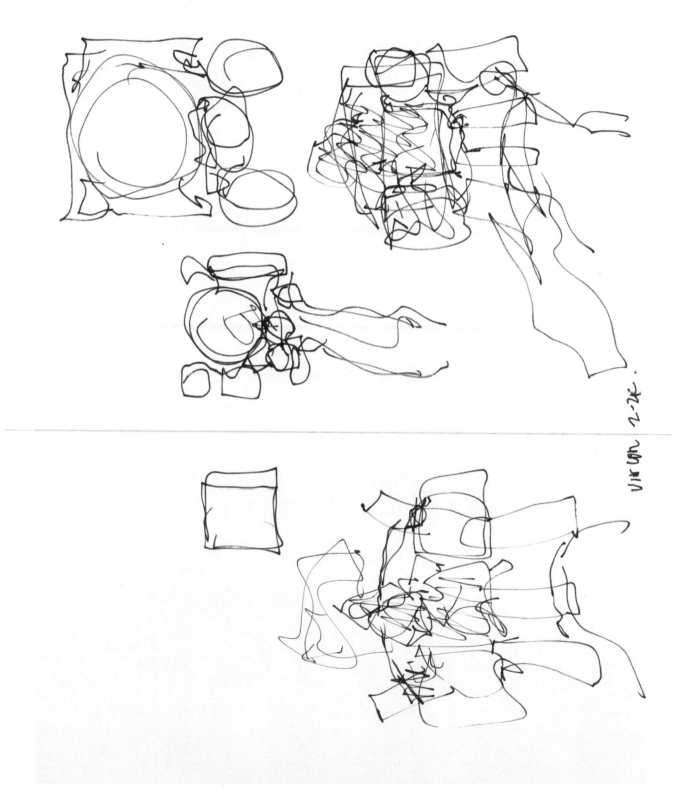

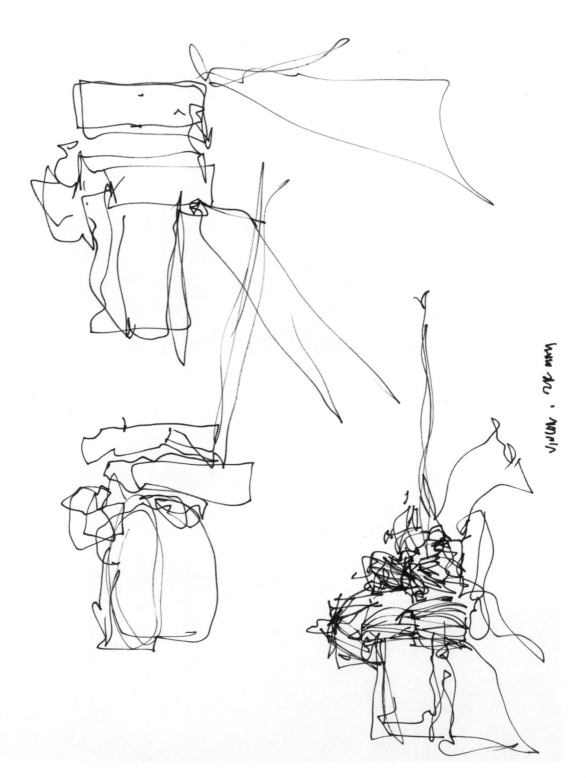

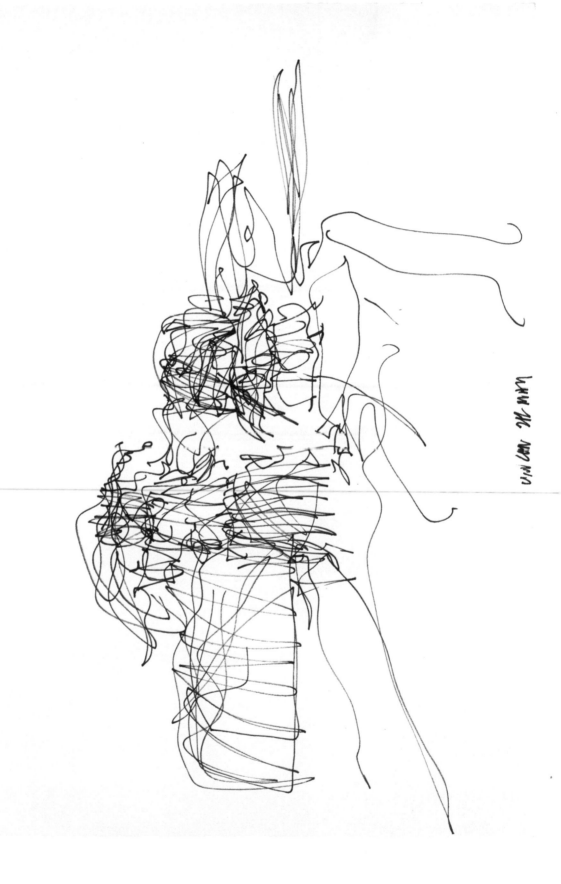

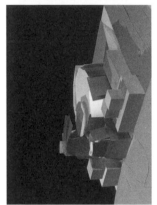

M15.05
05.08.00

M15.06
05.08.00

M15.07
05.08.00

262 | 263

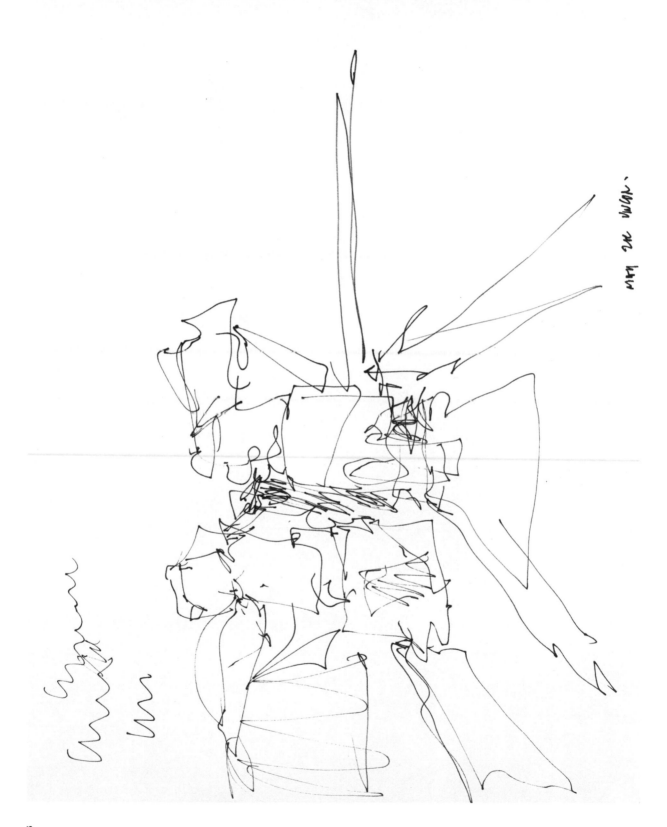

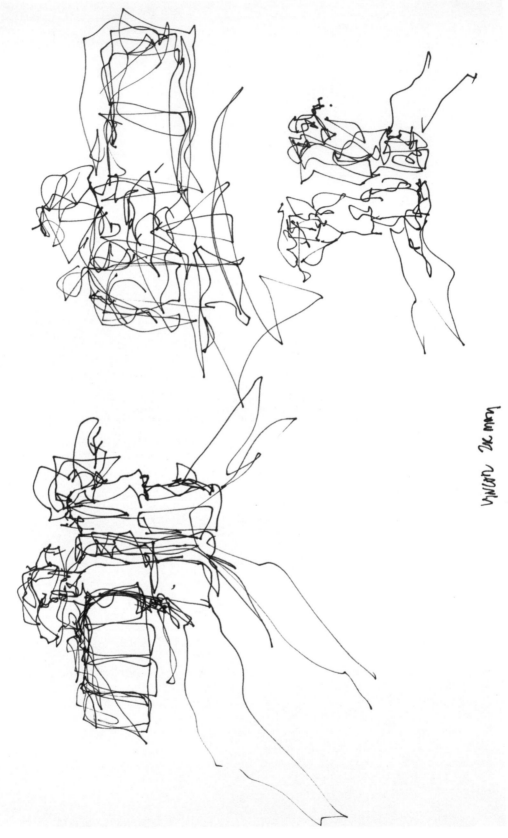

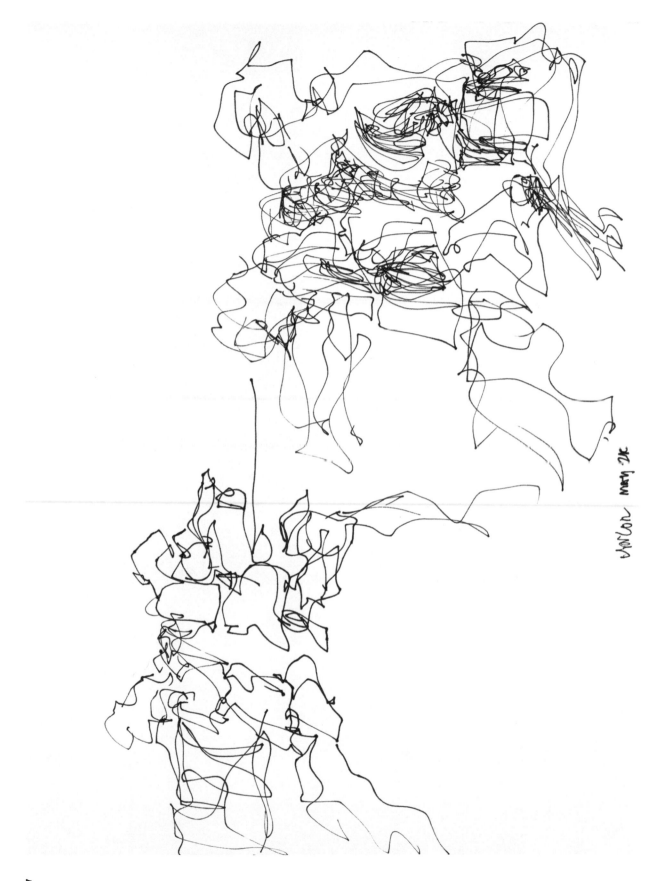

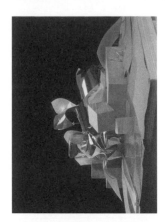

M15.08
05.08.00

M15.09
05.08.00

266
267

D15.08

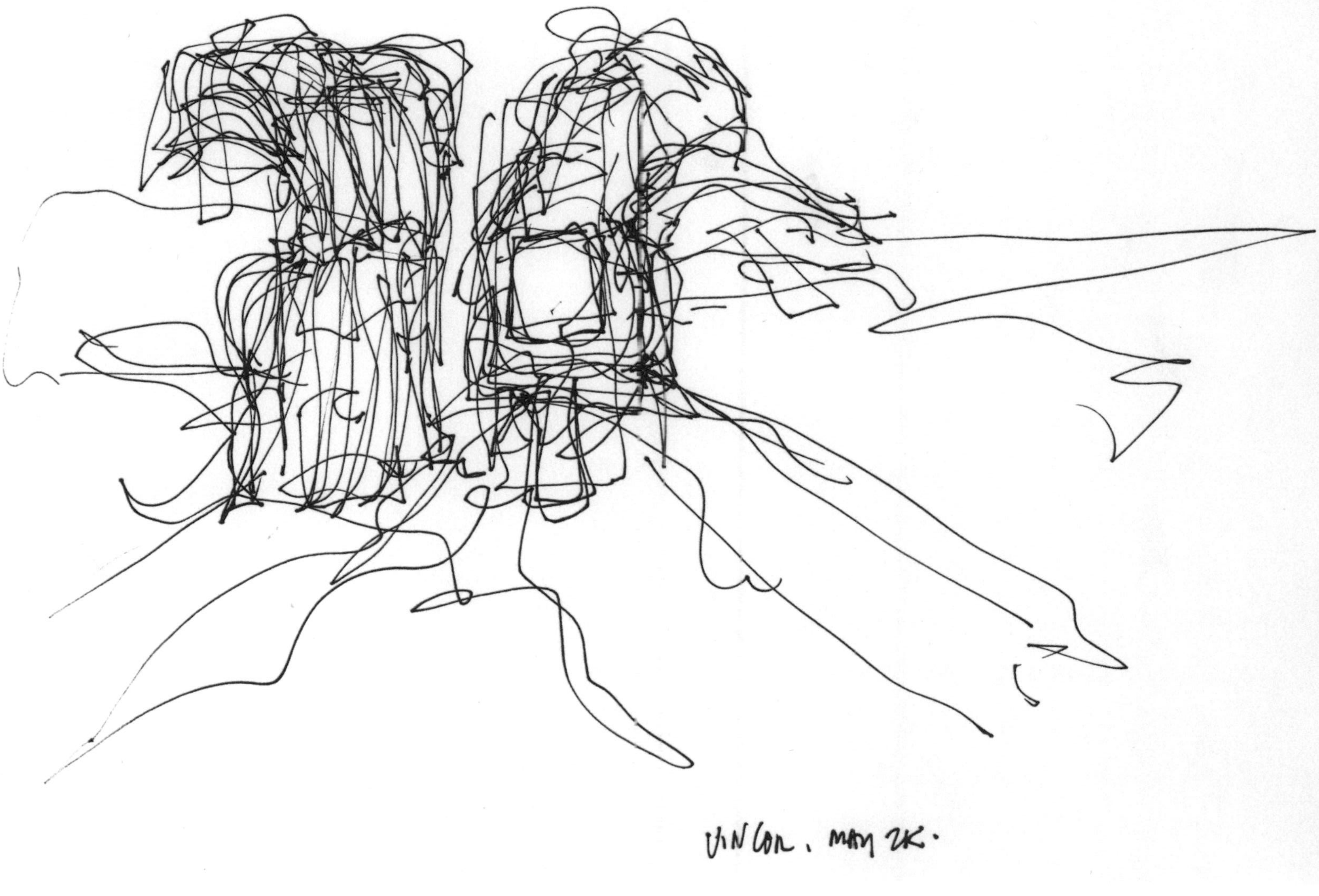

I always work on things in sets, like some of my artist friends who work in series. In architecture, though, it takes a longer time. FG

VINCN dkn 2001

unknown / 2001

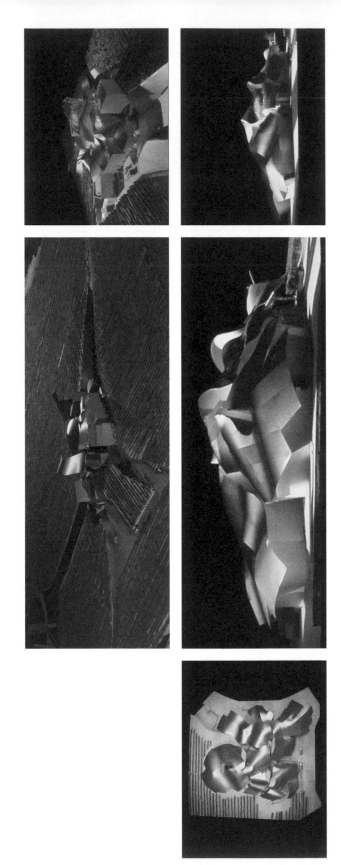

M15.10
07.26.00

M15.11
07.26.00

M15.12
08.02

M15.13
08.02

M15.14
08.02

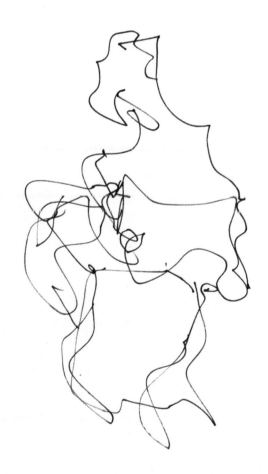

Vivian. omv/2001

Project 16

Maggie's Centre
Ninewalls NHS Hospital,
Dundee, Scotland
1999–2003

Maggie's Centre
Ninewalls NHS Hospital,
Dundee, Scotland

Design: commenced 1999
Construction: commenced 2001
Status: completed 2003
Number of drawings illustrated: 12

Maggie's Centre in Dundee is Gehry's first building in the UK and one of a series of small cancer care centers pioneered by his close friend Maggie Keswick Jencks, who died of breast cancer in 1995. The architecture aims at complementing the purpose of the building by working with the surrounding landscape to provide an environment of tranquility and calm.

The center occupies 2,150 square feet and includes a communal therapy room, a kitchen, an information area, and a circular library. A staircase leads to a more private room above, offering views out over the Tay estuary. The final design is based around two key elements, a tower, inspired by lighthouses, and an asymmetrically folded roof, based on the shawl worn by a woman in a portrait by Vermeer that Gehry had seen with Maggie. The roof itself is constructed of Finnish pine and laminated plywood, and covered with stainless-steel shingles.

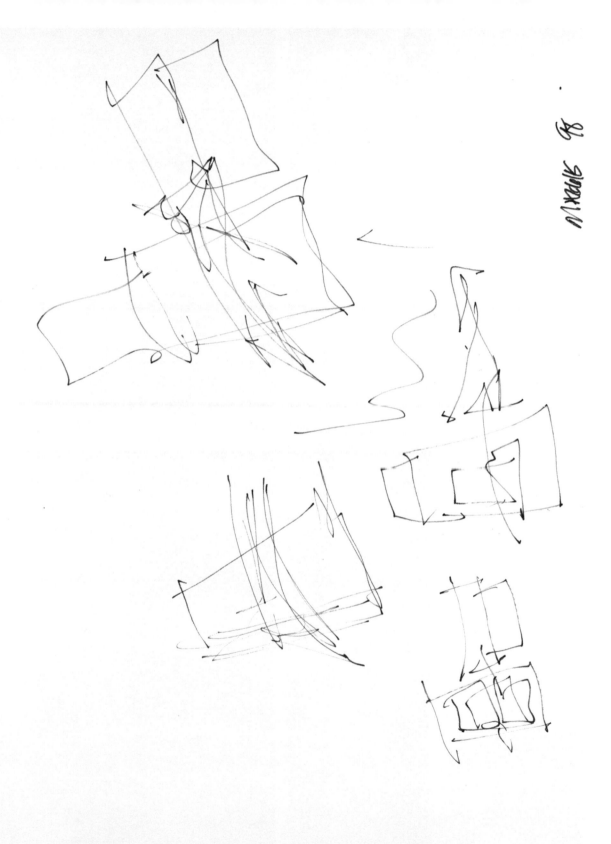

M16.01
04.13.99

M16.02
04.13.99

M16.03
04.13.99

M16.04
04.13.99

M16.05
08.11.99

M16.06
08.19.99

278
279

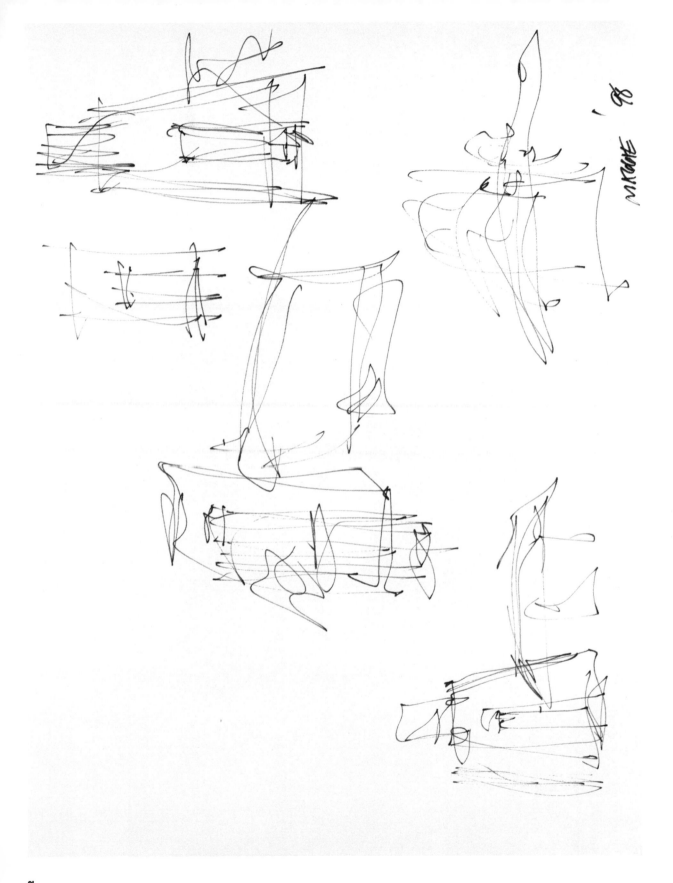

For some projects Frank doesn't really draw that much. There might be a lot more happening on the models. Frank makes a lot of these drawings on airplanes, flying to different projects, and if he's not travelling for a little while then maybe drawings don't get done. Hard to say. I don't see a lot of the drawings. I don't really know how much Frank has been drawing at any given time. Sometimes I'll ask Frank to see the drawings for a particular job and all these drawings come out that I never saw before. How few or many

drawings Frank produces might also have something to do with how quickly Frank "gets" a project design, or how complex a project is. If he's struggling with the design then we might make model after model and he'll draw like mad. If Frank "gets" it right away then maybe he'll go straight to making models and skip the drawings altogether. Like Maggie's Centre, for instance. Frank's instruction was verbal. He got it straight away. He said take this Vermeer painting and make a model of it. cw

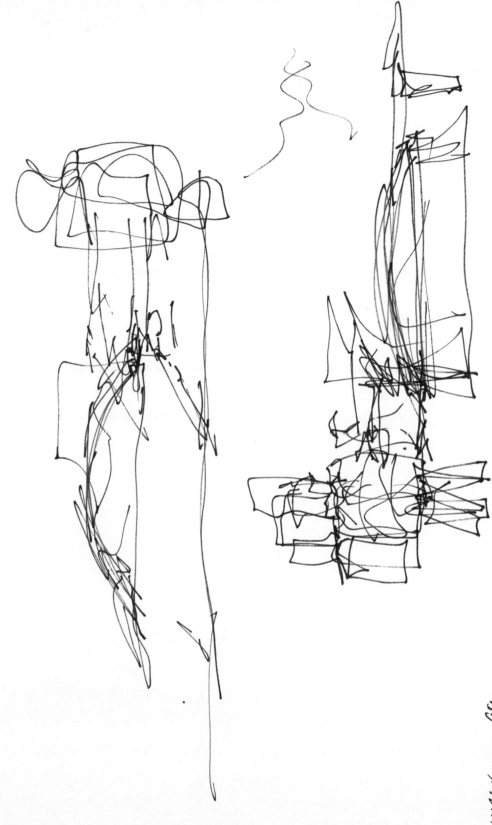

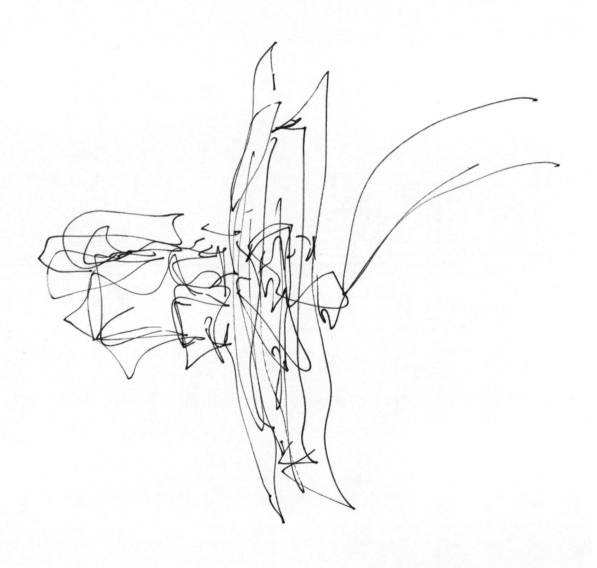

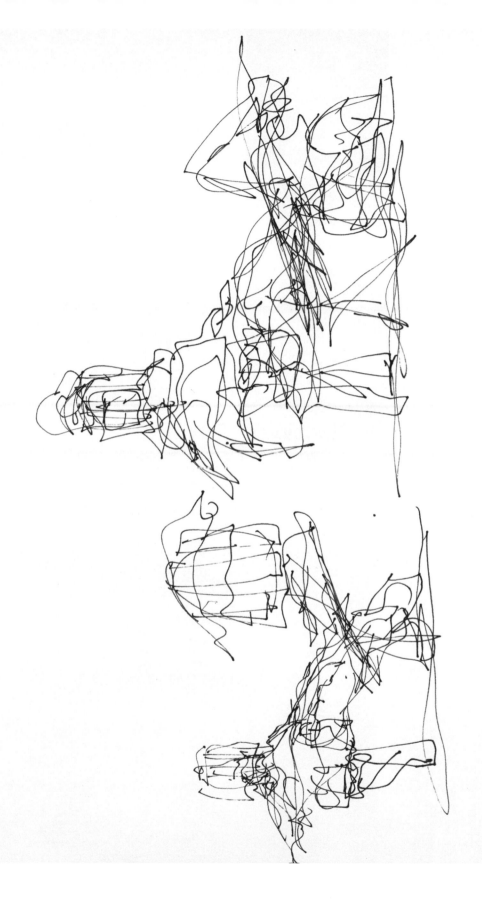

MAGGIE . AUG '99

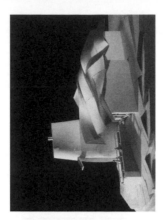

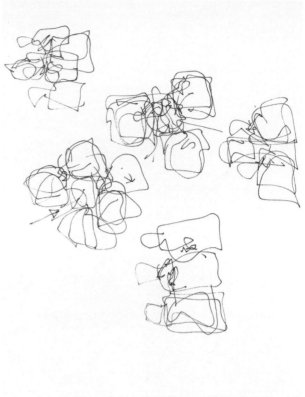

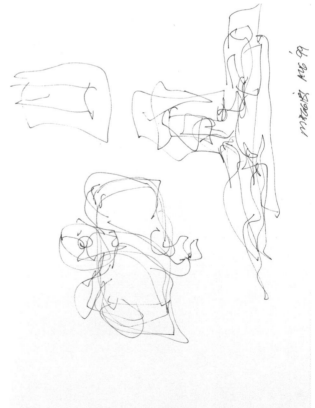

M16.07
12.01.99

M16.08
12.01.99

D16.06

D16.07

284
___
285

MARGOT ~ Malaga

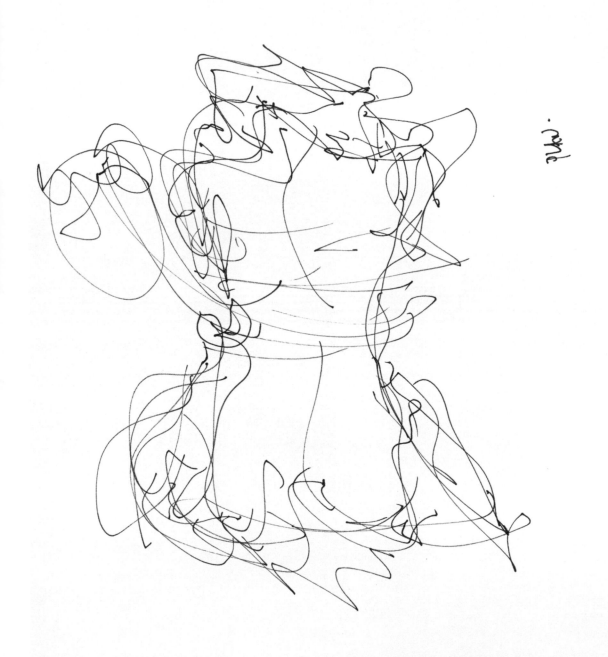

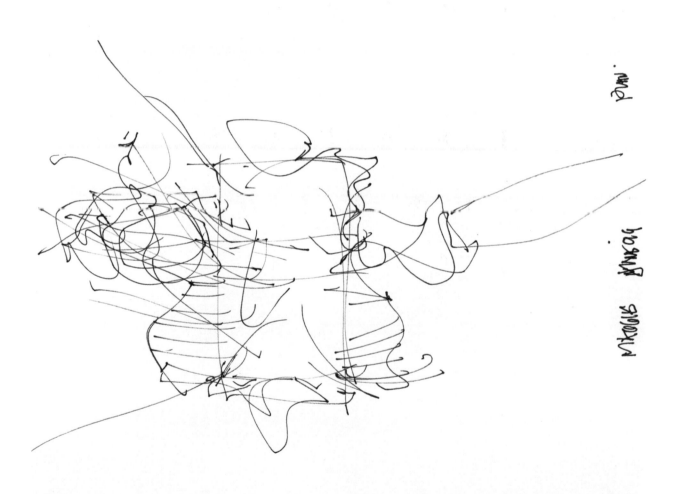

Painting and sculpture can engage you emotionally, and architecture has the potential for doing it when it's done with that intention. But there is so much stuff to hide behind, such as function and context. How do I make it? We are really struggling here, but that is the kind of detailing I do, and that is different from the way other architects work. I don't know if that's better or worse. It's just different. FG

MATGOK - MAY 94

Samsung Museum of Modern Art

Seoul, Korea
1995–1997

Samsung Museum of Modern Art
Seoul, Korea

Design: commenced 1995
Status: unbuilt (project terminated 1997)
Number of drawings illustrated: 2

This proposal for the Samsung Museum of Modern Art was for a building that would house collections of traditional Korean art as well as contemporary art from both Korea and Europe. It was to be located between an ancient imperial palace, a university, several office buildings, and a main road on an irregular L-shaped site in the congested Un-Ni Dong district of Seoul.

The concept of a spiral of galleries, starting low in the ground and growing into a continuous spiral, stepping gently vertically around a central square to the highest point in the museum, 200 feet above the ground, was developed in order to supply natural light to all of the galleries of this high-rise museum while complying with strict, local zoning requirements.

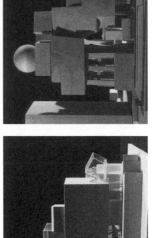

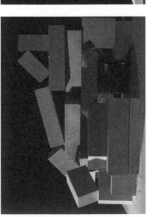

M17.01
07.07.95

M17.02

M17.03

M17.04
11.06.95

When I start a project, I inform myself a lot about the project requirements and the people involved. And then I work in the models—trying things, trying forms, looking. I try something and I take it off, then I try it again, and the work slowly evolves, a piece at a time. If I too consciously premeditate, I don't enjoy it. I don't find it as exciting, and the end result isn't as good. Sometimes when I'm presenting a project I don't know where I'm going beyond a certain point. FG

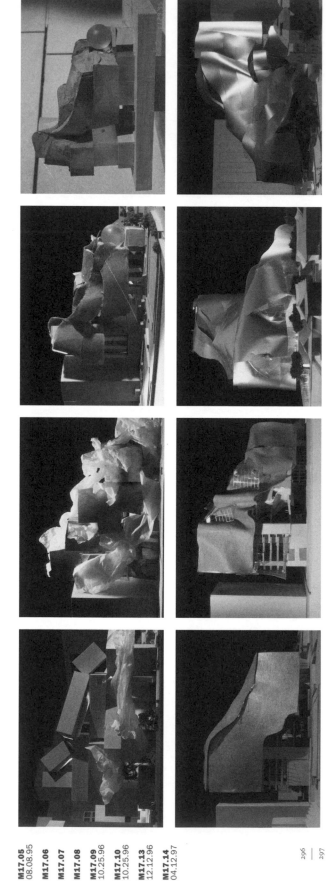

M17.05 08.08.95
M17.06
M17.07
M17.08
M17.09 10.25.96
M17.10 10.25.96
M17.13 12.12.96
M17.14 04.12.97

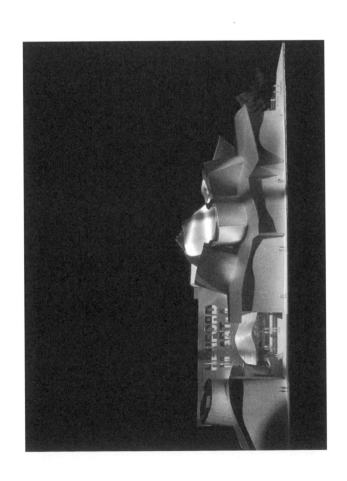

MARTa Herford
Herford, Germany
1998–

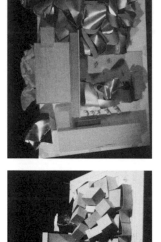

MARTa Herford
Herford, Germany

Design: commenced 1998
Construction: commenced 2001
Status: expected completion 2004/2005
Number of drawings illustrated: 2

The MARTa Herford provides galleries for the exhibition of art, furniture, and architecture. The fundamental design strategy involves the incorporation of a fragment of an existing industrial building into new buildings located to its south and north. In this way, the existing building, with its original character maintained, becomes the centerpiece of the new museum complex. The exterior of the new buildings will be clad in brick and stainless steel.

Visitors enter the complex through a new, central, entry plaza that is flanked on both sides by the new buildings. The existing building consists of 37,000 square feet and includes the lobby for the complex and a store on the ground level, as well as galleries and a furniture and design exhibition area on the upper levels. The building to the south includes a cluster of smaller galleries providing 8,000 square feet of multipurpose exhibition space surrounding a larger gallery providing an additional 4,800 square feet of multi-purpose exhibition space. The building to the north includes a gallery of 3,700 square feet devoted primarily to furniture design but which is also available to fulfill multiple exhibition and event uses. A restaurant located at the south–east corner of the complex overlooks a gentle bend in a river adjacent to the site.

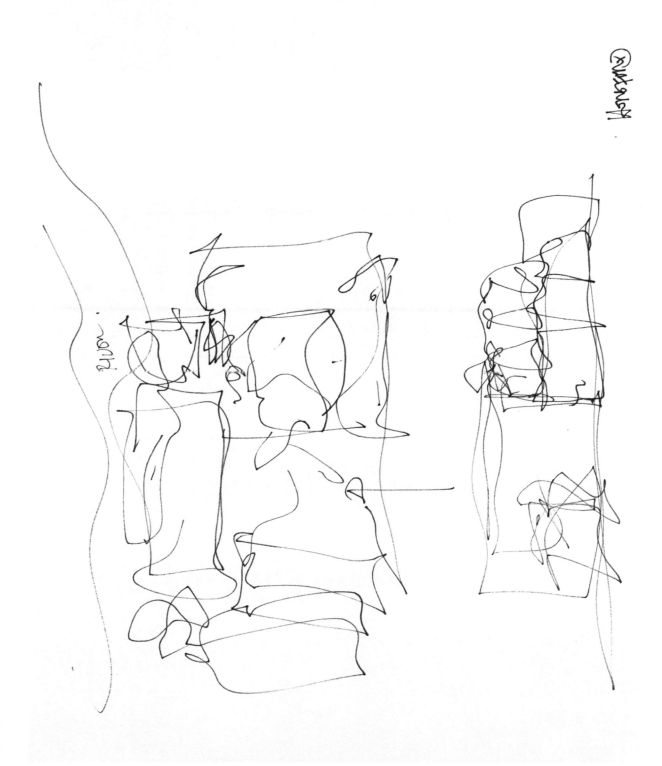

Project 19

Walt Disney Concert Hall

Los Angeles, California

1987–2003

Walt Disney Concert Hall
Los Angeles, California

Design: commenced 1987
Construction: commenced 1999
Status: completed 2003
Number of drawings illustrated: 48

Located on a historically and culturally prominent site in downtown Los Angeles adjacent to the Music Center of Los Angeles County, the Walt Disney Concert Hall serves as the permanent home of the Los Angeles Philharmonic. The majority of the site is devoted to gardens, accessible not only from the concert hall itself but from adjacent streets as well. The concert hall lobby is accessible from the street and remains open during the day; large operable glass panels provide maximum accessibility to various amenities including a gift shop, a restaurant and café, an underground parking garage, and a pre-concert performance space, which will be used for performance-related lectures, educational programs, and other scheduled and impromptu performances throughout the day.

The focus of the design is the 2,265-seat main concert hall, whose interior and form are a direct expression of acoustical parameters. Seating surrounds the orchestra platform. The wood walls and the sail-like wooden ceiling forms give one the impression of being within a great ship inside the walls of the hall. A pipe organ designed in conjunction with the interiors occupies a central position between the seating blocks at stage rear. Skylights and a large window at the rear of the hall allow natural light to enhance daytime concerts.

The exterior of the concert hall is clad in stainless-steel panels. The building's orientation, combined with the curving and folding exterior walls, present highly sculptural compositions as viewers move along adjacent streets and through the surrounding gardens and plazas. An extensive backstage technical area surrounds the concert hall and opens onto a private garden for musicians. The Roy and Edna Disney 250-seat multi-use theater for California Institute of the Arts (CalArts) programs is included in the base of the building with direct street access surrounding streets. This facility, together with its separate lobby, art gallery, and café, is a major venue for CalArts in the city of Los Angeles. A 2,500-car garage on six levels is located below ground with access from three surrounding streets.

M19.01
11.98

M19.02
11.98

306
307

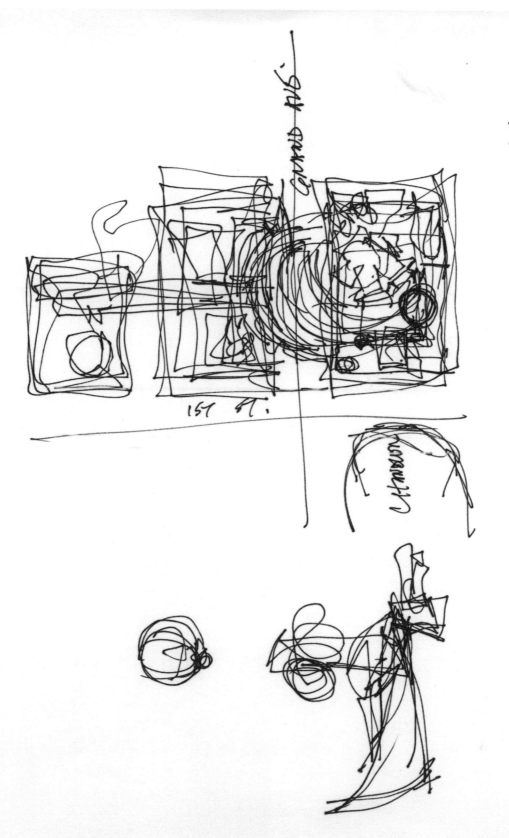

F. Cesmy

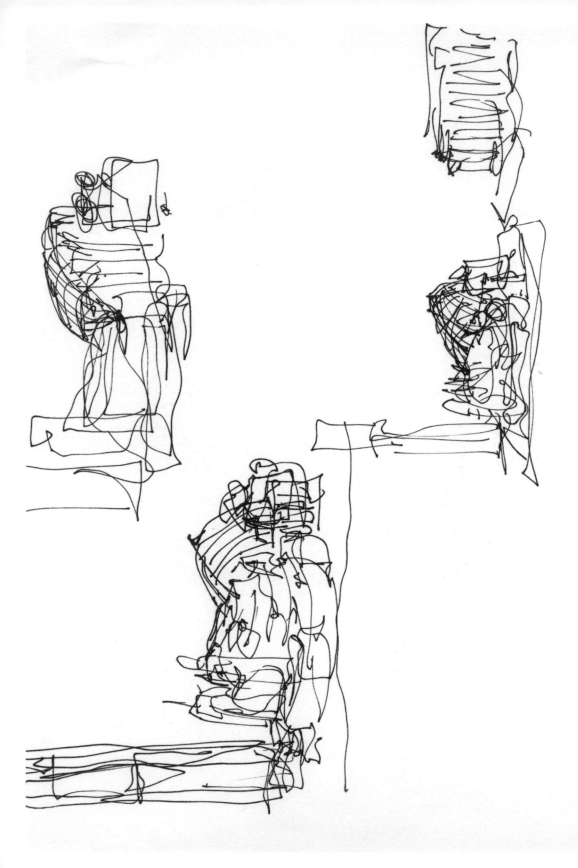

Bilbao Plan

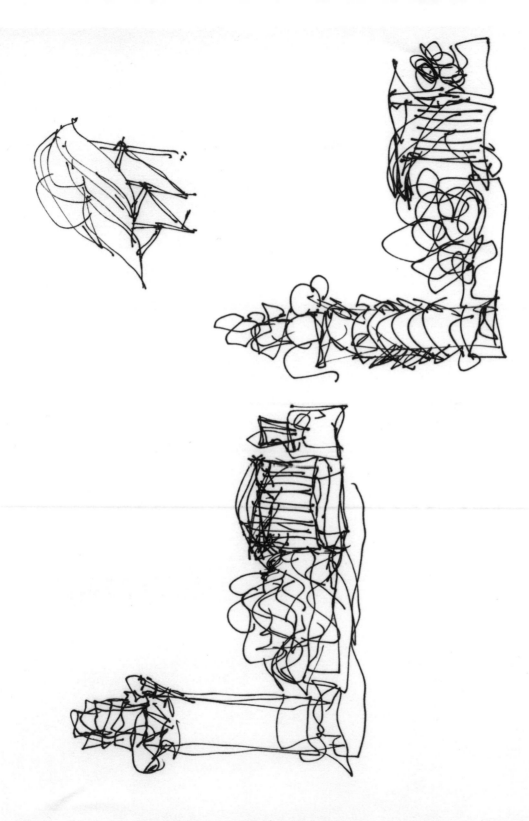

Disney new by man

The architecture of Disney Hall doesn't get in the way of people walking in and out. It's inviting. Accessibility is a big priority in all of my work. The key issue for me is, what does the building say to the people on the street, how does it welcome them? I don't think that destroys or negates an artist's position. I want people to be able to interact with my ideas and not be intimidated by them. This is very important, particularly today. I also think there is a freer spirit here on this site in downtown Los Angeles: there is no context to speak of and we built in the middle of nowhere. This allows for a much freer expression.

I wanted this building to be one idea, inside and outside, one aesthetic, unlike traditional concert halls. I wanted it to express the joy and feeling of music. FG

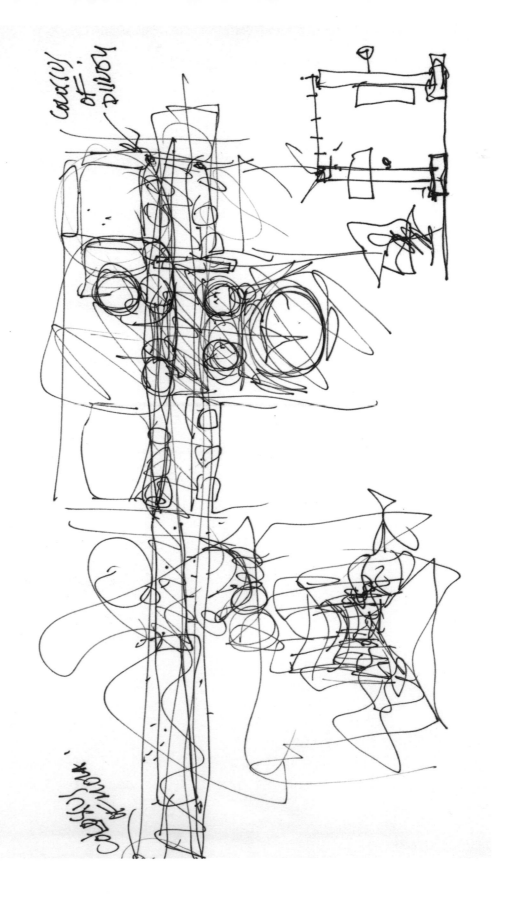

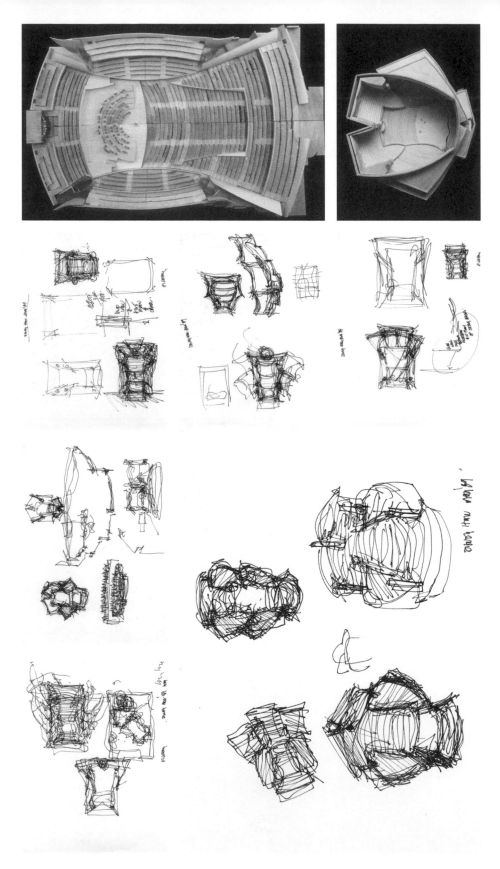

D19.06
D19.07
D19.08
D19.09
D19.10
D19.11
M19.06
M19.07
11.98

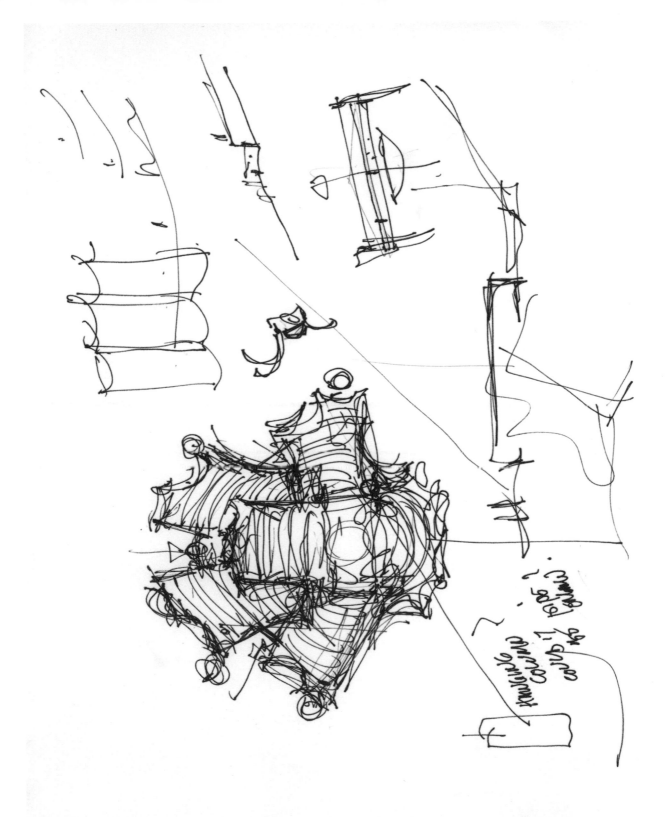

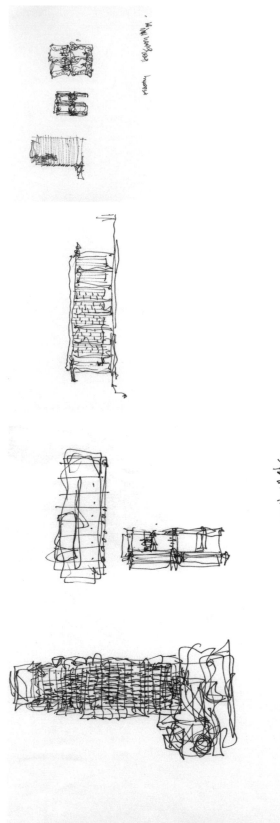

D19.13
D19.14
D19.15

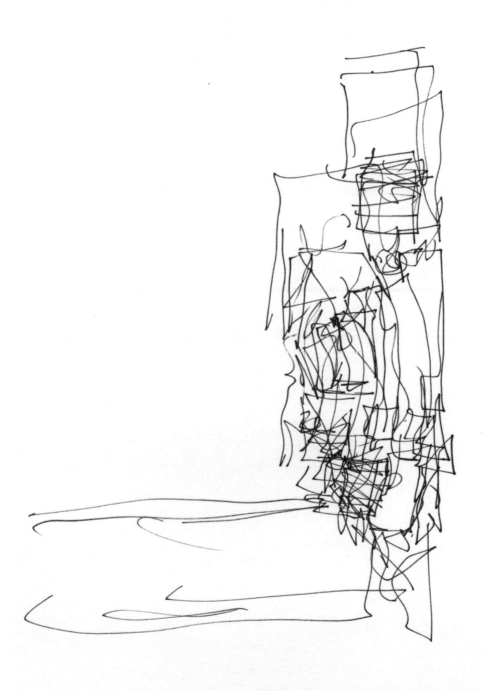

observatory (museum)
roof hangar
fitout

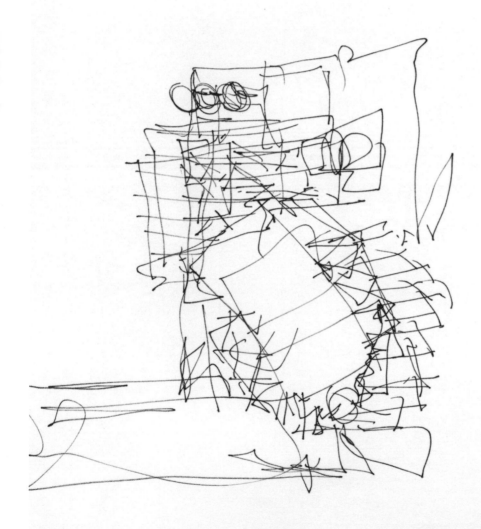

Barcelona Art Museum / House of G.

Flotzny   D1/201 Hall   Monett '80

M

We're making buildings for people and you have to fight for that. And it's not only the computer screen that you have to fight. There are so many forces that can screw it up, that can make a project less than what it should be. FG

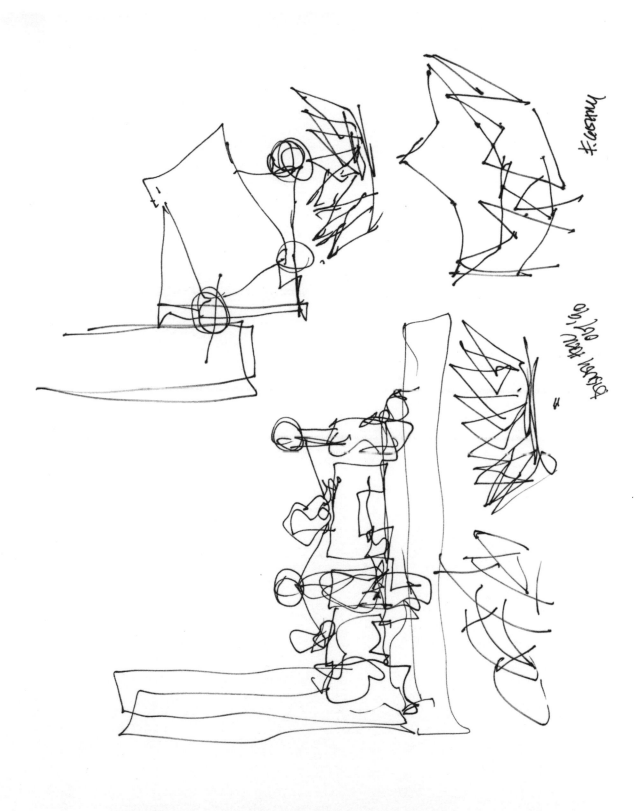

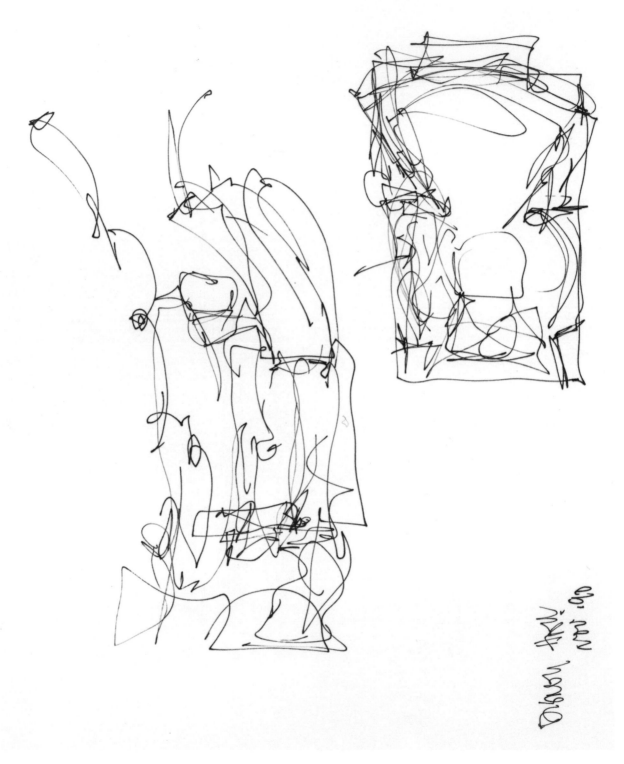

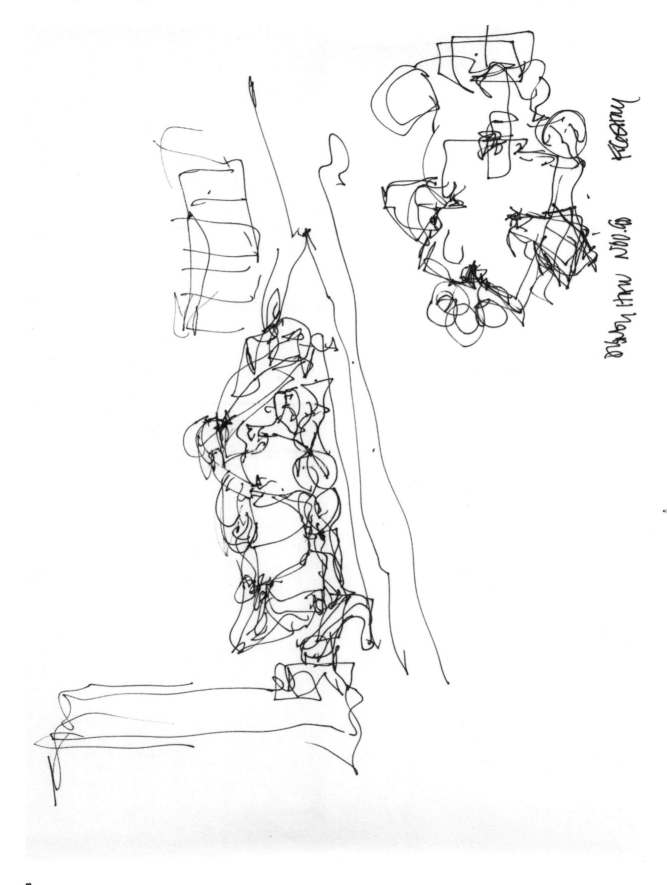

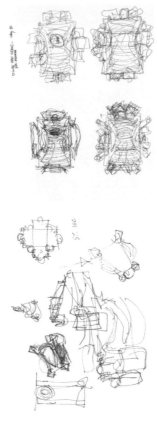

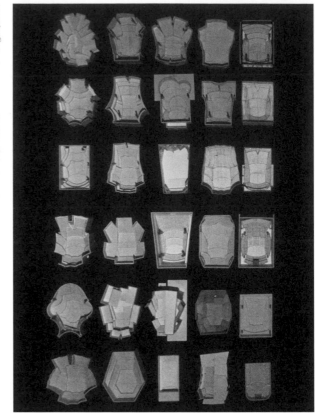

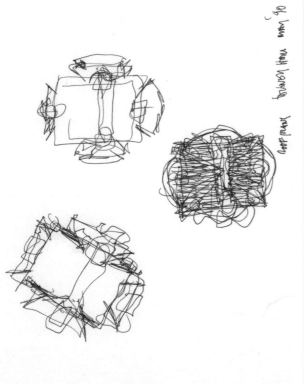

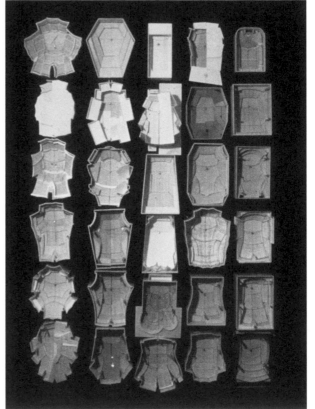

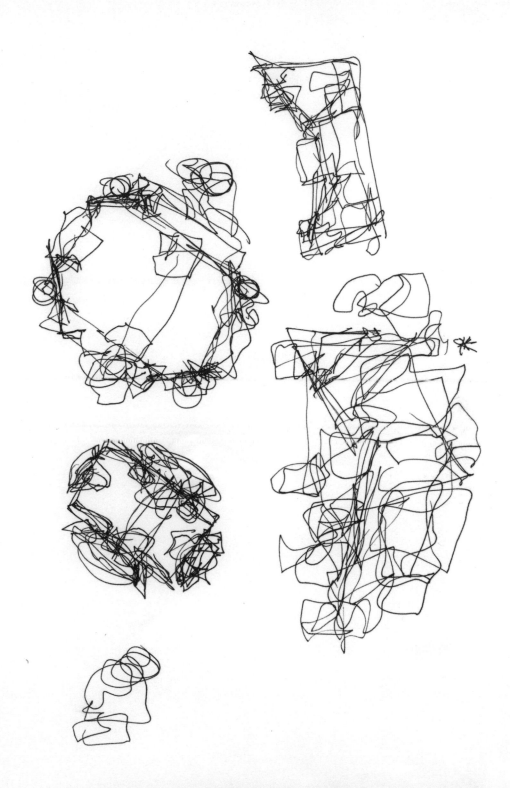

More than any other kind of project, theaters really do start from the inside out. You don't even look at the outside of the building until you figure out the stage and the performance space and the relationships between the performers and the audience. And then you really do just build the building around it. It's a concentric process that starts with the stage at the center. Most other buildings are aggregations of parts.

Theaters have a more linear, even concentric, logic to designing them. It was interesting to work on Janáček opera sets at Bard College, for example, to get on the other side of the proscenium and figure it out that way. Working with of contact with the client, easier than dealing, say, with scientists, who live in a completely different universe to architects and designers. Establishing a common ground is important. CW

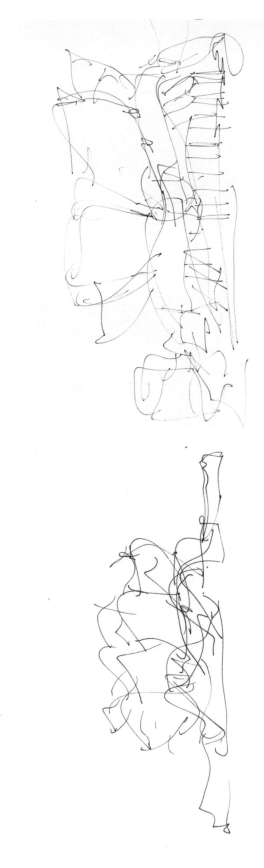

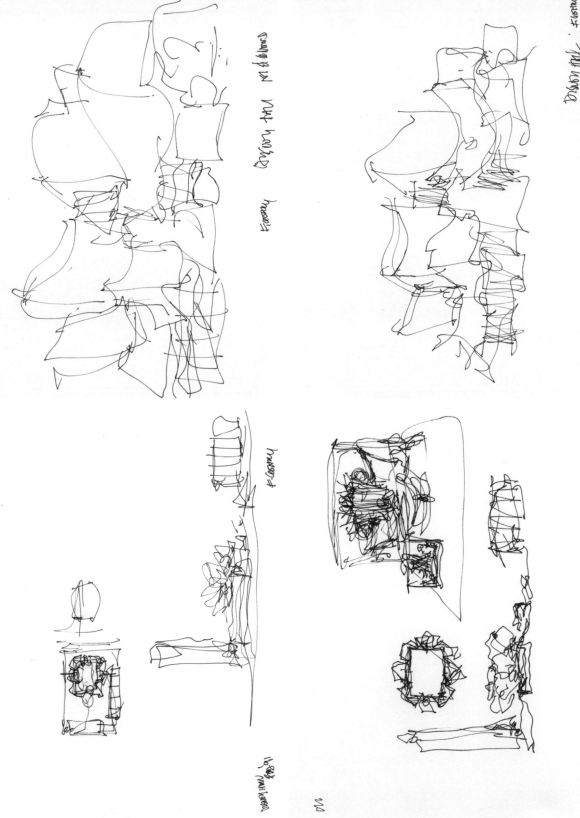

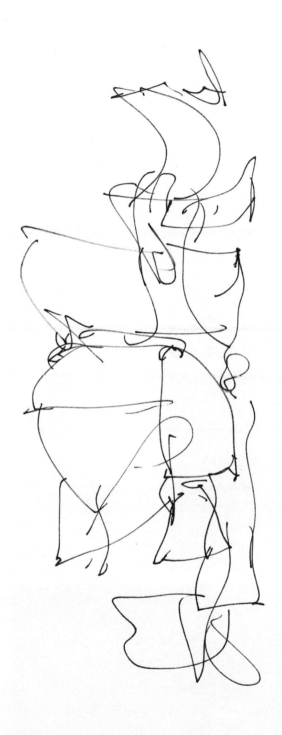

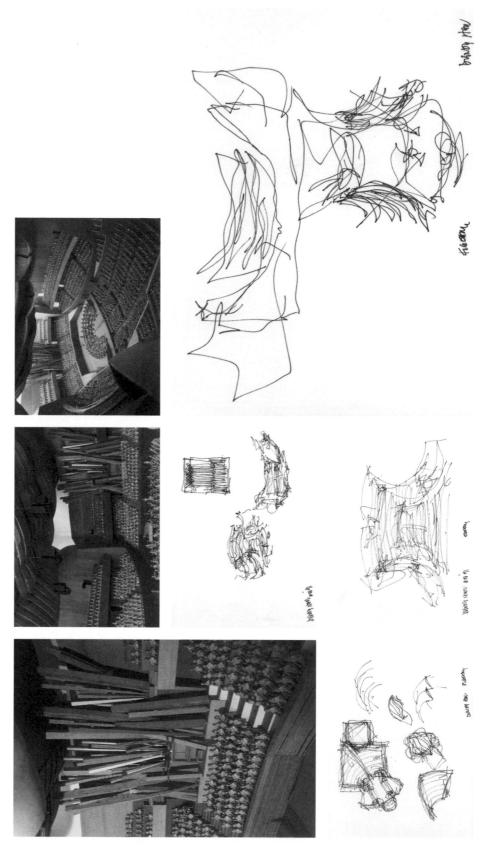

M19.10
02.25.94

M19.11
06.17.95

M19.12
10.01.98

D19.36

D19.37

D19.38

D19.39

332
___
333

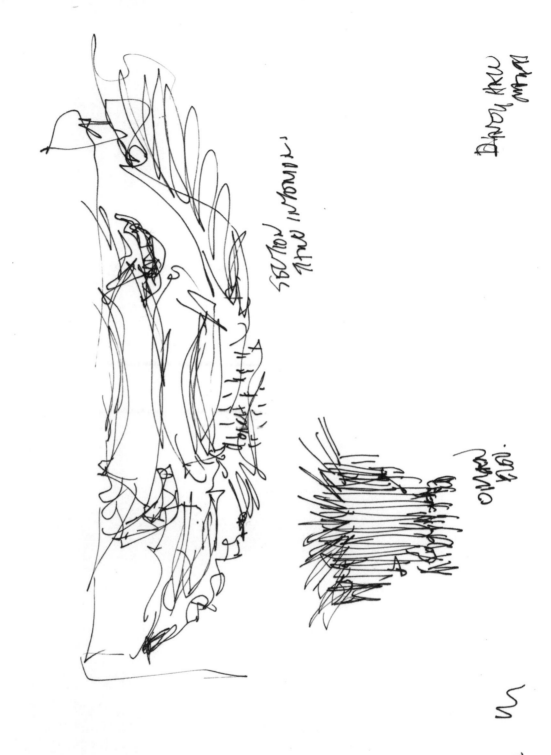

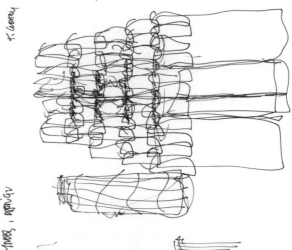

F. Gehry

M19.13
05.28.98

M19.14
05.28.98

D19.41

D19.42

334
—
335

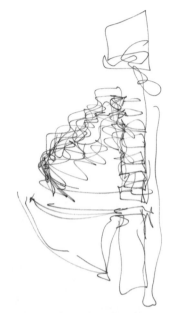

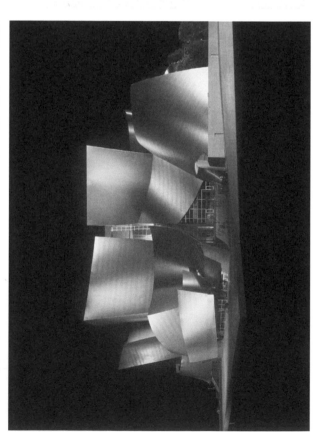

M19.15
2000

M19.16
2000

D19.44

D19.45

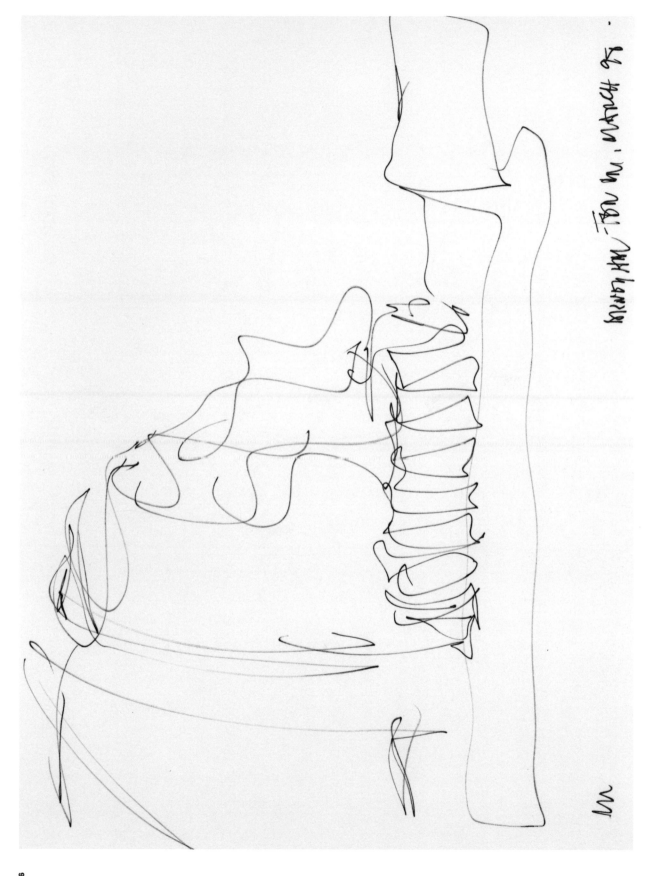

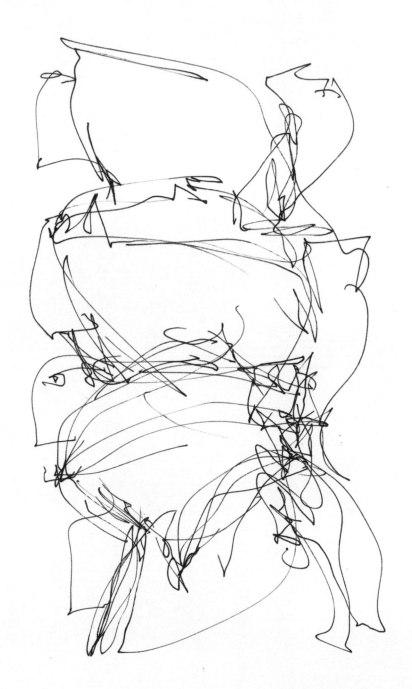

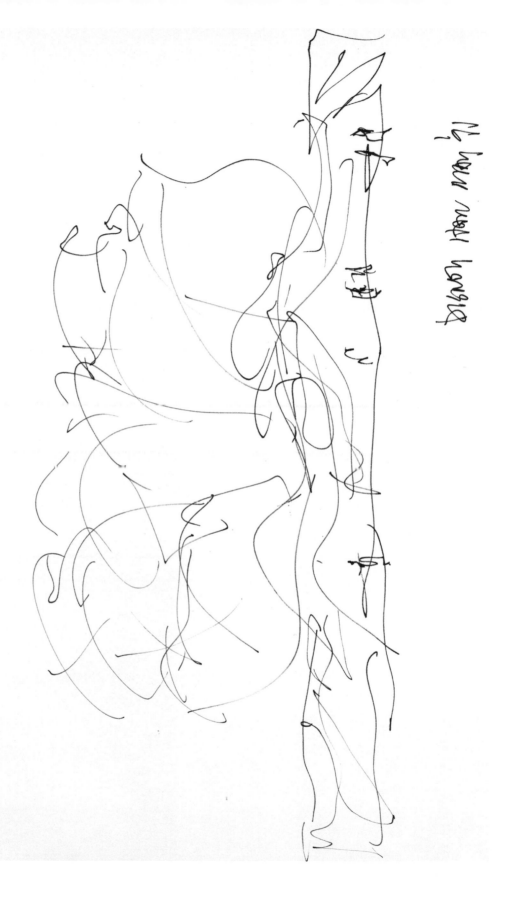

Project 20

The Ray & Maria Stata Center

Massachusetts Institute of Technology, Cambridge, Massachusetts 1998–2004

The Ray & Maria Stata Center
Massachusetts Institute of Technology,
Cambridge, Massachusetts

Design: commenced 1998
Construction: commenced 2001
Status: completed 2004
Number of drawings illustrated: 17

The Stata Center provides research laboratories and offices for the Laboratory for
Computer Science (LCS), the Artificial
Intelligence Laboratory (AI), the Laboratory
for Information and Decision Systems
(LIDS), and the Linguistics and Philosophy
Department (L&P). In addition, the center
houses more general facilities for use by
the MIT community as a whole.

While the building needed to combine
semi-private research areas and offices
with more accessible educational and
public facilities, the research community
needed to express two distinct identities
while remaining a cohesive whole. As a
result, the Stata Center rises from its base
in the form of two tower wings. The William
H. Gates Building is located on the Eastern
edge of the Stata Center and houses facilities for the LCS. The Alexander Dreyfoos
Building is located on the Western edge of
the Stata Center and houses facilities for
the AI Laboratory, the LIDS, and the L&P
Department. The building as a whole works
rather like a city: research laboratories
are located within the tower wings and are
divided into neighborhoods, generally
of two levels each, within which groups
that share a common area of research
can assemble. Each neighborhood
includes a central elevator core, a central
double-height lounge, and double-height
laboratories that create a visual and
physical connection between the two
levels of the neighborhood.

The neighborhoods are generally organized
with laboratories at the core and offices
at the perimeter. Laboratories are open
or enclosed according to the intended
research activity, while the overall neighborhood plan radiates from the double-
height lounge, the most public space,
to a band of offices on the perimeter, the
most private spaces. The lounges stack
behind the vertical extension of the light
courts and provide views of the upper
terrace. Within this organization, additional shell and core building systems have
been designed to accommodate maximum
flexibility for research groups that must
adapt regularly to changing research
topics and methods. The Stata Center
is clad in various materials, creating
a range of colors and textures that emphasize and reinforce the depth of the overall
architectural composition.

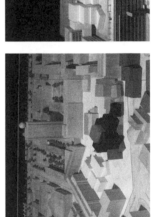

M20.01
06.04.98

M20.02
06.04.98

M20.03
07.29.98

342
—
343

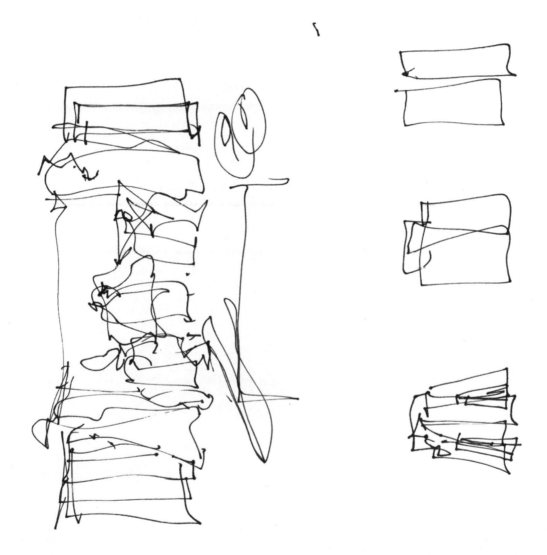

Bob Lee · Liu

M20.04
10.15.98

M20.05
10.23.98

M20.06
11.09.98

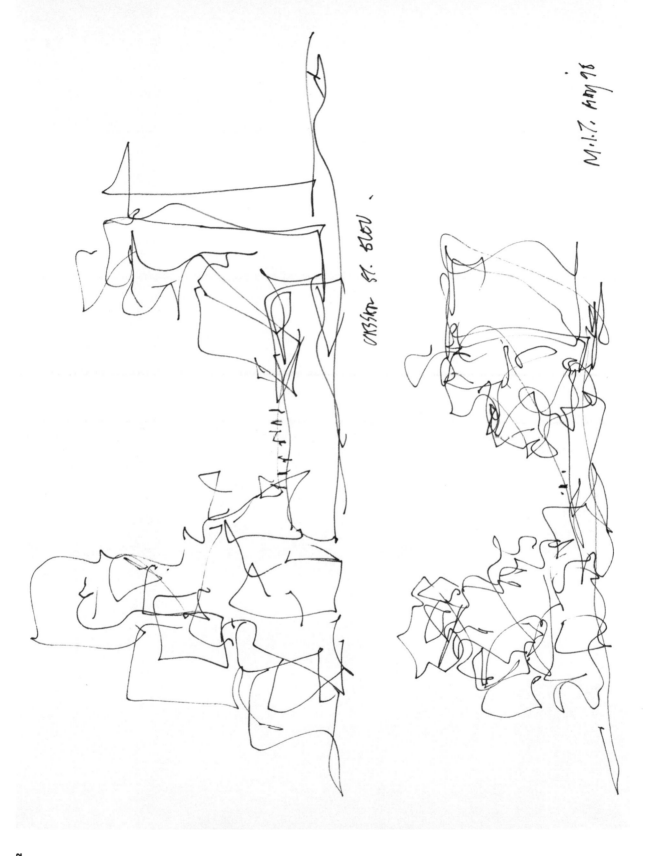

I secretly had my office prepare a dossier on each of the faculty members and their offices at MIT. And, sure enough, when the faculty members started talking to us about what they wanted, they described their offices just as they already were. When I showed them the dossier they were surprised. We then made models showing them the ways different cultures might deal with this problem. We had a scheme based on a traditional Japanese house with panels that could open up to combine spaces and close shut for privacy. They hated that because there was no hierarchy. Then we gave them a scheme based on a colonial American house with a central hall and rooms around the bottom and rooms around the top. But they didn't like that either; it was too formal. Then one of our team members made an "orang-utan village" around a tree with elders higher up and the children below. At first they were insulted. They thought we were calling them apes. But in the end they chose the orang-utan village. FG

M20.07
05.05.98

M20.08
05.05.98

M20.09
06.05.98

346
347

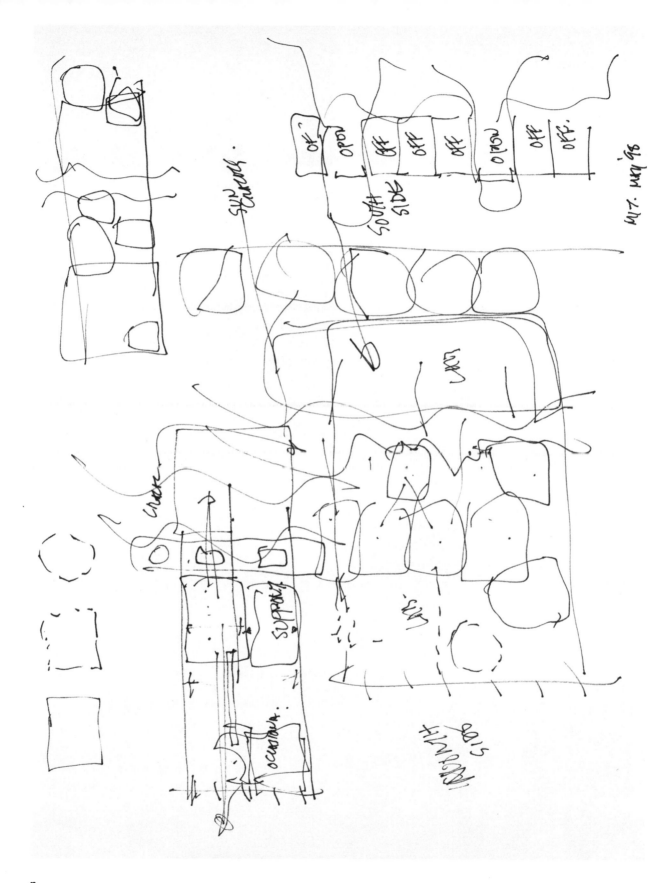

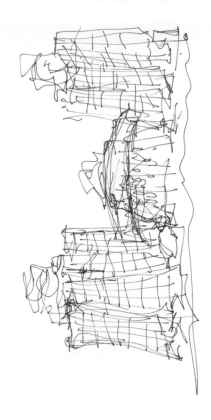

D20.04

D20.05

M20.10
11.09.98

M20.11
11.09.98

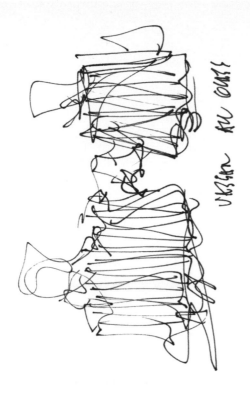

URBAN RW CONSE

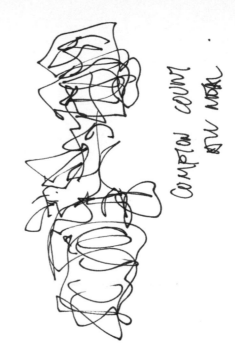

COMPTON COUNT
RW MOAL .

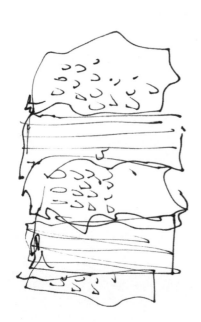

D20.07

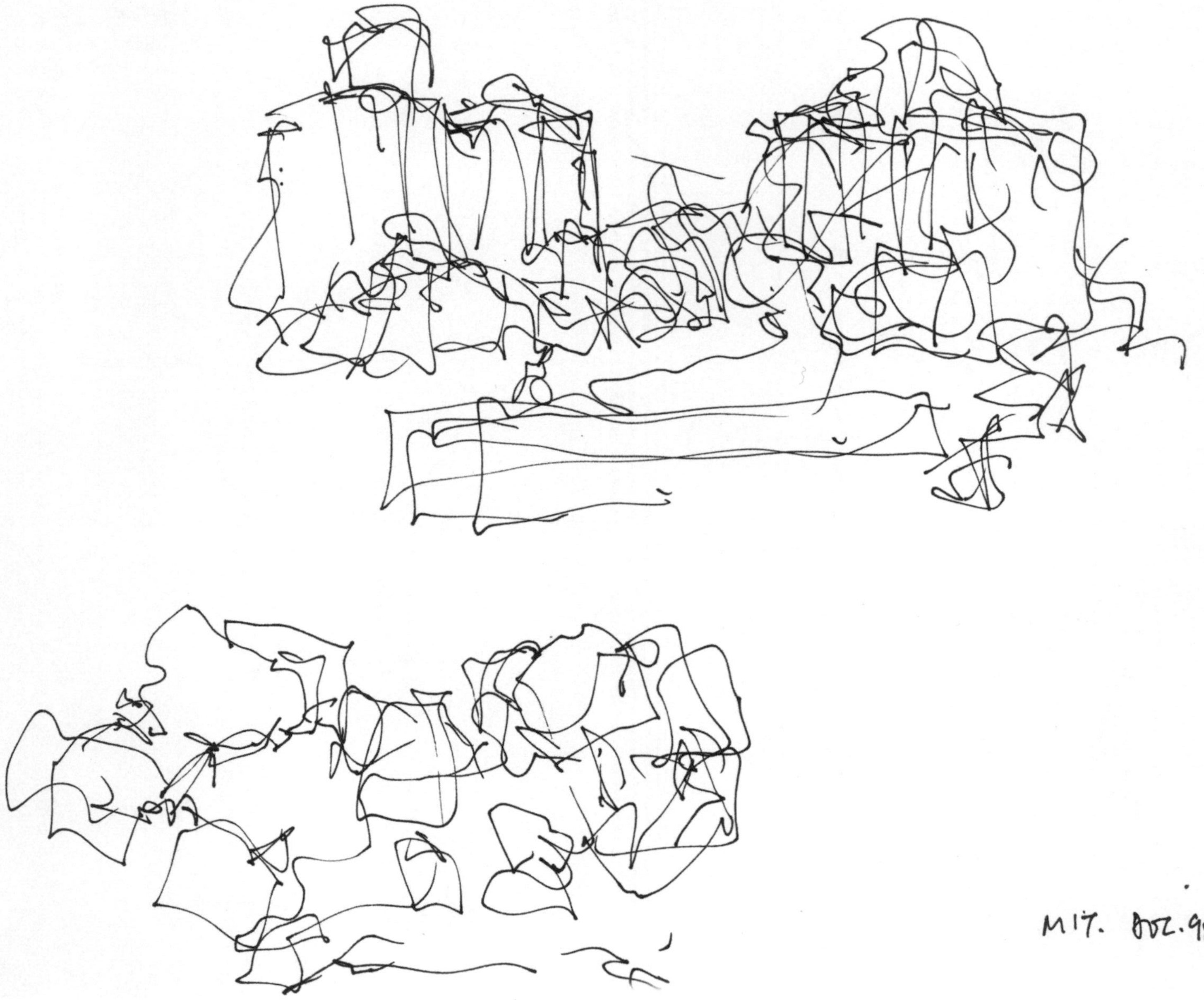

D20.08

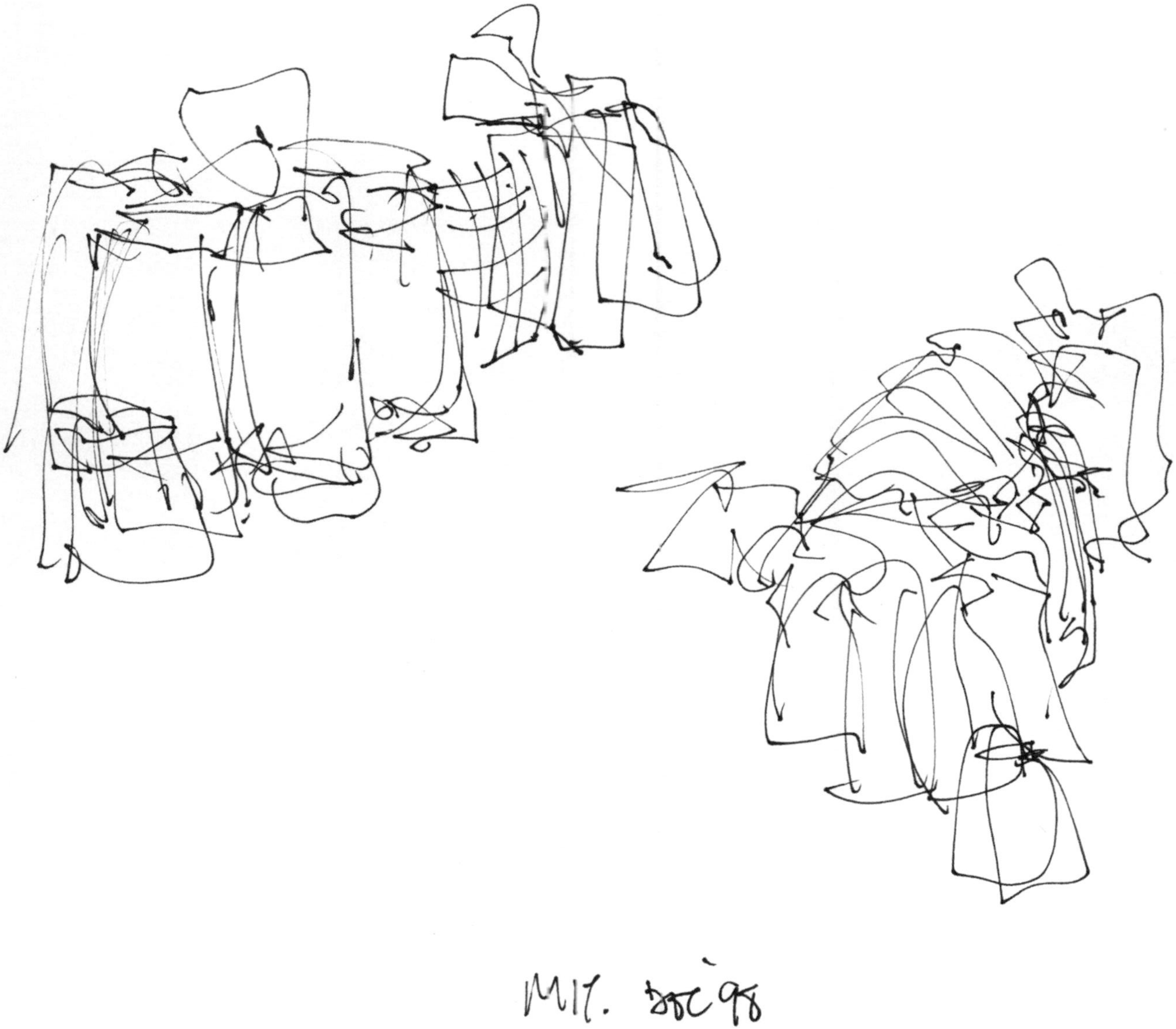

M20.12
12.18.98

M20.13
12.23.98

M20.14
12.23.98

M20.15
12.29.98

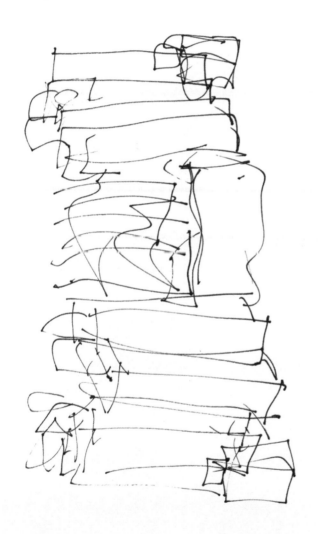
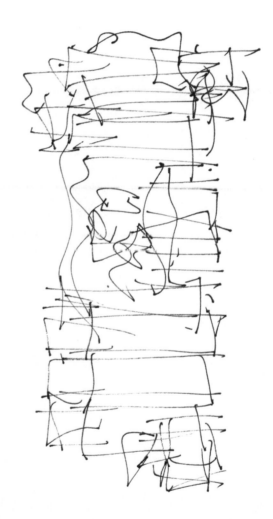

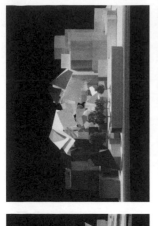

M20.16
01.06.99

M20.17
01.06.99

M20.18
01.18.99

M20.19
01.18.99

D20.10

D20.11

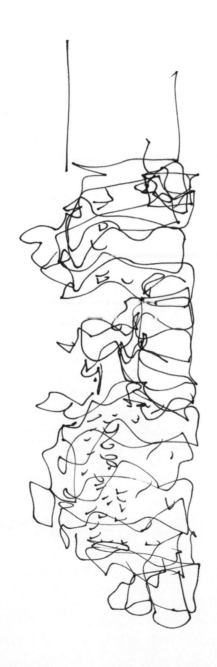

Mitt. 2494. 86

D20.12

MIT · March 1996

NY. 99

M20.20
01.06.99

M20.21
02.02.99

M20.22
02.02.99

M20.23
02.17.99

M20.24
02.18.99

M20.25
012.18.99

M20.26
05.27.99

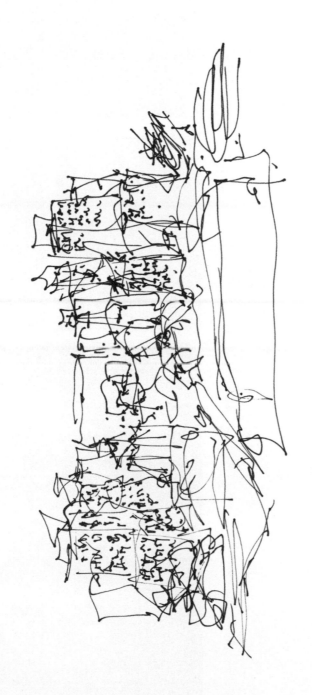

M2027
04.26.99

M20.28
05.26.99

M20.29
05.26.99

M20.30
06.25.99

M20.31
06.25.99

360 | 361

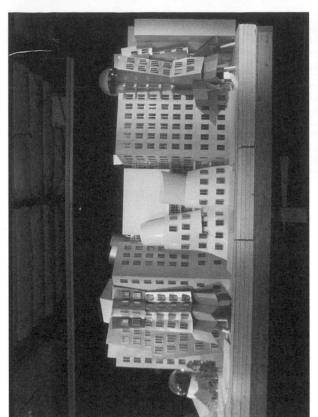

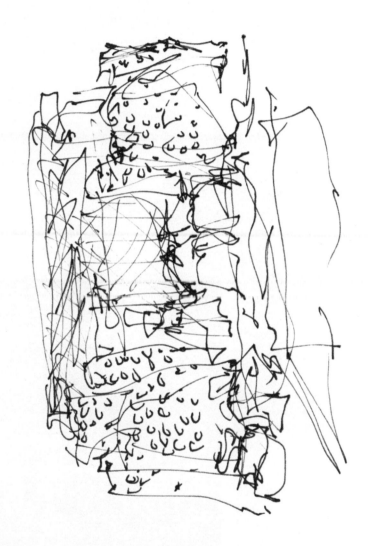

Project 21

Corcoran Gallery & School of Art
Washington, D.C.
1999–

Corcoran Gallery and School of Art
Washington, D.C.

Competition: June 1999
Design: commenced 1999
Status: ongoing
Number of drawings illustrated: 11

Founded in 1869, the Corcoran Gallery of Art is located in Washington, D.C., on 17th Street North West at New York Avenue, adjacent to the White House and the National Mall. It is Washington's oldest art museum and its only college of art and design. The Corcoran's current facilities include a building designed by Ernest Flagg and opened in 1897, as well as an addition designed by Charles Platt and opened in 1928. Both the original building and the addition currently contain two floors of galleries, administrative offices, and support facilities, as well as facilities for the college of art and design. The original building plans for the existing facilities were never fully realized, and because the existing facilities cannot accommodate the Corcoran's growing permanent collection or its recent increase in student enrollment, an international design competition was held and the design of a new and final addition was commissioned.

This extension of the museum creates a new main entrance on New York Avenue that leads to a new atrium, placed on an axis with the existing 17th Street North West entrance and atrium. The central location of the new atrium creates a unifying element between the existing facilities and the addition. Two distinct types of gallery space will be included. A series of traditional gallery spaces will be located within a cluster of rectilinear volumes located in the new atrium. A series of more sculptural galleries will be located within three sculptural volumes that animate the facade along New York Avenue.

In order to insure that the college of art and design would have an equally strong identity within the institution, a second new atrium, devoted exclusively to use by the college of art and design, is located below street level along New York Avenue. Large skylights at street level flood the atrium with natural light. Studios for the college of art and design are located within a series of elements in the atrium that relate to the forms of the facade above. Additional facilities for the college of art and design are located adjacent to the atrium. The new main entrance to the museum passes between the skylights at street level, thus providing an equal presence to the museum and to the college of art and design as visitors arrive.

M21.01
05.14.99

M21.02

M21.03
04.24.00

366
367

CARC. MAY 2K

D21.01

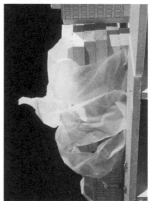

M21.04
05.27.99

M21.05
03.31.99

M21.06

D21.03
D21.04

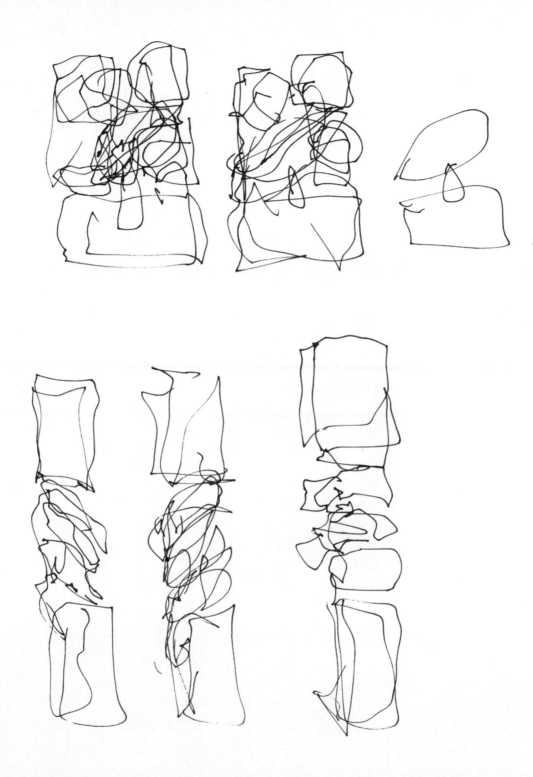

M21.07
05.27.99

M21.08
05.18.00

D21.06

D21.07

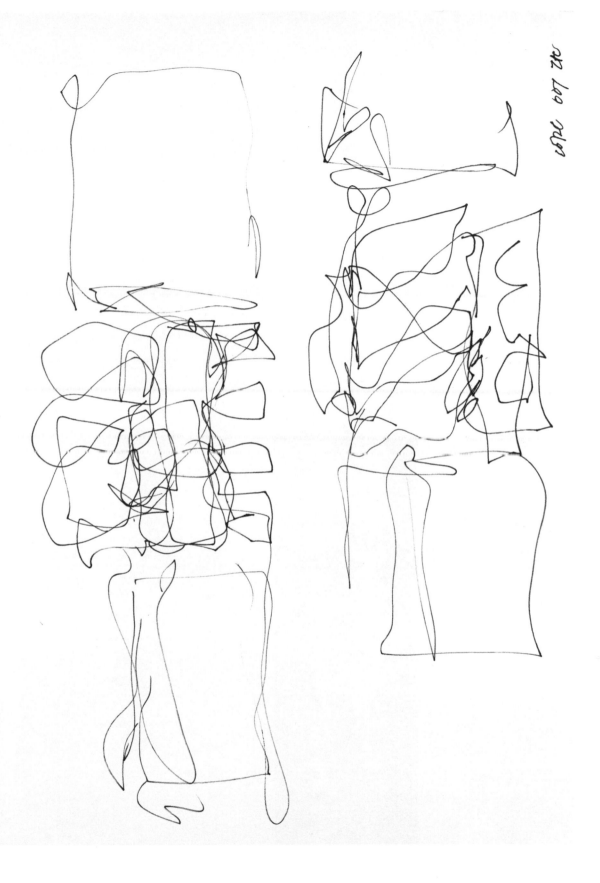

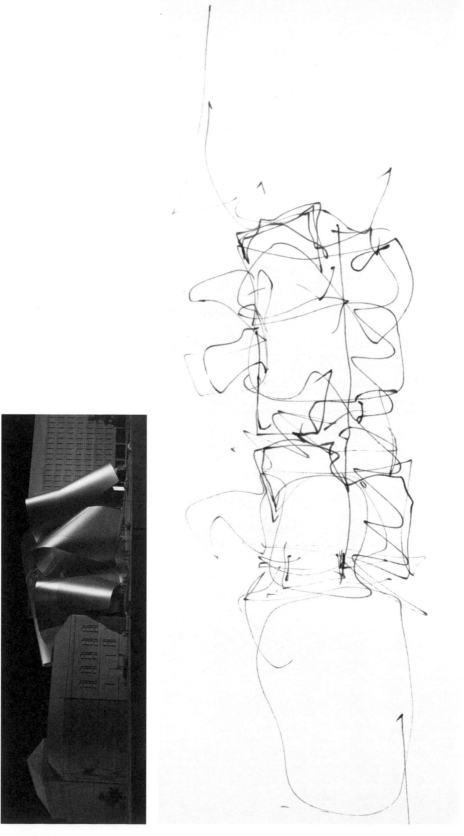

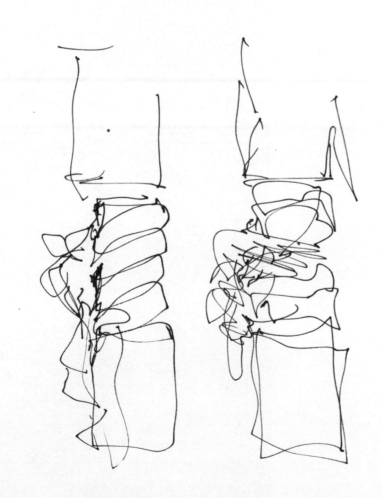

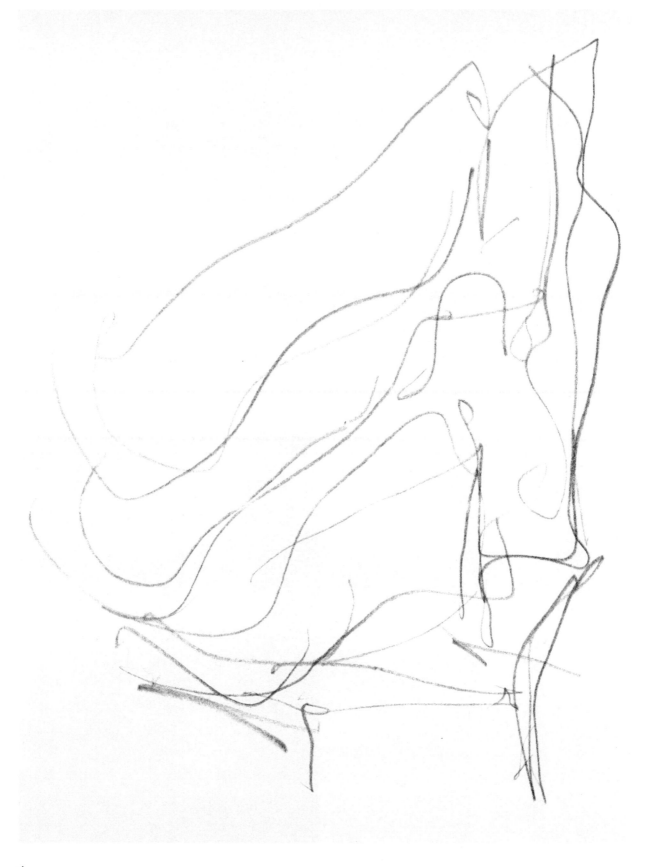

D21.11

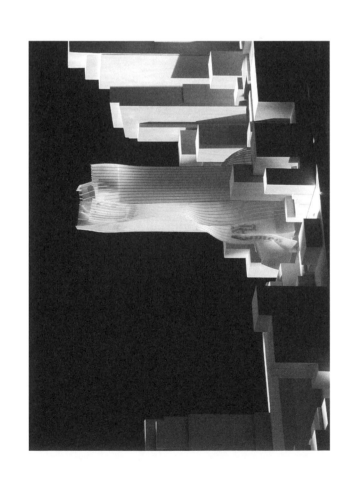

Project 22 (unbuilt)

The New York Times Headquarters
New York, New York
2000

The New York Times Headquarters
New York, New York
2000

Status: competition entry
Number of drawings illustrated: 16

In the summer of 2000, *The New York Times* and Forest City Ratner Companies conducted an invited competition to select an architect for the design of an office building located on 8th Avenue between 40th and 41st Streets in Manhattan. Gehry Partners, working in collaboration with the New York office of Skidmore, Owings & Merrill, was invited to participate.

The brief required that the building should provide between 700,000 and 900,000 square feet of office space created specifically to fulfill the unique needs of *The New York Times*, including a Newsroom of approximately 170,000 square feet, and approximately 600,000 square feet of speculative office space.

In response to zoning regulations, the overall massing of the building was developed as a series of setbacks, with larger floor plates at the lower levels of the building and a series of repetitive smaller floor plates at the upper levels. The lower levels of Gehry's designer were devoted exclusively to use by *The New York Times*, while the upper levels are devoted to speculative office space. A "crack" in the center of the 8th Avenue facade running from street level to mid-rise level, in conjunction with the massing setbacks, allows the lower levels of the building to be read as two mid-rise towers that are more appropriate in scale to the surrounding buildings. This "crack" also allowed the upper levels of the building to be read as a slender tower. A continuous glass curtain wall unified the lower and upper levels of the building.

The primary entry to *The New York Times* lobby is located on 8th Avenue. From this lobby, the newsroom—the heart of the company's reporting operations—was immediately visible and was articulated as a series of open spaces on multiple levels, culminating in a cafeteria and winter garden. The design of the newsroom permitted direct access from nearly all areas on the lower levels of the building and provided a visual presence befitting its significance. A private lobby serving the speculative office levels was accessed through primary entries on 40th and 41st Streets. Winter gardens were located at each massing setback, providing unique amenities for building tenants.

At the upper levels of the building a more sculptural architectural language was employed, articulating the crown of the building as an abstraction of *The New York Times* logo and providing a signature presence on the Manhattan skyline.

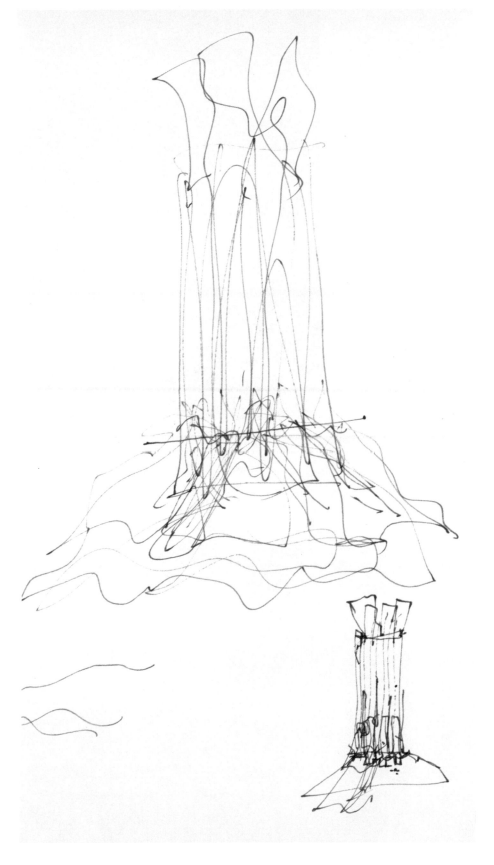

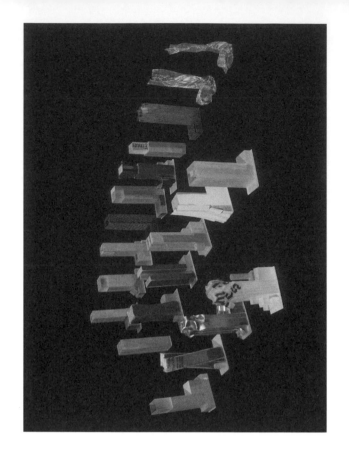

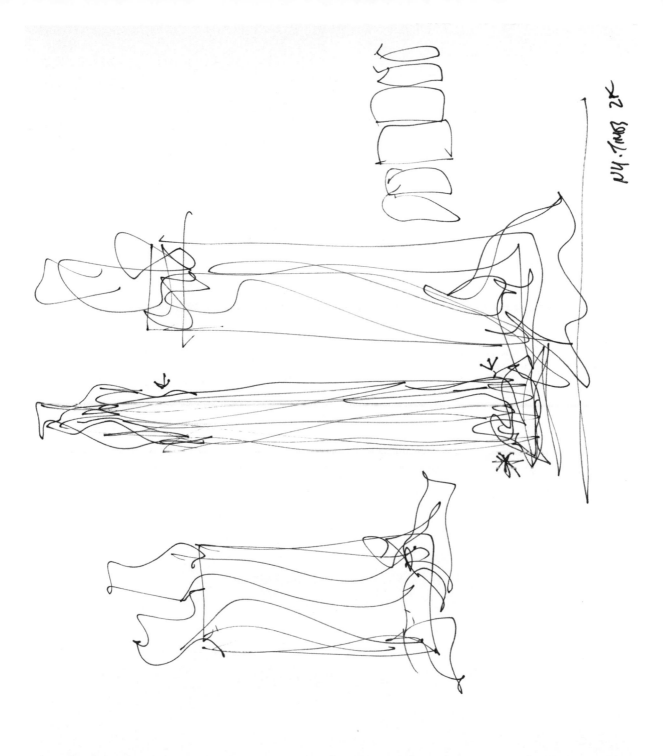

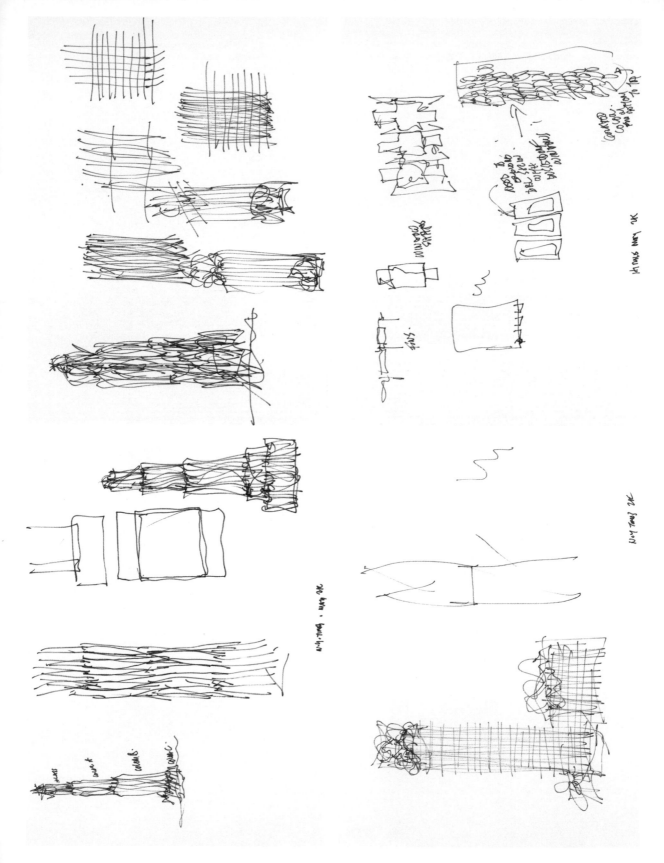

D22.03
D22.04
D22.05
D22.06

384
385

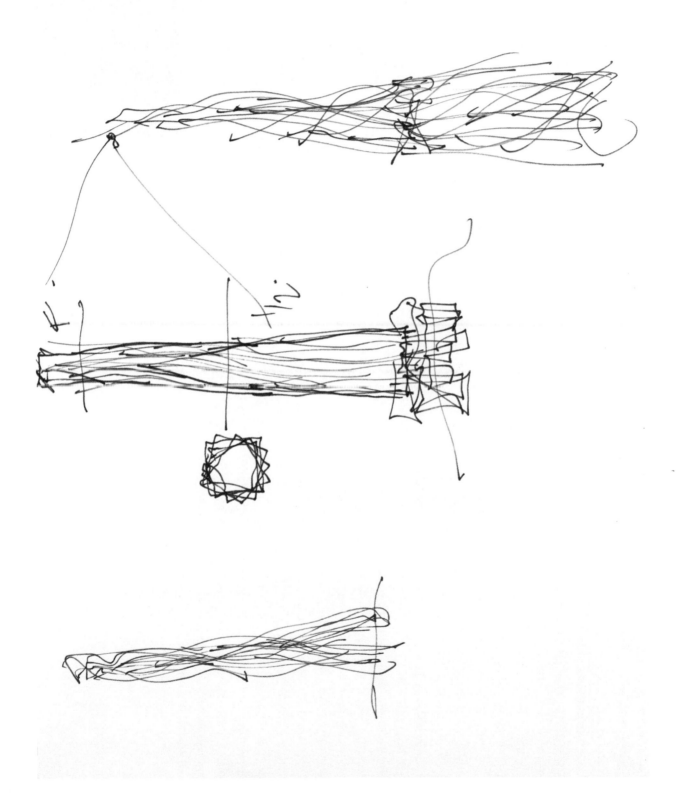

A lot of these drawings were done to facilitate conversations and discussions in meetings with the client. We would explore the "high rise," for example, and the drawings became analytical tools. In these meetings we would, say, make the massing of the model. That's the first thing Frank wants to see. This building would have been 40 stories high, stepped back, as you would imagine a New York high-rise building would have to be. So the first set of drawings basically talks about stuff related to the program of spaces and their uses.

Once we had done that part of the design process, then we started to say, "Alright, within this kind of profile, what are the opportunities?" Number one is that we could make the bottom simple, and then put the articulation at the very top, just like every other New York high rise. There were a series of these kinds of discussions, here in the studio, about what the top would be like. Then we considered the fact that this would probably have been a glass building, in which case we could have a grid on it. Or you could say that because of this, we could also have broken up the building into three pieces, so that the tower itself is articulated with two other parts. Because the building was actually kind of wide, we wondered what would make the building look taller. Although it's not really a twin tower, we could break it into two vertical elements.

Then we thought about branding for *The New York Times*, and signage, near the bottom and near the top. It was through the articulation of the architecture that this building itself became a sign. That was part of our idea. And that raised issues about materials again. For the longest time, we weren't too sure whether this building would be glass or metal. Glass buildings are tricky because a lot of times when you make a model it's an abstraction. When you look at a glass building, it looks black. If you drive around New York looking at glass buildings, most of them look black, not white. So what do you do with the glass and the texture of the skin?

I was very interested in doing this skyscraper and I know that Frank was interested too, especially if you could reinvent the rules a little bit and have some freedom to play with the curtain walls. EC

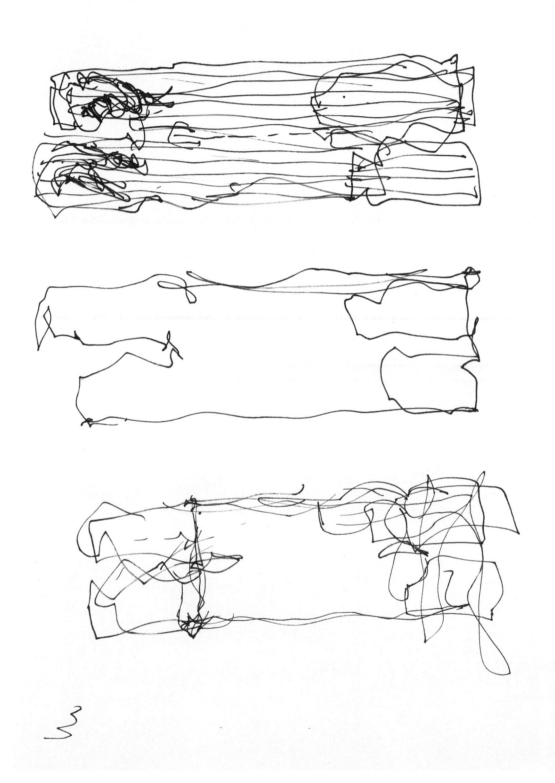

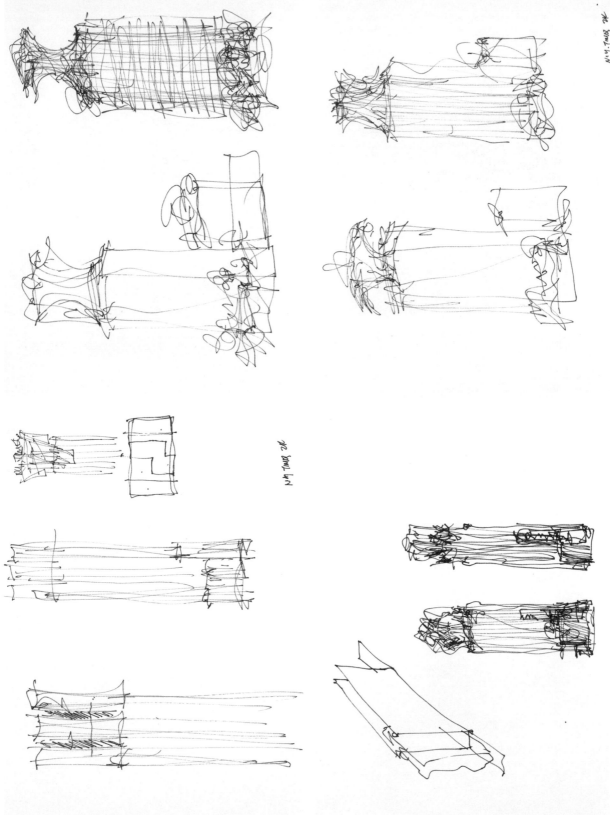

New York. Twist. 2H.

2H. Twist. New York

D22.09
D22.10
D22.11
D22.12

388
389

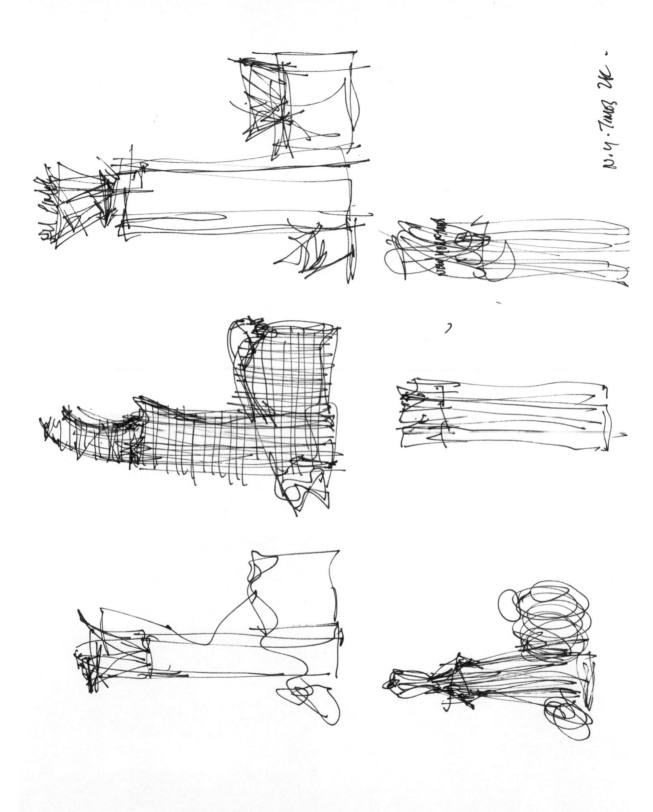

N.Y. Times 2K

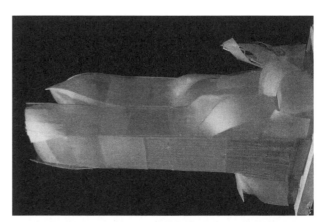

M22.03
08.25.00

M22.04
09.09.00

390
391

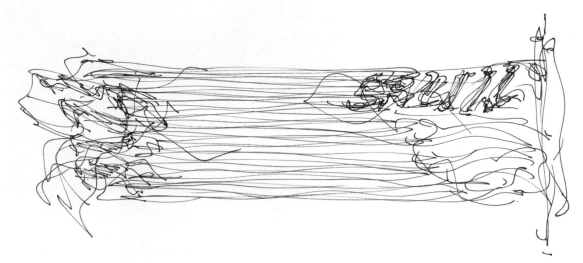

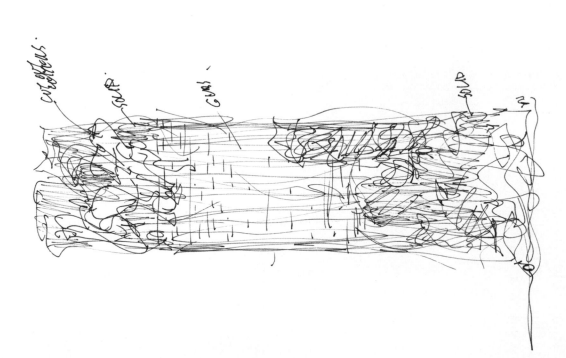

This project was like sculpting in marble. You have to find the sculpture in the block of stone. You see it in Michelangelo's Slaves, for example, where he left rough marble untouched. He didn't have a picture to work from, he found the form in the marble. It's the same in my drawings. I have a freedom in my drawings that I love to express in my architecture. FG

M22.05
09.09.00

M22.06
09.09.00

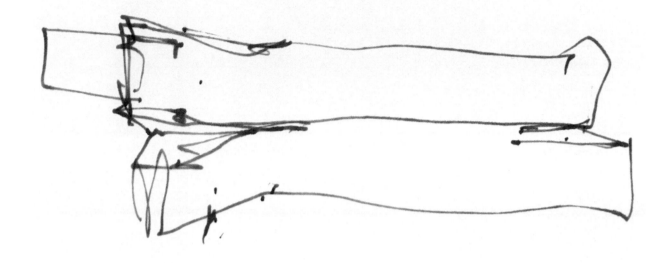

Project 23

Ohr–O'Keefe Museums
Biloxi, Mississippi
1999–

Ohr-O'Keefe Museums
Biloxi, Mississippi

Design: commenced 1999
Construction: commenced 2003
Status: expected completion 2005
Number of drawings illustrated: 11

Dedicated to the American ceramicist George E. Ohr and the cultural legacy of African Americans, the Ohr-O'Keefe Museums campus is located in Biloxi, Mississippi, in the newly created Tricentennial Park adjacent to the Mississippi Sound and the Gulf of Mexico. It is intended to provide facilities for art exhibition, art research and education, and cultural and community events.

The site is set within a grove of ancient Live Oak trees. The project was developed as a series of six small pavilions woven among the trees and connected by an open brick plaza, creating an inviting and lively arts campus that maintains the existing park setting and encourages pedestrian circulation throughout the site and throughout Tricentennial Park as a whole. The entire project will employ a micro-pile foundation system intended to minimize impact on the root systems of the oaks.

The pavilions that comprise the Ohr-O'Keefe Museums are the Welcome Center, the Exhibition Gallery, the Museum of African American Arts, the George E. Ohr Museum, and the Center for Ceramics. In addition, the Pleasant Reed House, which is the first home built in Mississippi by a former slave and which is now a designated historical landmark, has been moved to the campus and is being restored to serve as a cultural resource depicting African-American life in the nineteenth century. The wood frame, tin-roofed house in the shotgun vernacular (so called because the doors of all the rooms are lined up so that a gunshot fired into the front door would go through the house and out the back door without hitting a wall) will be placed on the campus between the Welcome Center and the Center for Ceramics.

The Welcome Center serves as the primary entry building to the campus. The main volume consists of a large brick and glass main hall housing the ticketing foyer, a café, and a mobile 35-seat lecture room that can be relocated when necessary to allow the main hall to function as a single open space for large events. A plaster element recalling the shotgun vernacular contains a kitchen, administrative offices, and support facilities, and a more sculptural element clad in stainless-steel panels houses the retail shop. Recalling the shoo-fly vernacular (the shoo-fly was a fan that swept back and forth to chase away flies, typically housed above the dining room table in a belvedere), the Welcome Center is topped by an overlook that is sheltered by a roof clad in stainless-steel panels, providing visitors with views of the campus, Tricentennial Park, and the Gulf of Mexico.

Exhibition spaces are provided in the pavilions for the Exhibition Gallery, the Museum of African American Arts, and the George E. Ohr Museum. Each of the gallery pavilions is residential in scale and in placement. The Exhibition Gallery is a white plaster pavilion with a roof and entry canopy clad in stainless-steel panels. The Exhibition Gallery provides 1,050 square feet of flexible exhibition space intended to accommodate works of varying size and in varying media. The Museum of African-American Arts is a pavilion clad in brick and stainless-steel panels. The Museum of African-American Arts provides 1,700 square feet of exhibition space divided between a main gallery and a collection of smaller alcoves intended for the display of smaller works. The George E. Ohr Museum consists of four gently sculptural volumes clad in stainless-steel panels and connected by a central glass-enclosed gallery. It provides 2,900 square feet of exhibition space devoted to the display of pottery created by Ohr in the late nineteenth and early twentieth centuries. Each of the gallery pavilions includes hardwood floors and receives indirect natural light via skylights. In addition, each of the gallery pavilions includes a front porch where didactic text describing each of the current exhibitions will be displayed, allowing the works on display to be presented in environments entirely free from distraction.

The Center for Ceramics serves primarily as a resource for ceramic arts education. It is clad in brick, white plaster, and stainless-steel panels, and provides a full working studio and work yard joined with large glass overhead doors, an arts research library, and an art conservation area. An exhibition preparation area is housed in a brick storage vault intended to provide a safe haven for artworks in the event of a flood or a hurricane. Administrative offices, research spaces, and glass-enclosed conference facilities occupy the upper floors.

The use of local materials, references to the southern vernacular, and the scale and placement of each of the pavilions on the site, represent sensitive responses to the conditions of the site and to the context of the surrounding area.

The thing that attracted Frank to the Ohr–O'Keefe Museums was the similarity of the organic, folded shapes of Ohr's pottery to what we were doing here. We went around and around working on it and then decided to do just the opposite. If we made this building in the same shapes as the pottery, then it's going to dilute the pottery. So we made something much more neutral.

We also broke the project down into a campus of buildings, dodging the oak trees, to work on a residential scale. It's like a small village plus the shotgun house in the middle, which is a comment on what's happening in Biloxi: they're building giant casinos and wiping out the town that was once there. We were trying to do the opposite and to fit in. cw

M23.01
07.10.00

M23.02
11.26.00

M23.03
12.20.00

398 | 399

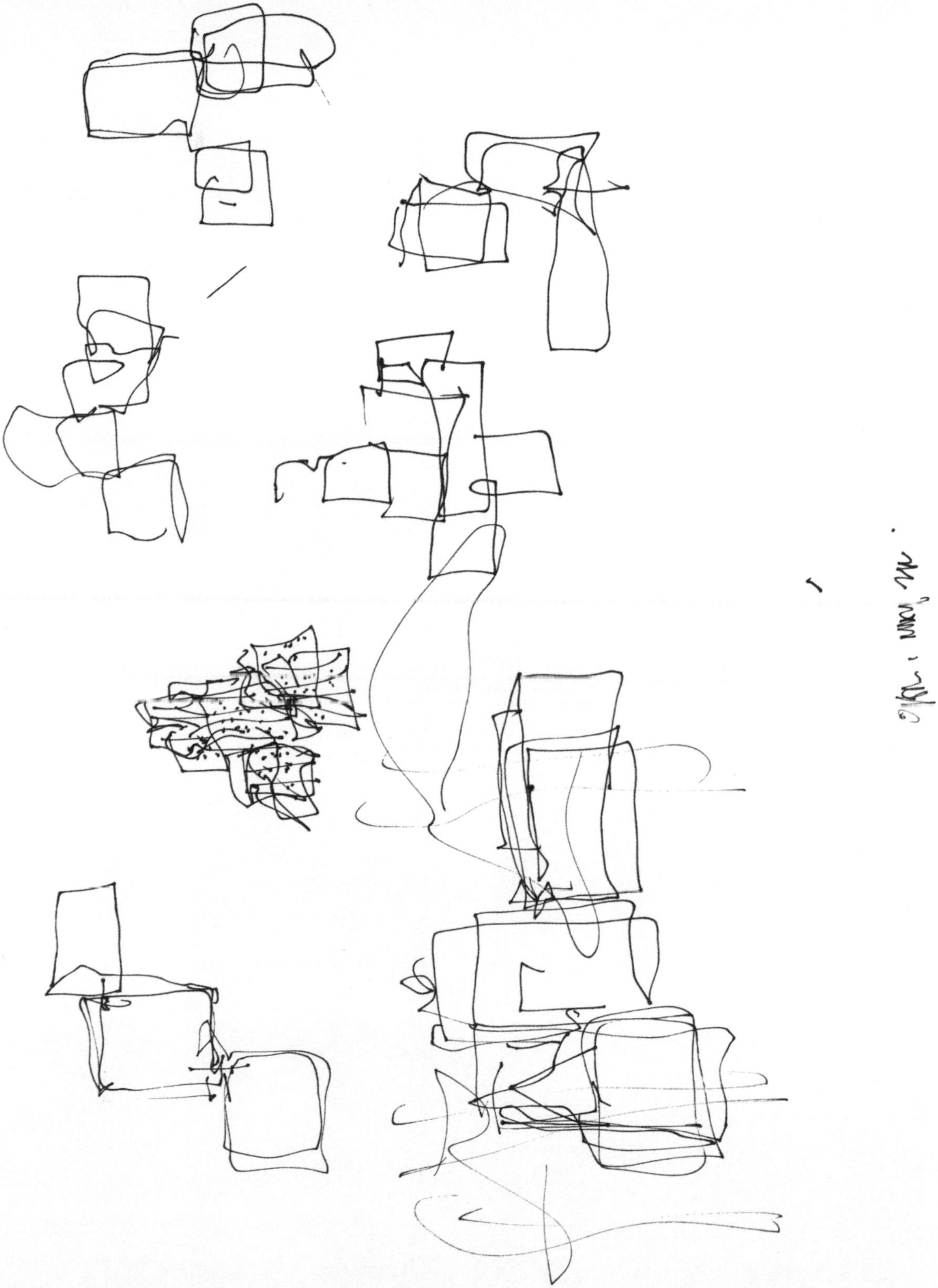

D23.02

I'm very careful about the people I work with. It's a five-year partnership. And a small thing takes just as long as a big thing. I just assess the reality of it. If someone comes and says they want another Bilbao, or something like that, and they have no real program—they just need something to fix the town—I'll refuse it. FG

ELEVATION

ohh - 09/2K

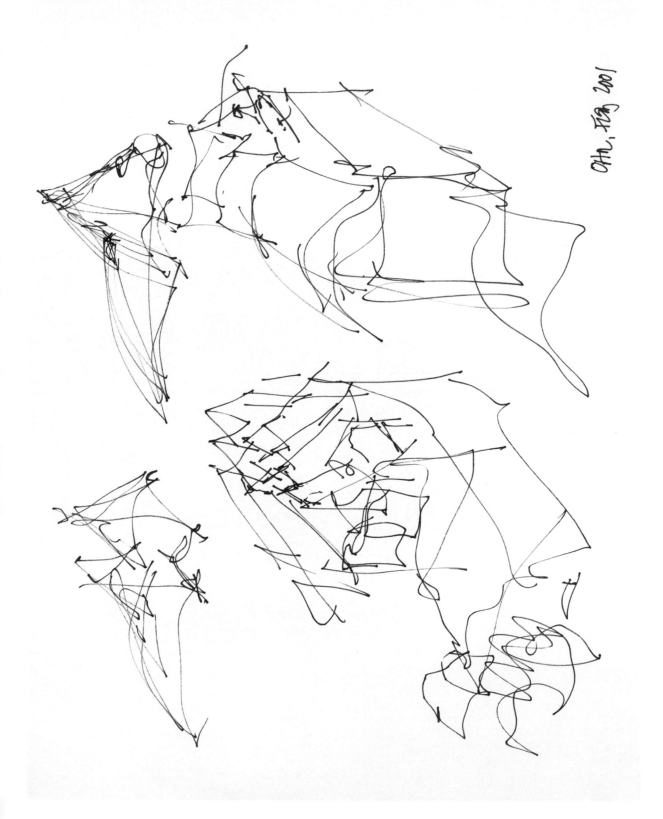

Otto, Frei 2001

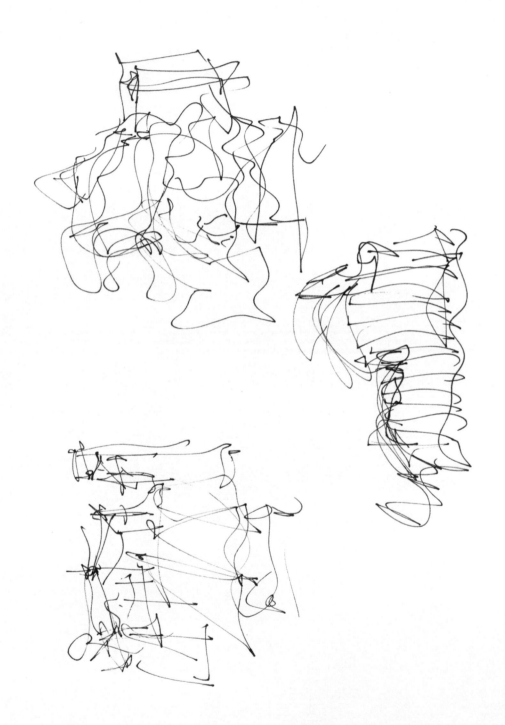

M23.04
01.18.00

M23.05
01.18.00

M23.06
01.18.00

M23.07
01.18.00

oth Heb 2001

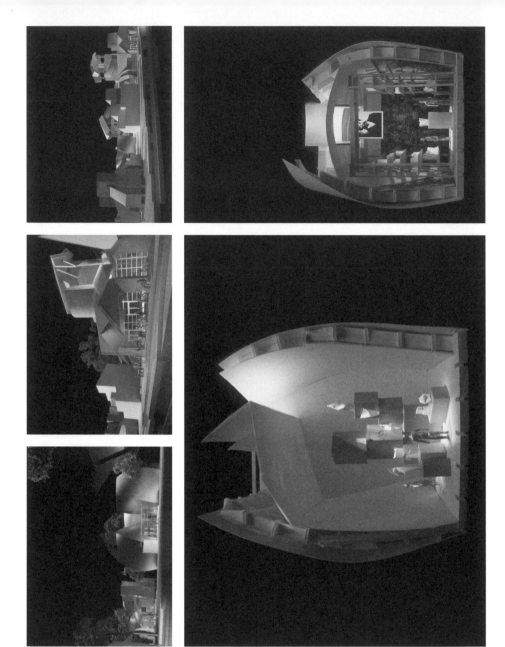

M23.08
M23.09
M23.10
M23.11
M23.12

408 | 409

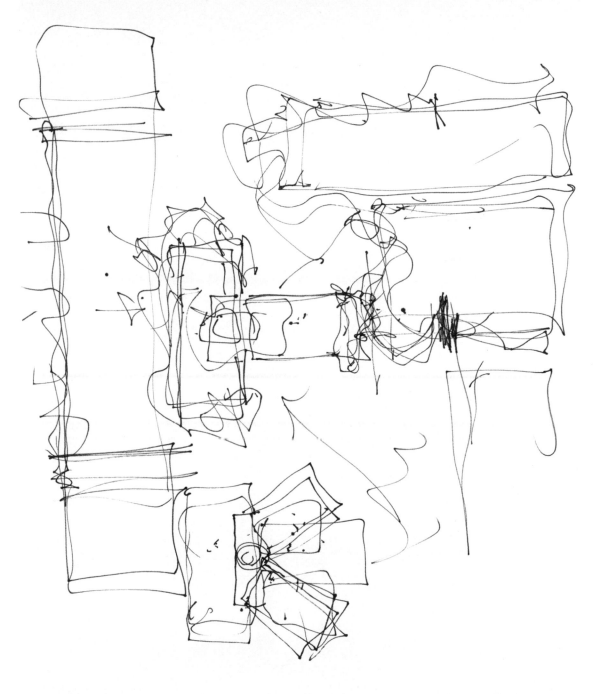

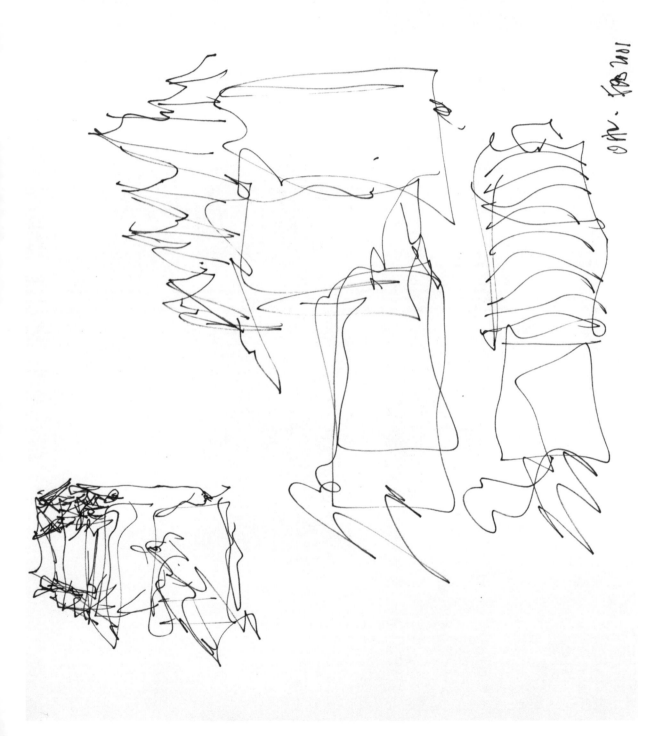

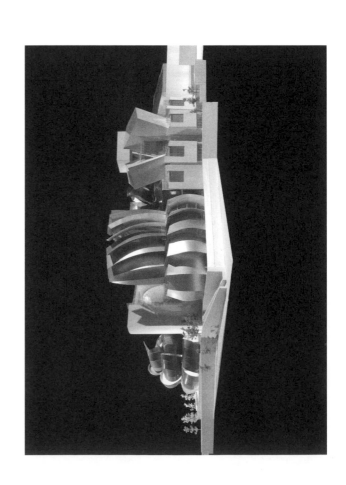

Museum of Tolerance, Jerusalem

Center for Human Dignity, a Project of the Simon Wiesenthal Center

Jerusalem, Israel

2000–

Museum of Tolerance, Jerusalem
Center for Human Dignity,
a Project of the Simon Wiesenthal Center,
Jerusalem, Israel

Design: commenced 2000
Construction: commenced 2004
Status: expected completion 2005/2006
Number of drawings illustrated: 22

The site for the Museum of Tolerance, Jerusalem, occupies a prominent location in the heart of West Jerusalem. It is within a short distance of the Jaffa Gate and the Old City, and bordered by Hillel Street, Moshe Ben Israel Street, Mamila Cemetery, and Independence Park. This site includes two land parcels, linked by a bridge over Hillel Street. The larger of these is on the south side of the street, directly adjacent to Mamila Cemetery, the smaller, on the north side, is within Cats Square, bordering on a dense and active commercial neighborhood filled with shops and restaurants.

The primary intention of the project is to provide exhibition and conference facilities to support programs that promote the ideals of awareness, tolerance, and civility among diverse cultures. It includes a museum, conference facilities, a multipurpose Grand Hall, an auditorium and related support facilities. The components of the project are expressed as distinct objects grouped together in a tight composition. The museum, the conference center, and the Grand Hall occupy the southern parcel of the site and are unified by a central atrium that is sheltered by a glass roof. The auditorium occupies the northern site within Cats Square.

The museum includes individual galleries that are clustered and arranged against a more simple, semi-circular form reminiscent of an amphitheater and opening toward the central atrium. The galleries are visible both from the atrium and from the adjacent conference facilities and the Grand Hall, providing presence to the issues of awareness and tolerance in all areas of the building. The exterior of the museum will be clad in Jerusalem stone.

A spiraling snake-like children's museum, clad in titanium, is located adjacent to the museum on the southern side, creating a link between the building and Independence Park. A retail store clad in Jerusalem stone is located adjacent to the museum on the northern side. The conference center consists of two distinct buildings: the Conference Theater and the Educational Center. The Conference Theater includes a 250-seat primary conference facility with a research center above and will be clad in blue titanium panels on the exterior and wood on the interior. The Educational Center includes nine smaller conference rooms for lectures and smaller conference sessions with a library above and is articulated as a cluster of boxes that will be clad in Jerusalem stone on the exterior and wood on the interior.

The strong, vertically spiraling form of the Grand Hall is intended to serve as an icon for Museum. The Grand Hall is intended to function as a multipurpose space, accommodating temporary exhibitions, banquets, conferences, or lectures. The Grand Hall will be clad in titanium panels on the exterior and in wood on the interior. The 350-seat auditorium of the performing arts center will be made available for community programming to encourage access and use by diverse local groups. The auditorium is intended to serve as an integral aspect of the life of the surrounding neighborhood and will be clad in Jerusalem stone. Another glass-enclosed café is located adjacent to the auditorium.

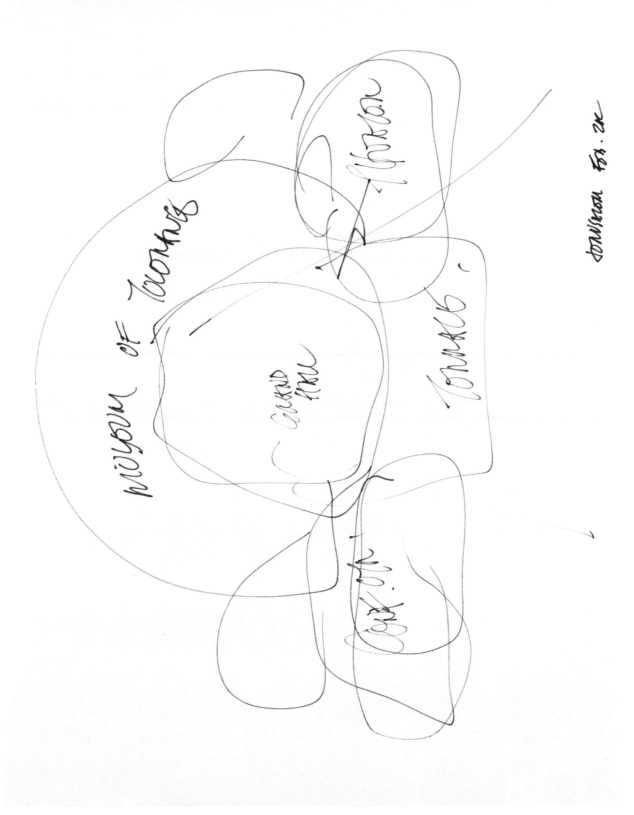

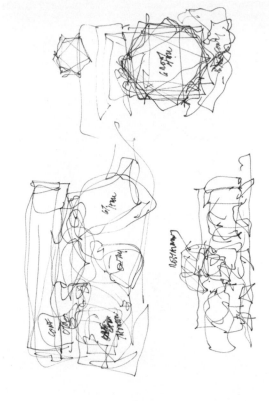

D24.02
D24.03
D24.04
M24.02
04.04.00

I think that if architecture wants to be relevant, it should necessarily relate to the period it's in and take it into account. FG

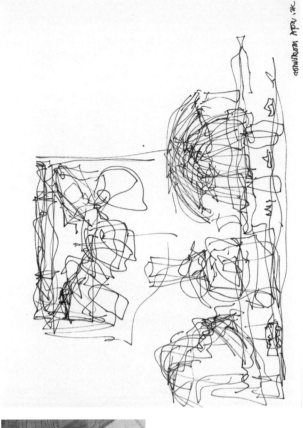

M24.03
06.05.00

D24.06

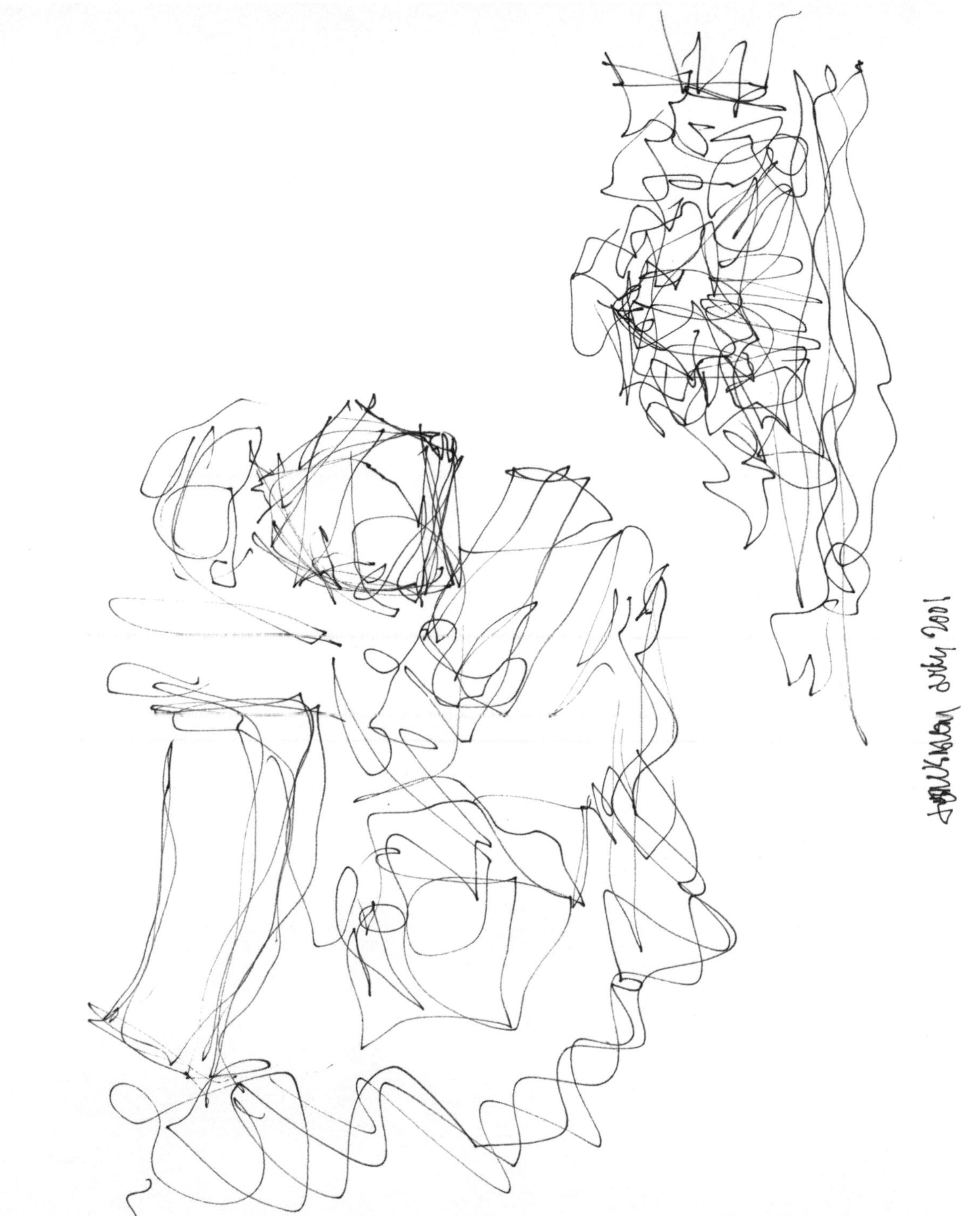

D24.09

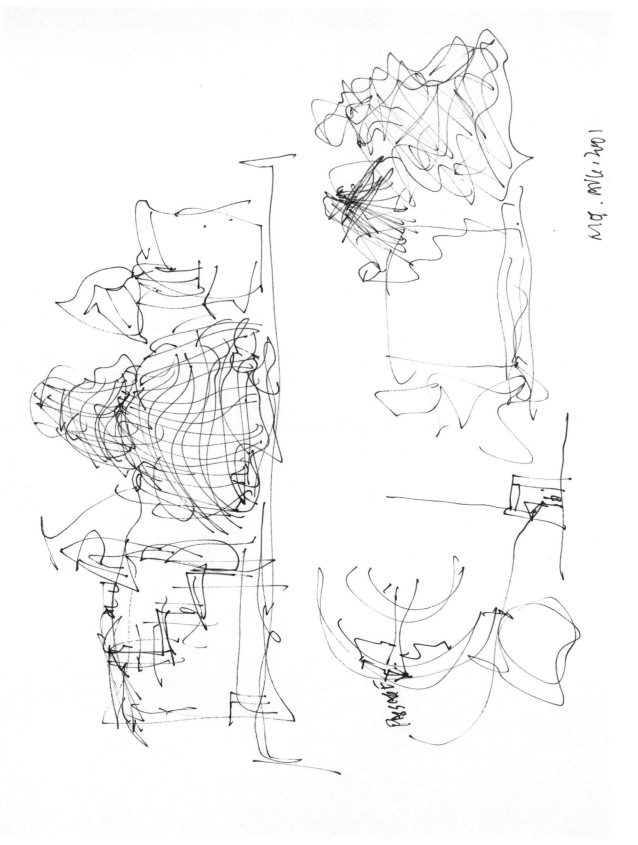

Liu Aug. 2002

HOT · NOV · 2012

MM · KJV. 2001

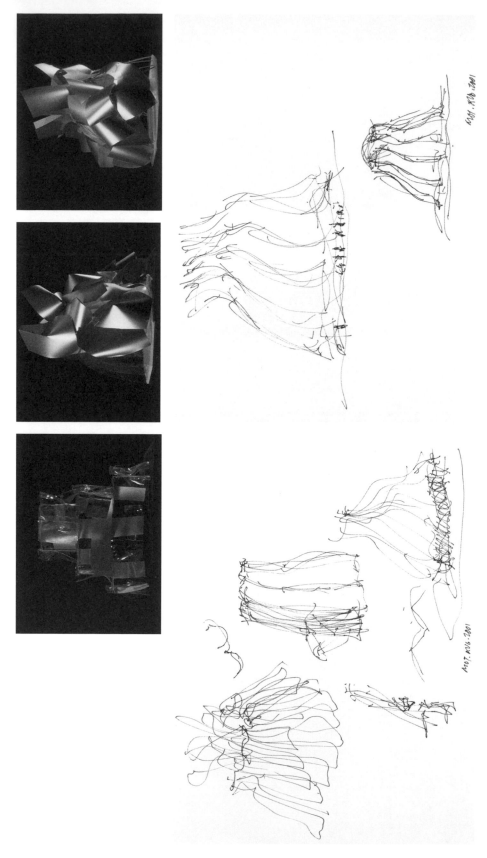

M24.04
M24.05
M24.06
D24.14
D24.15

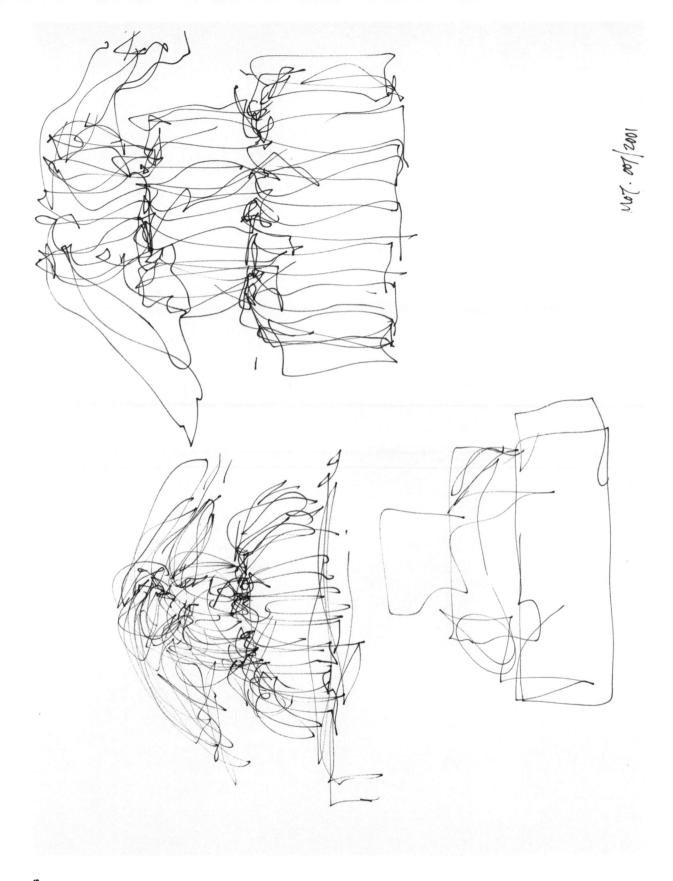

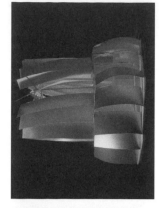

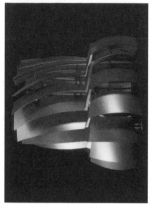

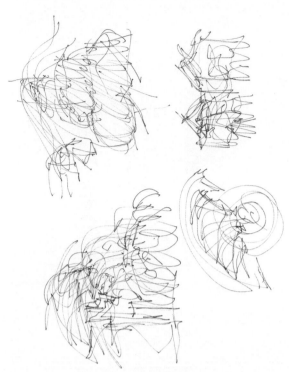

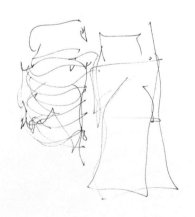

M24.07
M24.08
M24.09
M24.10
D24.17
D24.18

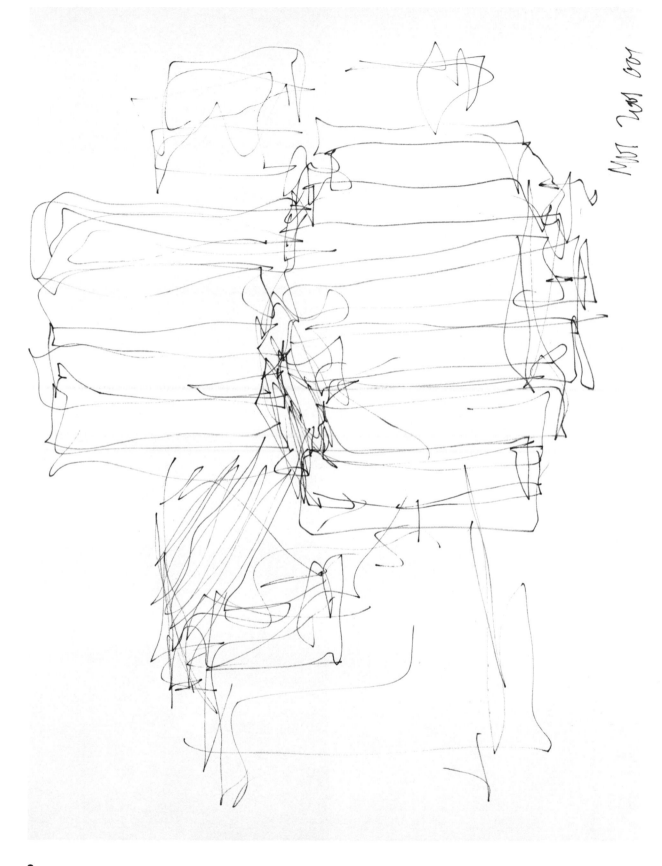

MUST NOT GO

D24.19

We looked hard for a shape that was right for the Museum of Tolerance, a shape that has a centrally radial plan. We looked at the Star of David, but we just couldn't do that, and then we looked at the Dome of the Rock too. We went around and around and tried symmetrical, geometrical shapes. And then we tried organic shapes, going back and forth between the two geometries. Finally, we decided to try to do both. cw

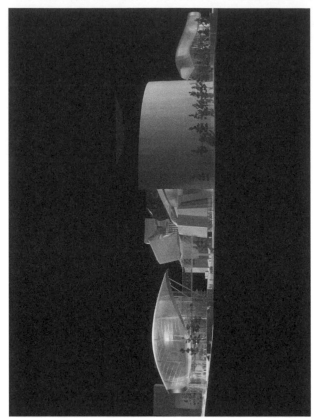

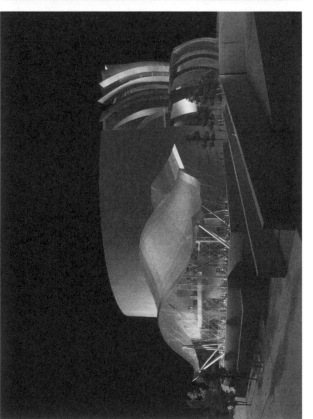

M24.11
M24.12

D24.20

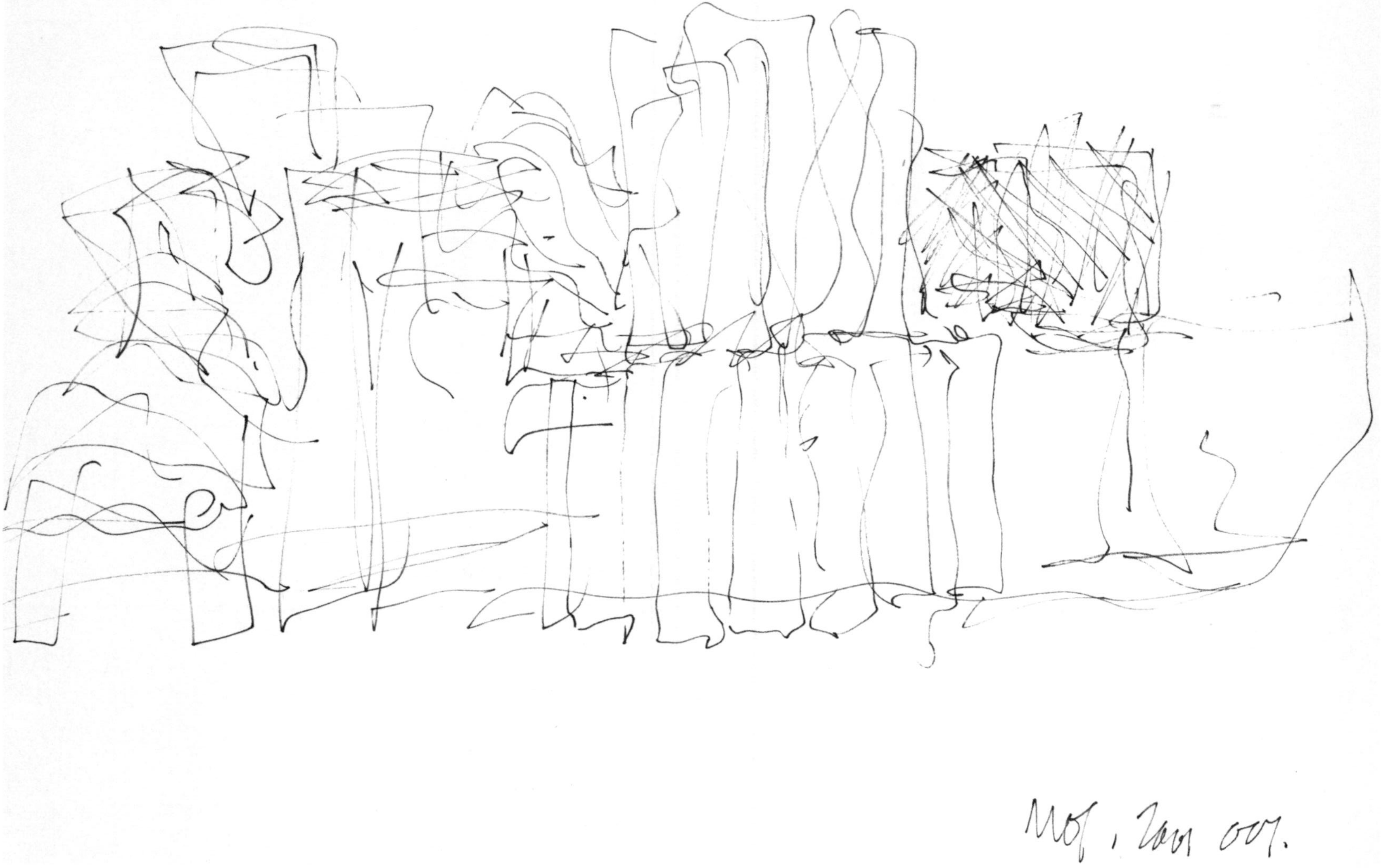

Once I've designed a building and we've finished the development package, I'm pretty much out of it. During the preparation of working drawings for contractors, my team will come to me with inevitable things you can't do, or with technical problems, and we resolve them. I'm involved in those visual things. When construction starts, I usually have to go for the ground-breaking ceremony and the client always makes me give a lecture—that's a given. I don't really visit the site much until the finishing, toward the last three or four months of construction, when you have to deal with all the things that went wrong and the changes you couldn't control. And I don't look for the soft stuff, pretty stuff. Buildings under construction look better than buildings finished. FG

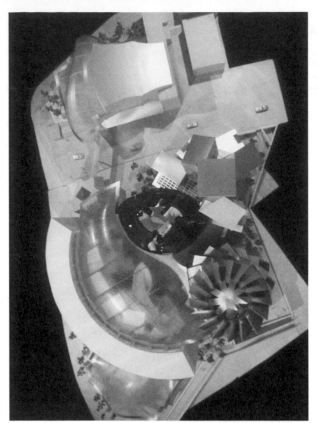

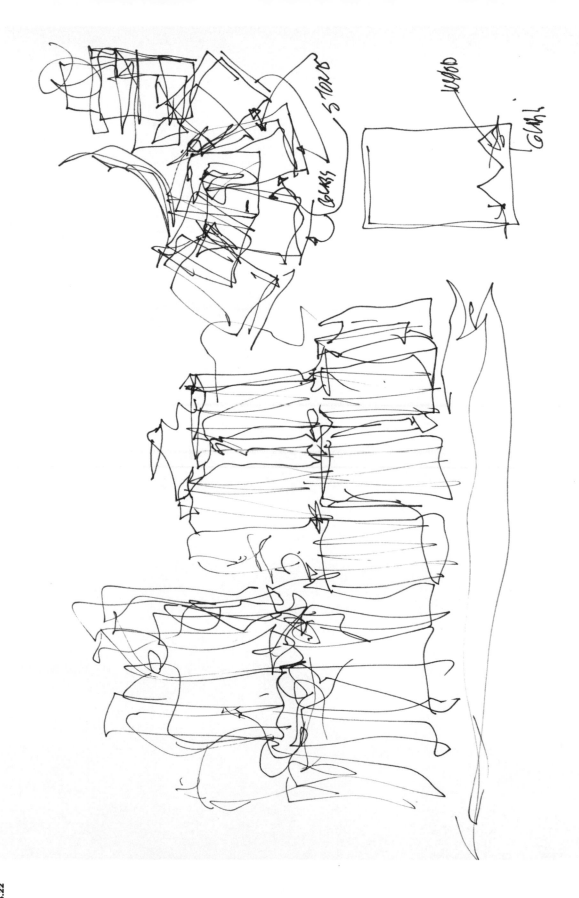

GLASS

GLASS

wood

Glass

n.o.T. nov. 2001

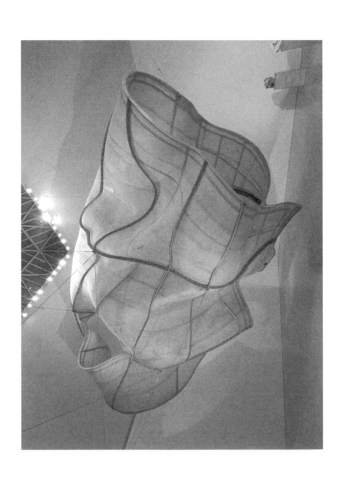

Project 25

Sculptural Study

2001

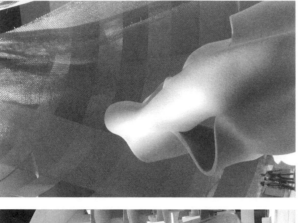

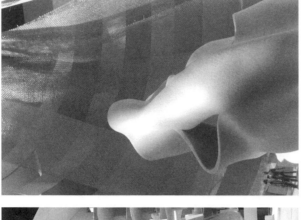

Sculptural Study
2001

Design: commenced in 2001
Status: never completed
Number of drawings illustrated: 4

M25.01
M25.02

This sculptural study was originally conceived as a central component of the exhibition of Gehry's work at the Guggenheim Museum, New York, in 2001. The structure was partially fabricated, but eventually unused. The study was developed using hand-drawn sketches and a hand-made fabric model. The model was digitized, and a three-dimensional surface model was created using the computer program CATIA. A series of formal and technical modifications were made to arrive at the final design. Several physical mock-ups were used to determine the approximate maximum curvature that could be accommodated by the intended cladding material. Computer analysis was used to limit the severity of compound curvature, based on information gathered from the physical mock-ups.

The study was designed to have a light steel frame and fiberglass skin clad in very thin titanium sheets. Formwork that included the breakdown panel joints for the study was CNC milled and assembled. The fiberglass skin for the study was laid to create a monolithic shell. Once the fiberglass skin was completed, the form-work was removed and a later structure was to have been assembled and attached to the monolithic shell. The steel structure would have provided support for the assembled structure, and dimensional stability for each panel when the study was disassembled for transportation. The fiberglass shell would then be cut into the pre-determined breakdown panels, and the titanium sheets were to be attached while the study was still fully assembled. A portion of the shell was later exhibited at the Museum of Contemporary Art in Los Angeles (see image on previous page), and another portion was used in stage sets designed by Gehry for an opera at Bard College.

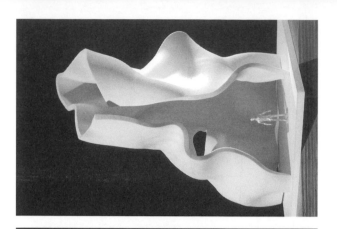

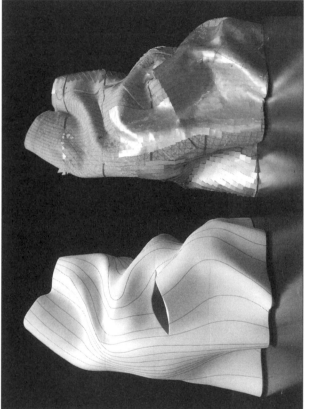

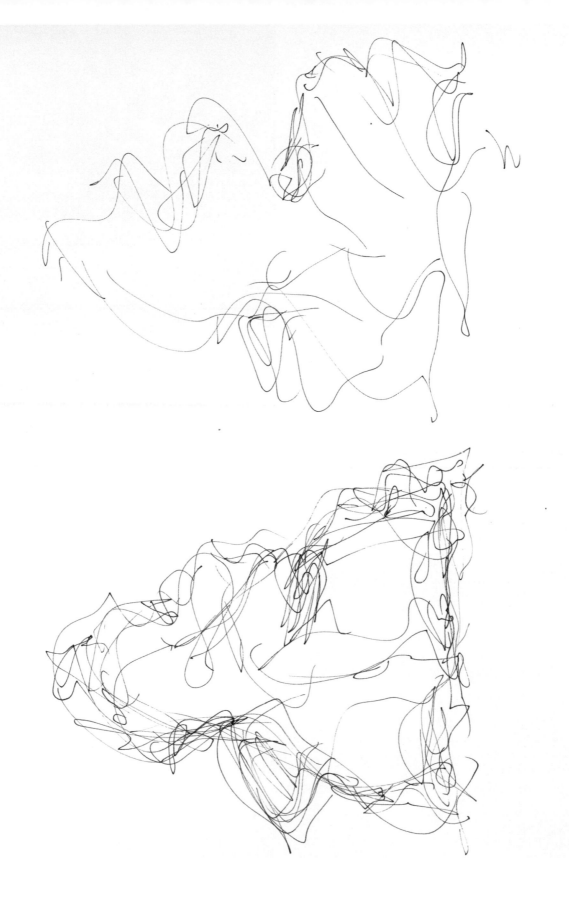

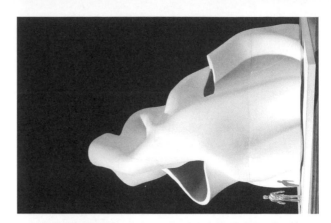

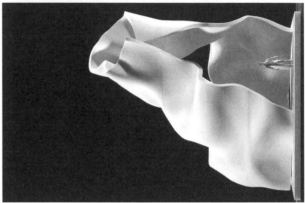

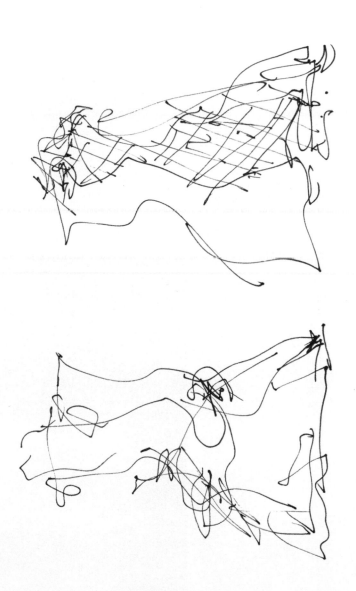

Florence, New York

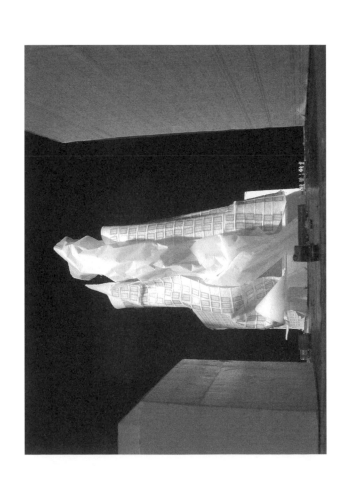

Project 26

Astor Place Hotel
New York, New York
2001

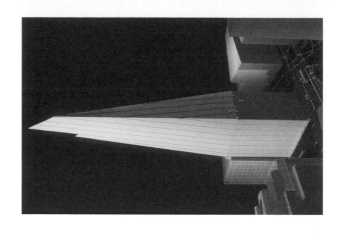

Astor Place Hotel
New York, New York

Design: commenced summer 2001
Status: concept only
Number of drawings illustrated: 15

The site for the Astor Place Hotel was located at the intersection of Astor Place, Lafayette Street, and 4th Avenue in New York, immediately adjacent to the Cooper Union for the Advancement of Science and Art.

Zoning regulations and site constraints suggested the development of a program in which the lobby, reception area, and additional public amenities, including a restaurant, a café, a bar, and a fitness center, would be located below ground, with the entire above-ground volume devoted exclusively to guest rooms. Many schemes were explored within a condensed design period, including an open courtyard scheme, a single tower scheme, a multiple tower scheme, and a mid-rise scheme based on a cruciform plan that ultimately appeared to be the most efficient option. Before any of the schemes could be fully developed, the project was placed on indefinite hold following the events of September 11, 2001. The client has since abandoned this project.

M26.01
08.03.01

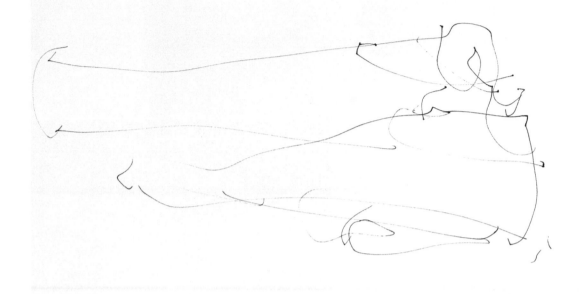

ATLAS PL. 2000 R13

ATLAS PL. 2000 R16

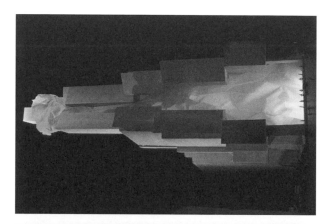

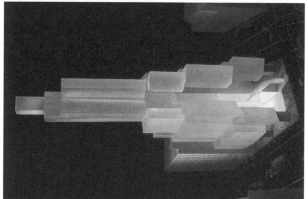

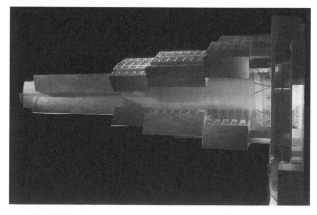

M26.02
08.03.01

M26.03
08.02.01

M26.04
08.02.01

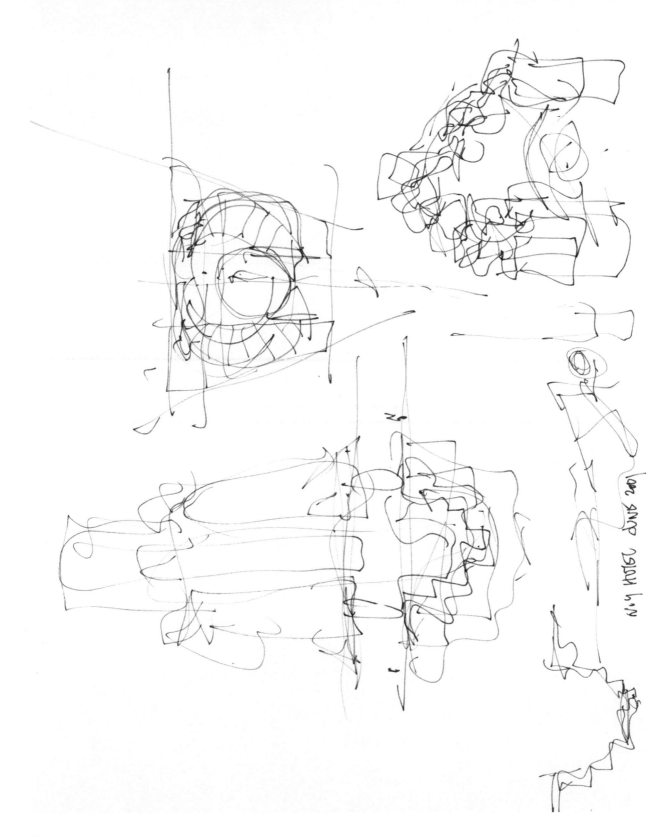

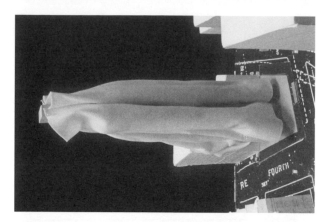

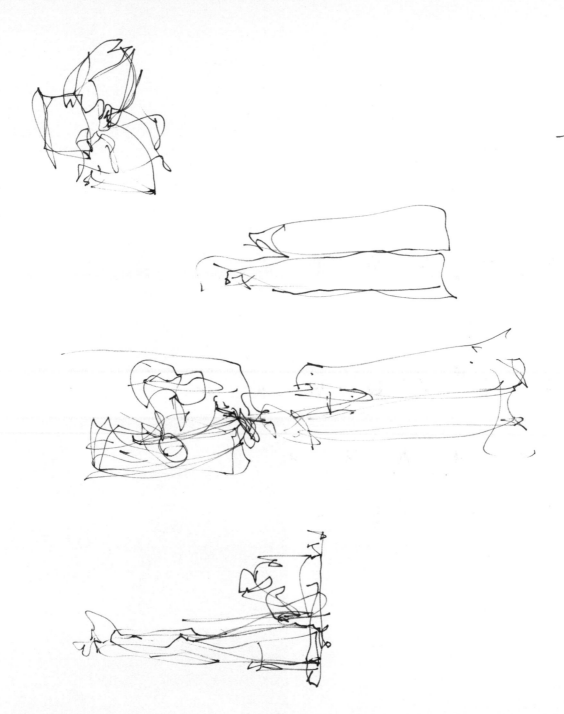

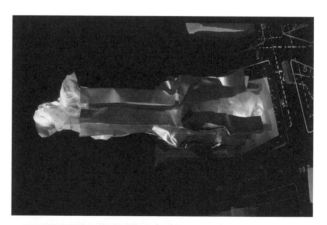

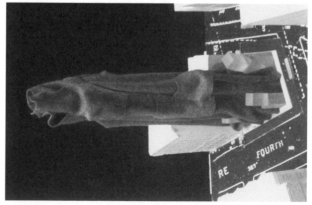

M26.07
2001

M26.08
08.02.01

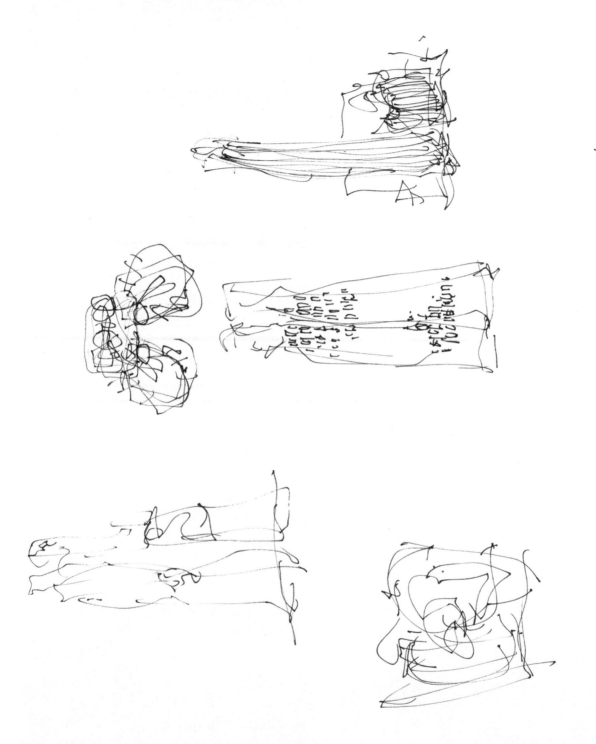

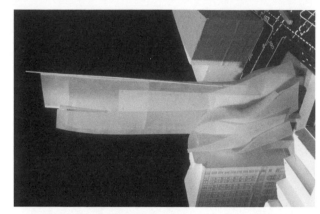

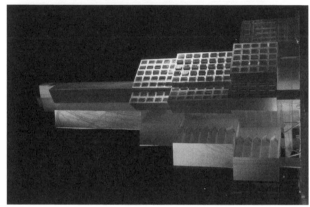

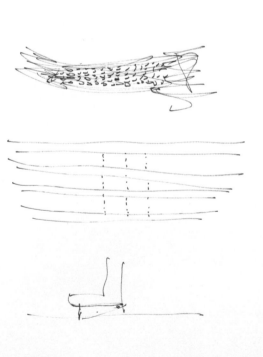

ASFOU 2001 007

D26.06
M26.09
08.03.01
M26.10
2001

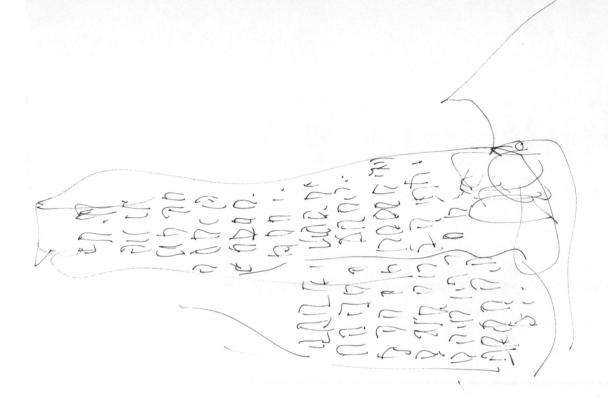

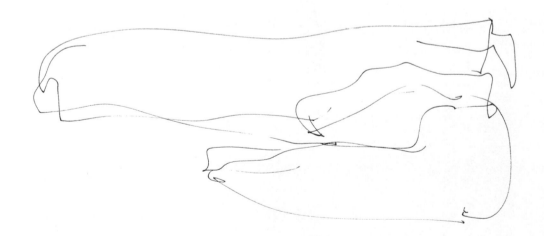

A lot of these drawings were done for discussions with Ian Schrager, for what would have been the first hotel he built from scratch. Schrager told us he likes what we call "Fred and Ginger," the Nationale-Nederlanden building in Prague, so we talked a little about doing this as a twin tower. But, in fact, this structure is less of a twin tower than it is a play on Dan Flavin's sculptures. The positive and the negative. It's really one building that has a space in the middle. I think of it as a sculpture, and I'd make a direct connection between this and Frank's Sculptural Study rather than the *New York Times* competition design.

Because this was to be a "hip" Schrager hotel, we thought we would connect the rooms up above with the lobby, which is actually underground; so it became necessary to create a vertical slot. This came out of understanding what a Schrager hotel is, as well as an interpretation of the site. By cutting this slot into the building you make a visual connection all the way down to the lobby. The elevators and services would have been on the back side. Architecturally it's an exciting design, but it also would have been an efficient building. And by making the building as efficient as we could, we basically eliminated the extra costs in creating extra elevator stops. I guess that the money we saved there allowed us to make a more exuberant skin. That was the idea. We were ready to go, except that 9/11 happened. EC

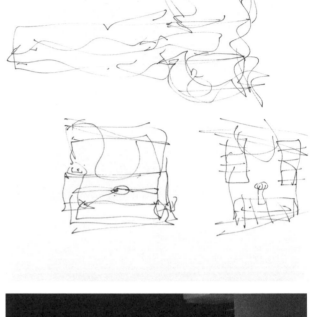

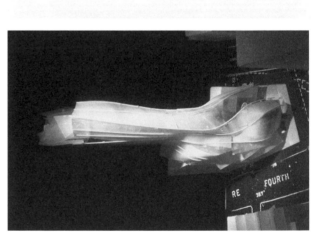

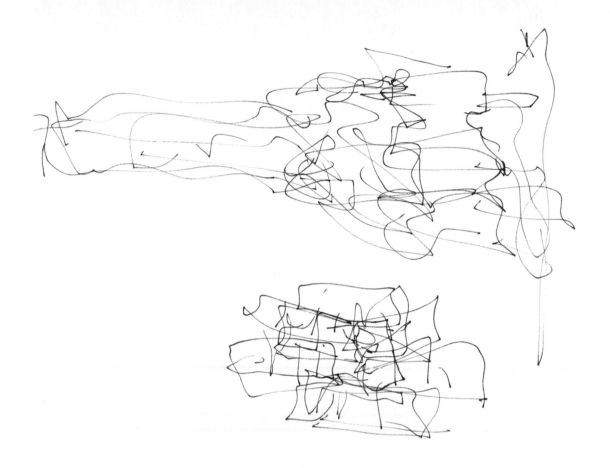

Avio, 2001 Basron

07. NOV. 2001

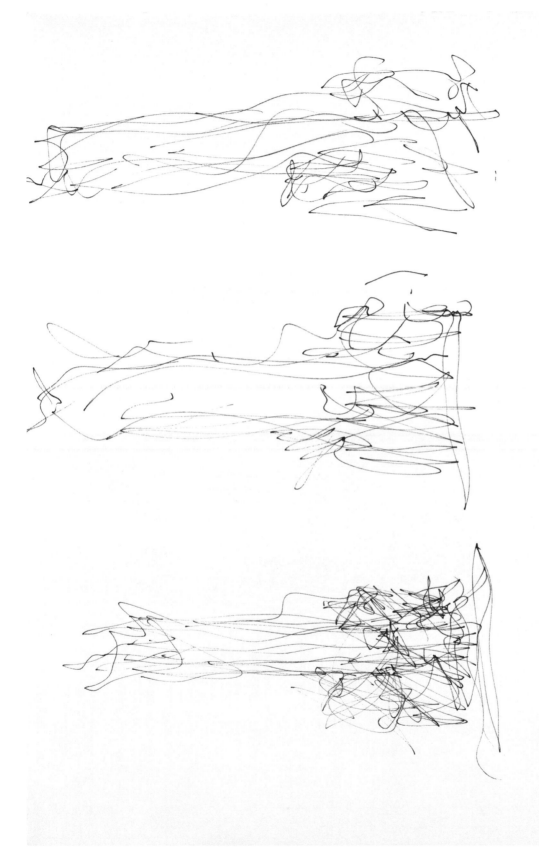

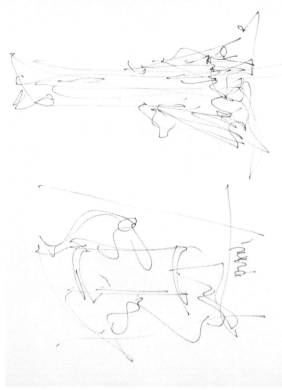

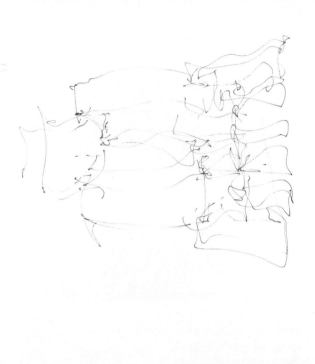

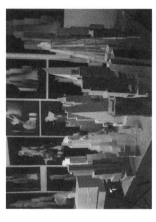

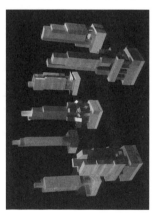

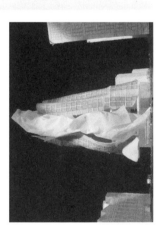

M26.12
07.30.01

M26.13
08.01.01

M26.14
2001

M26.15
2001

D26.13

D26.14

460 | 461

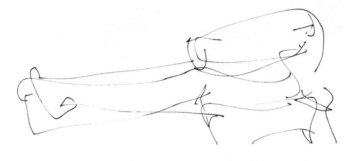

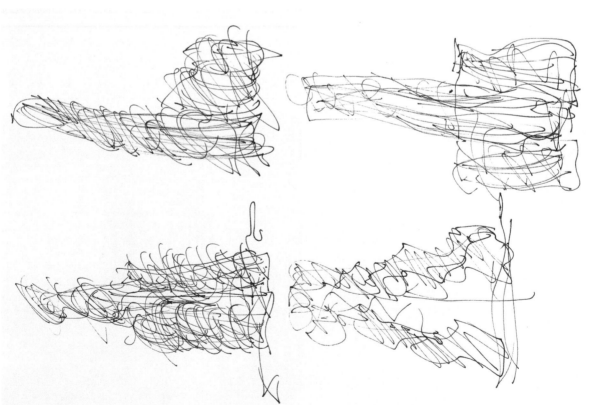

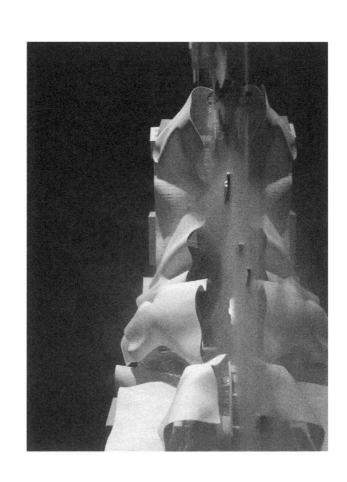

Project 27

Venice Gateway

Marco Polo Airport,
Venice-Tessera, Italy
1998–

Venice Gateway
Marco Polo Airport, Venice-Tessera, Italy

Design: commenced 1998
Status: ongoing
Number of drawings illustrated: 24

The Venice Gateway is a multi-purpose complex located at the Marco Polo Airport in Venice-Tessera, Italy. The airport is in the midst of an expansion program, which includes the construction of a new air terminal and runway, a supporting infrastructure, and parking facilities.

As a component of this overall expansion, the Gateway is intended to provide upgraded and expanded services to facilitate the exchange of travelers between the airport and boat and water taxi services, and to provide additional amenities, including a hotel, a conference center, retail facilities, and related support facilities. This complex aims at fulfilling a number of critical needs in the overall expansion plan for the airport, which is of particular importance as a result the recent increase in the number of travelers using the airport and the more general growth of the entire Veneto region.

The design currently demonstrates preliminary concepts concerning program, scope, volume, and scale. The overall objective underlying this design is to develop a project that fulfills the needs of the airport and of the surrounding region while at the same time celebrating the traditions and history of the area. The relationship of the complex to the water, and to the forms, materials, and colors of this complex, are intended to reinterpret these traditions within the context of current technologies, providing a joyful expression of contemporary Veneto culture.

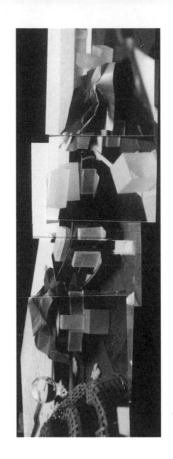

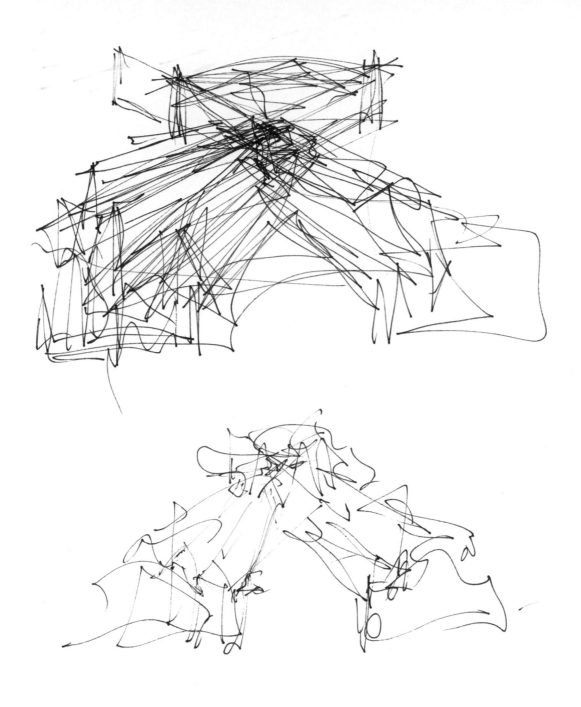

USONIE AUG. '98

VENICE July/98.

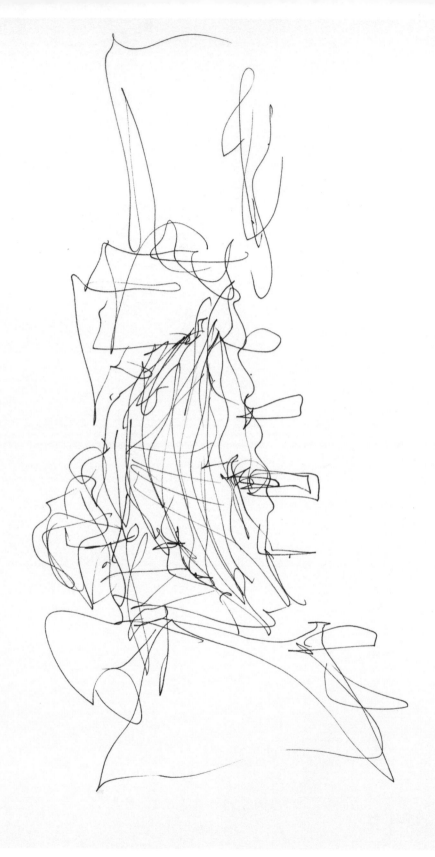

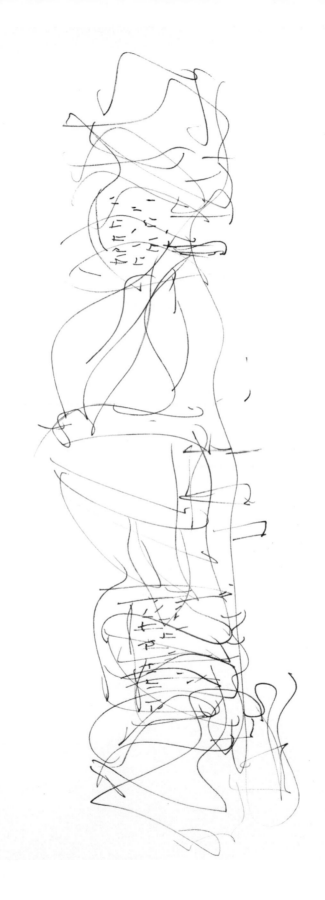

LUDWIG GODT · 62

D27.08

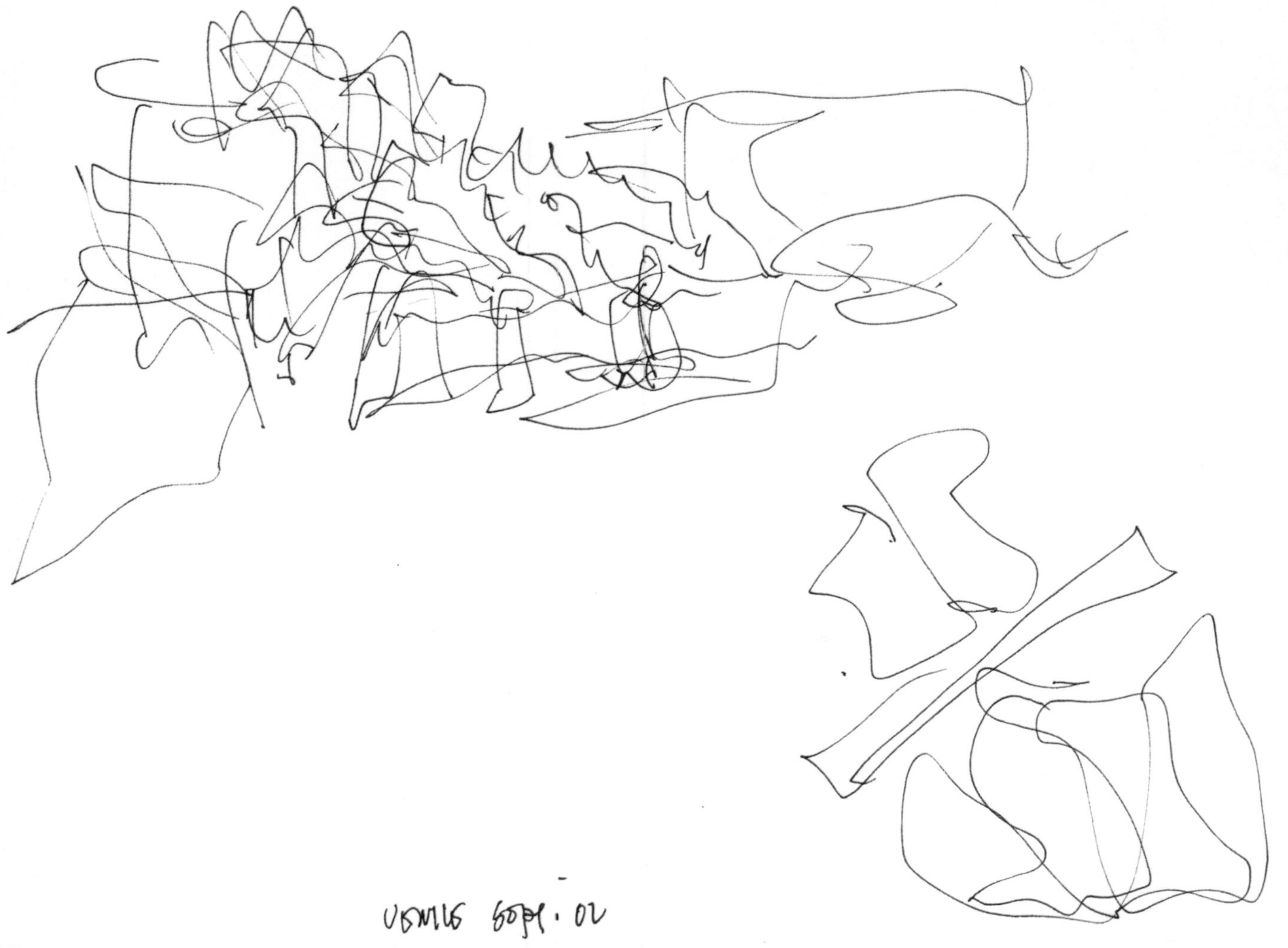

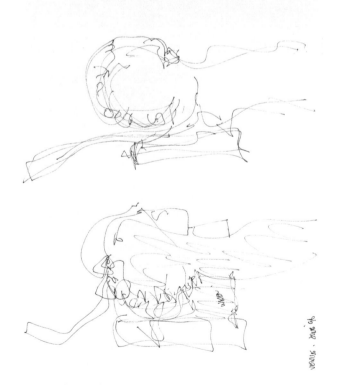

D27.10

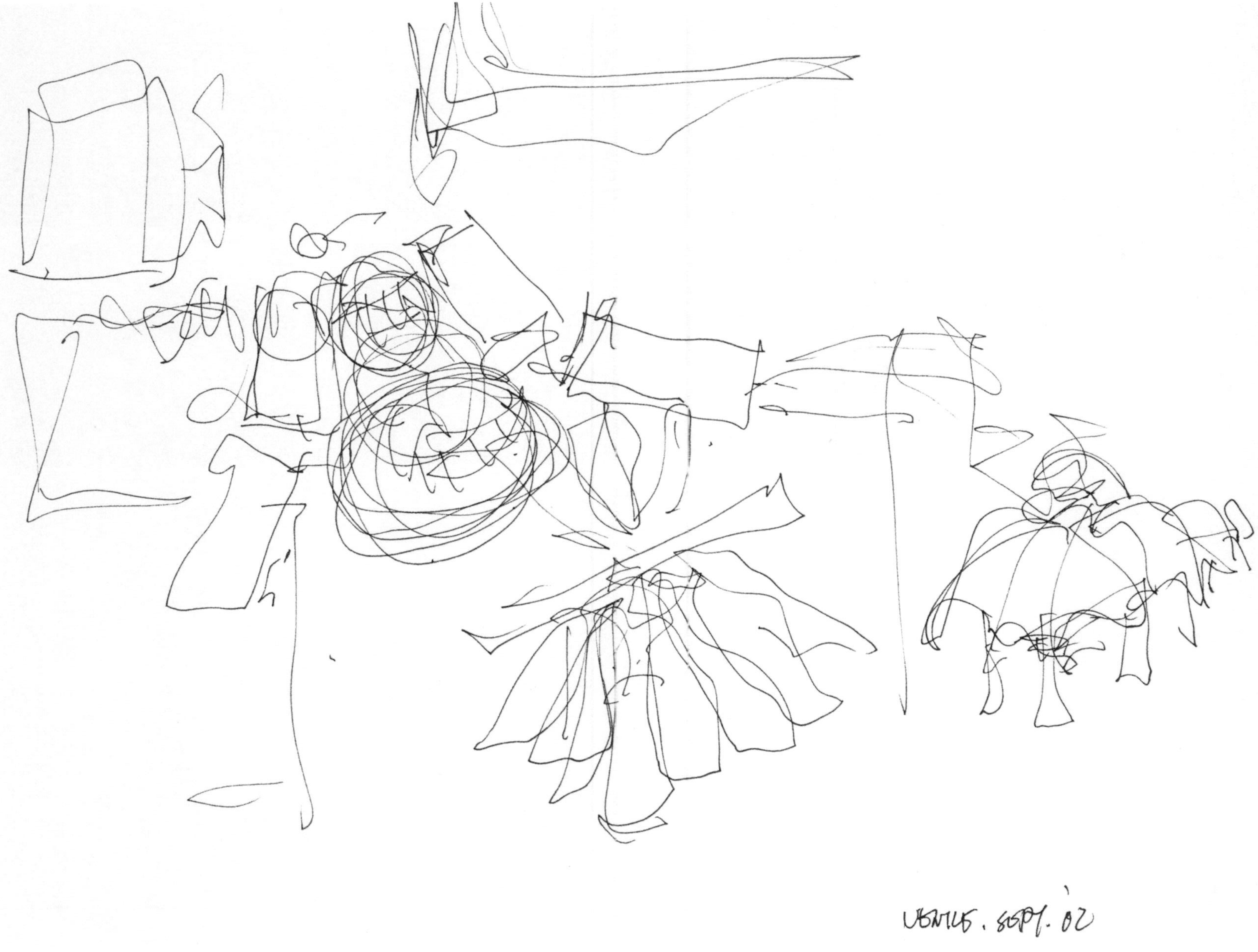

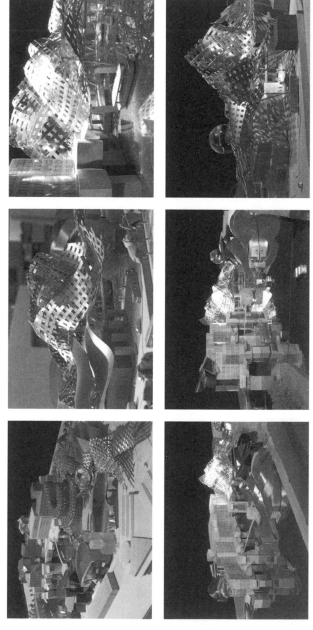

M27.04
09.04.98

M27.05
09.04.98

M27.06
09.04.98

M27.07
09.04.98

M27.08
09.04.98

M27.09
09.04.98

476
477

Danilo Dobri, 01.11.'02.

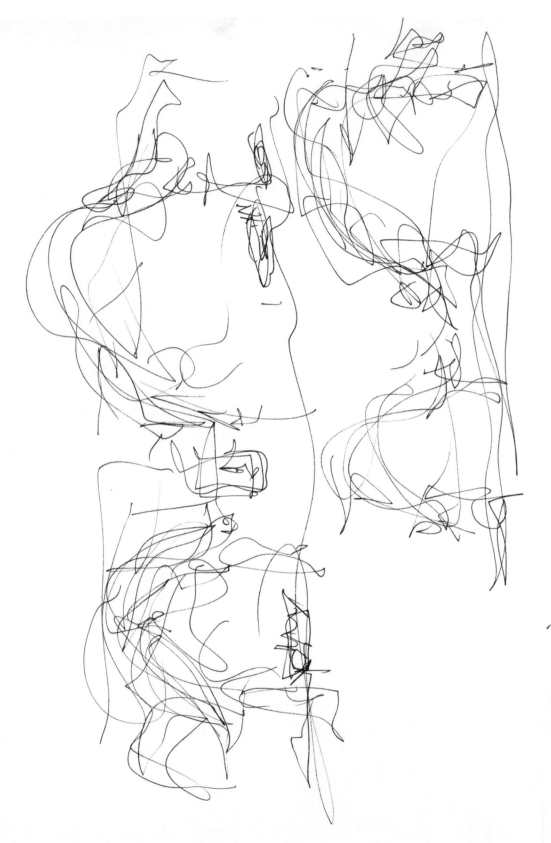

M27.10
02.02
M27.11
02.02
M27.12
02.02
M27.13
02.02
M27.14
02.02

480
481

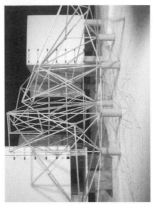

M27.15
11.02

M27.16
11.02

M27.17
11.02

M27.18
11.02

M27.19
11.02

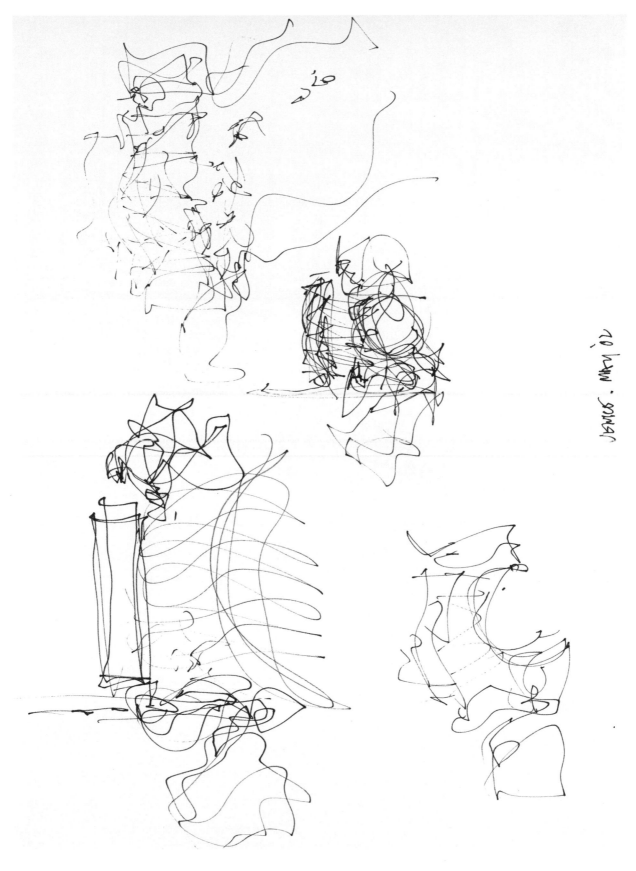

James · May 01

Orita Nagamichi 2007

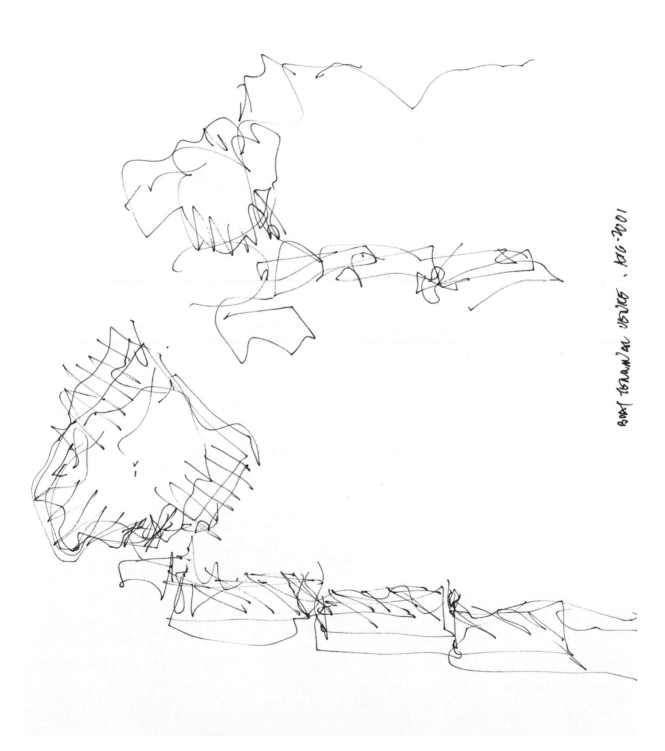

BOAT TERMINAL VENICE . AUG·2001

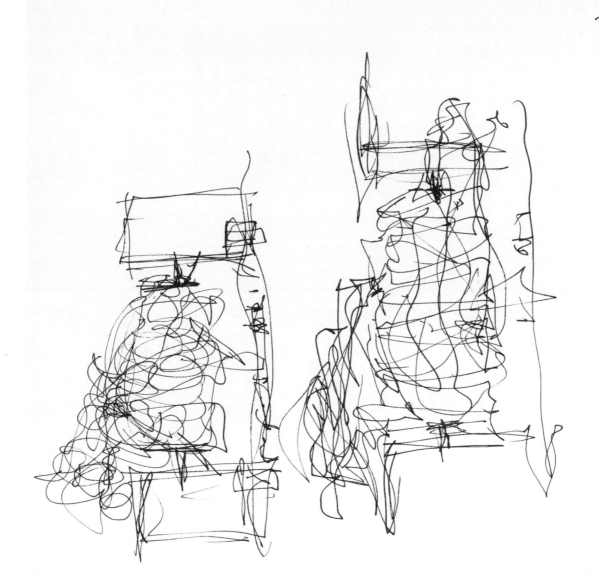

D27.19

D27.20

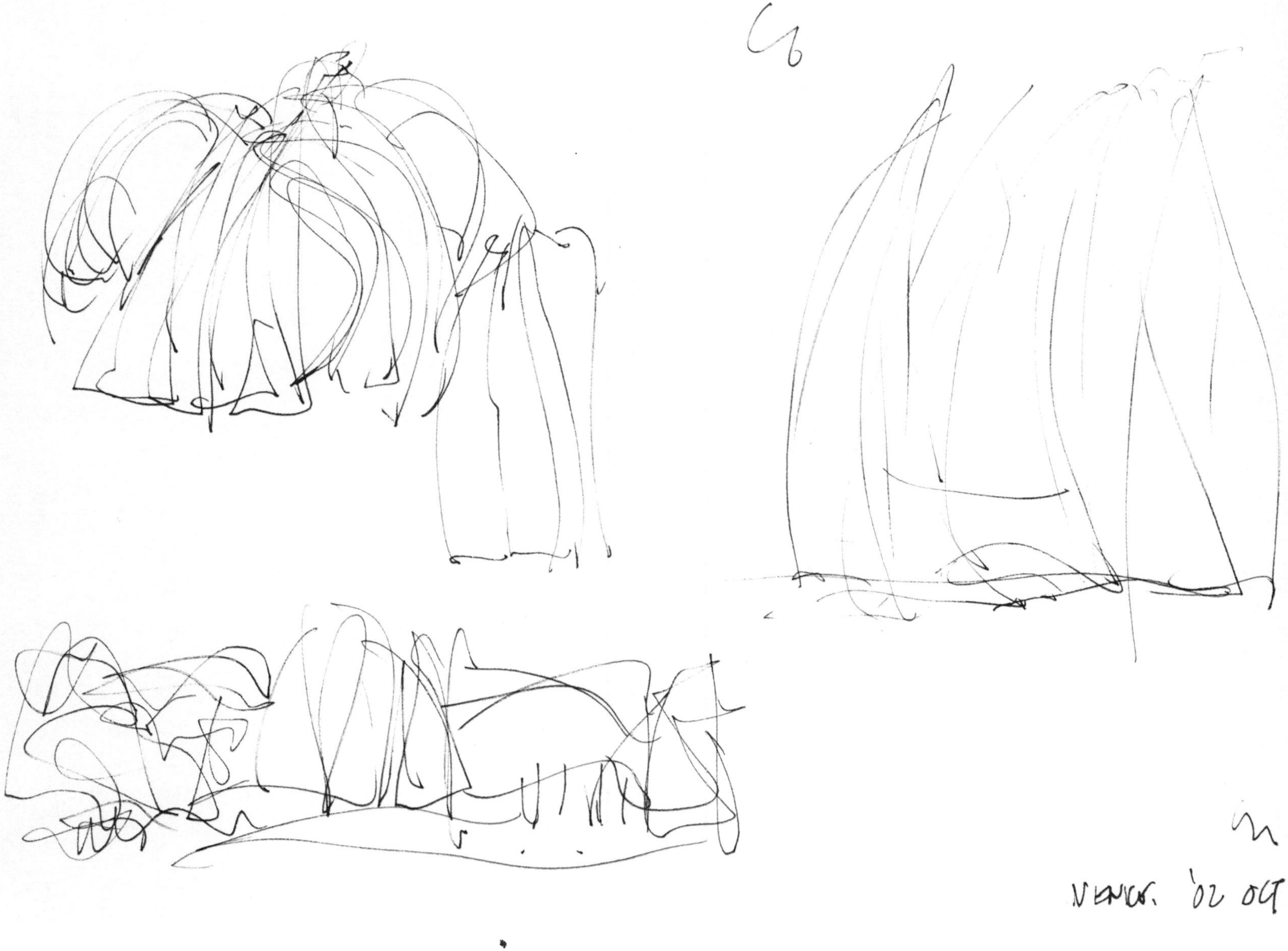

I'm just an architect, a dumb architect. I don't like to argue about the terms. I trained as an architect, I make buildings, so I'm an architect. Mostly I enjoy the process even better than the finale. I usually have some kind of love affair with the people, the things, the meetings—trying to live up to their dreams. FG

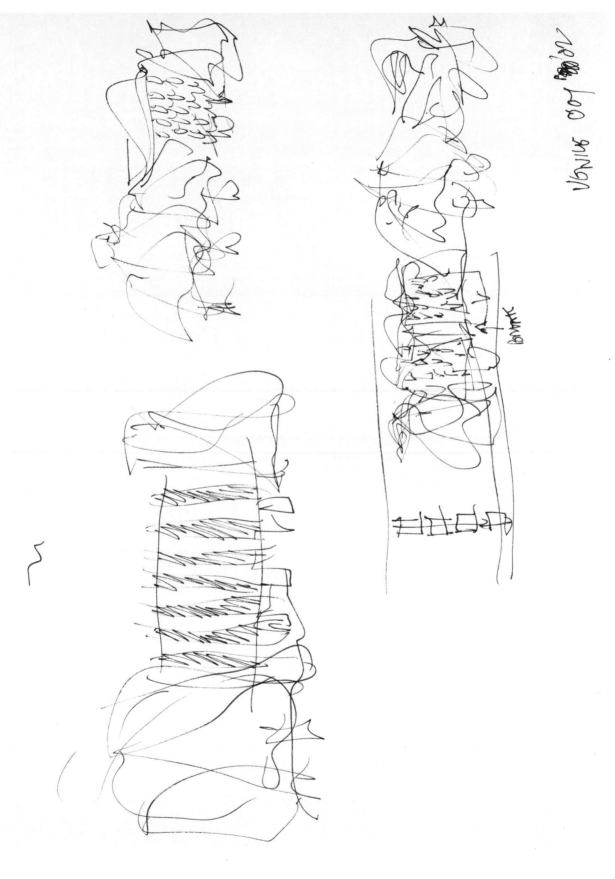

D27.21

Venus, oo, 69

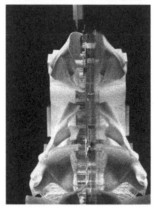

M27.22
M27.23
M27.24
M27.25

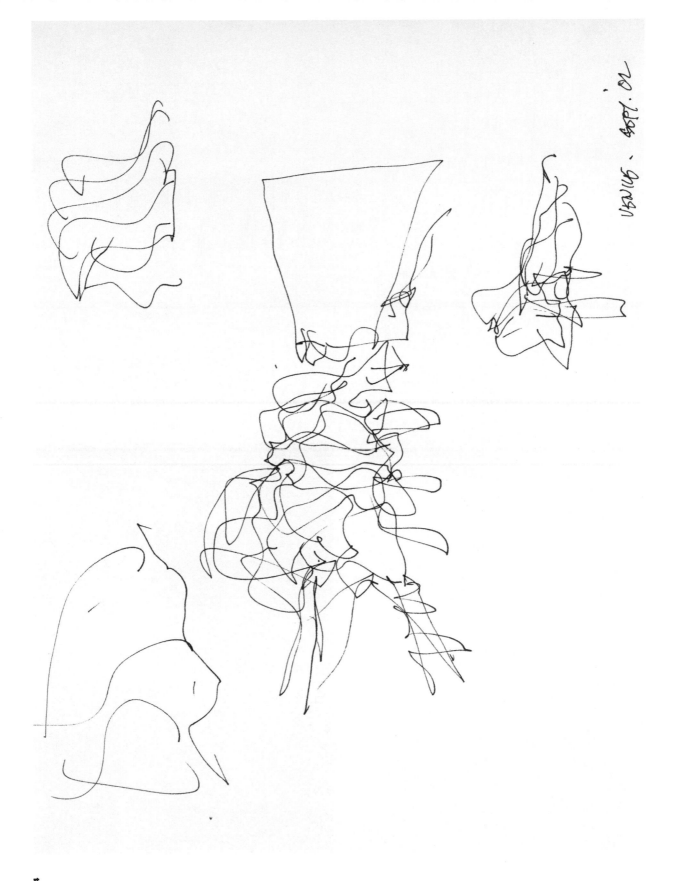

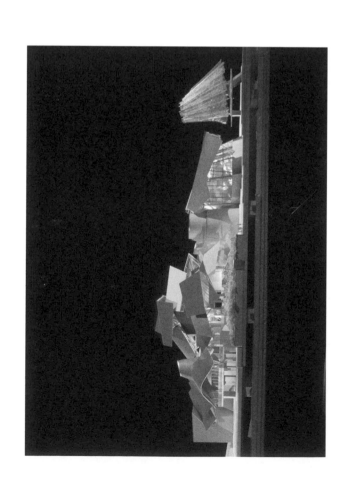

Project 28

Puente de Vida: Panama Museum of Biodiversity

Panama City, Panama

2000–

**Puente de Vida: Panama Museum
of Biodiversity**
Panama City, Panama

Design: commenced 2000
Construction: commenced 2004
Status: expected completion 2006
Number of drawings illustrated: 14

The Puente de Vida overlooks the Pacific
entrance to the Panama Canal and will
accommodate an exhibition display that
will link the geological rise of the isthmus
of Panama to significant changes in
aquatic and terrestrial plant and animal
life in the region.

The museum is organized around a central
open-air atrium with exhibition areas
located to the east and west. A retail
space is located to the north of the atrium
and is oriented to take advantage of
views toward Panama City. A temporary
exhibition area and a café are located to
the south of the atrium and are oriented
to take advantage of views toward the
Pacific entrance to the Panama Canal.

Primary exterior materials include brightly
painted aluminum panels. Primary interior
materials include brightly painted smooth
plaster walls set against an exposed steel
structure.

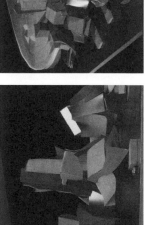

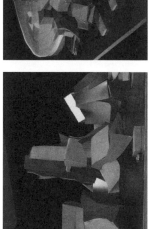

M28.01
12.15.99

M28.02
12.15.99

M28.03
12.15.99

PARKWK. many o'

D28.01

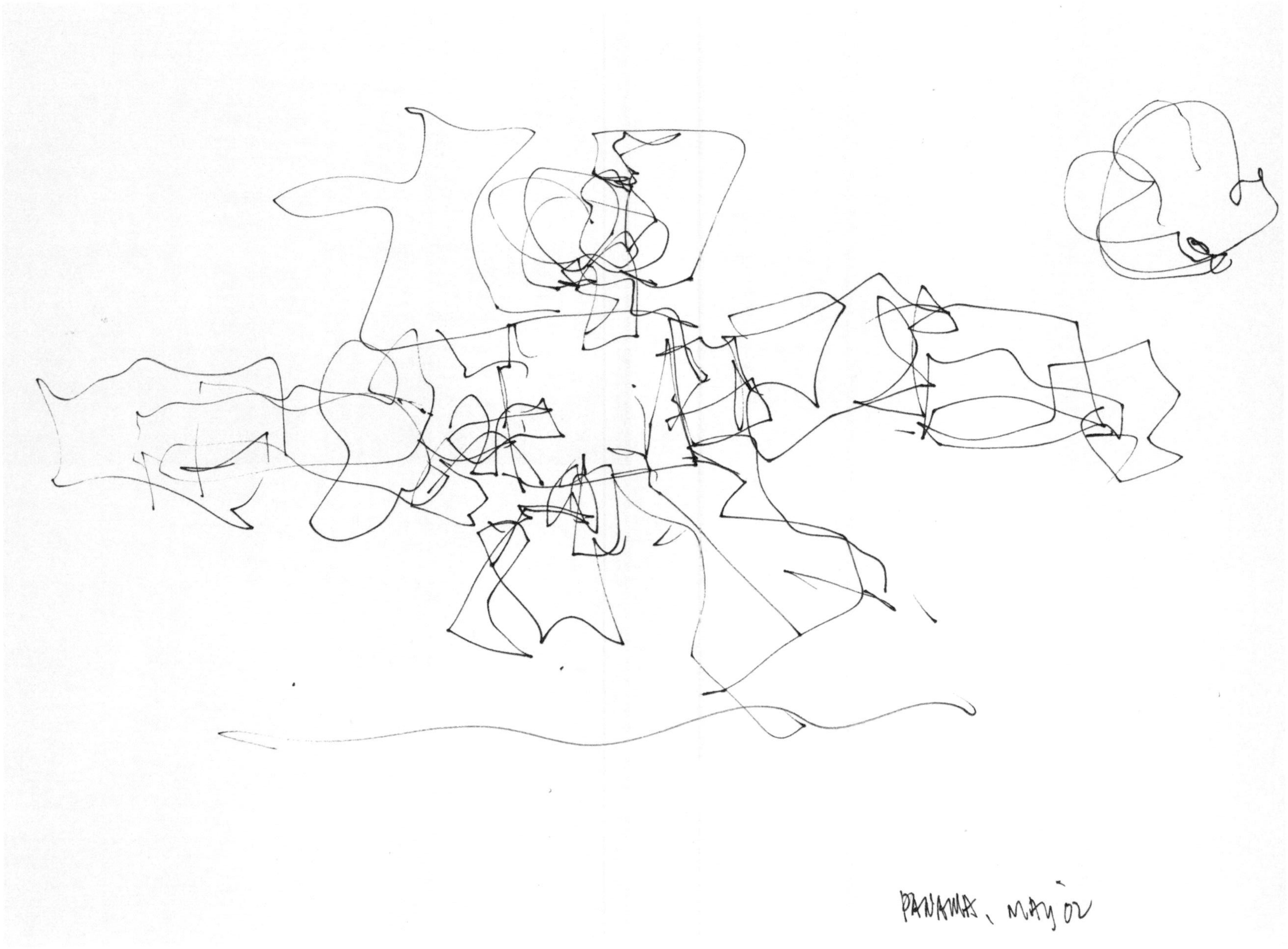

M28.04

M28.05
11.30.02

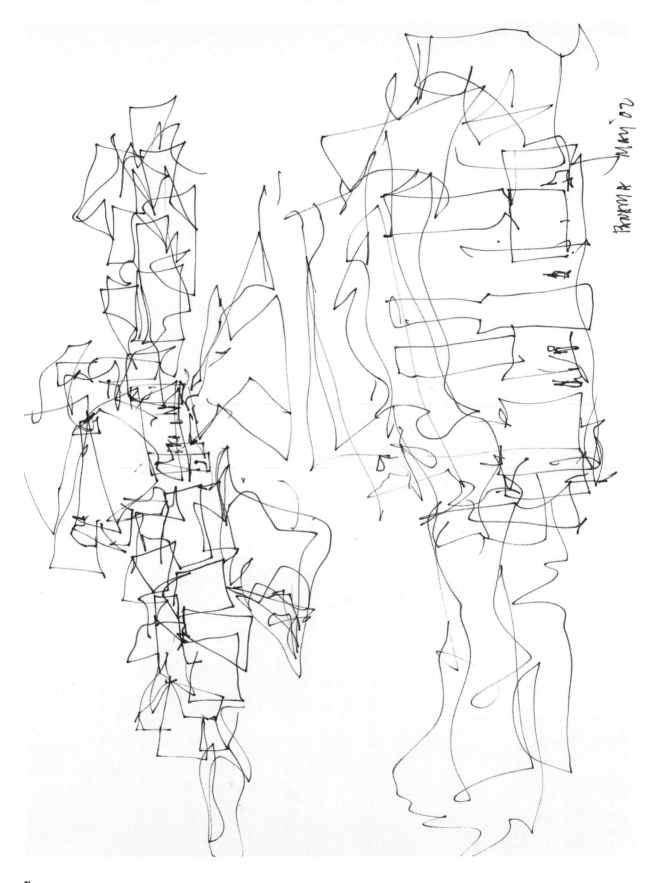

Barcelona, may '05

MIKYOUN ~ DEC. 2001

URBAN DRAWING
ON PAPER,
CONTINUED URBAN CONCEPT,
WATER AND THE UP'S
TO THE EARTH.

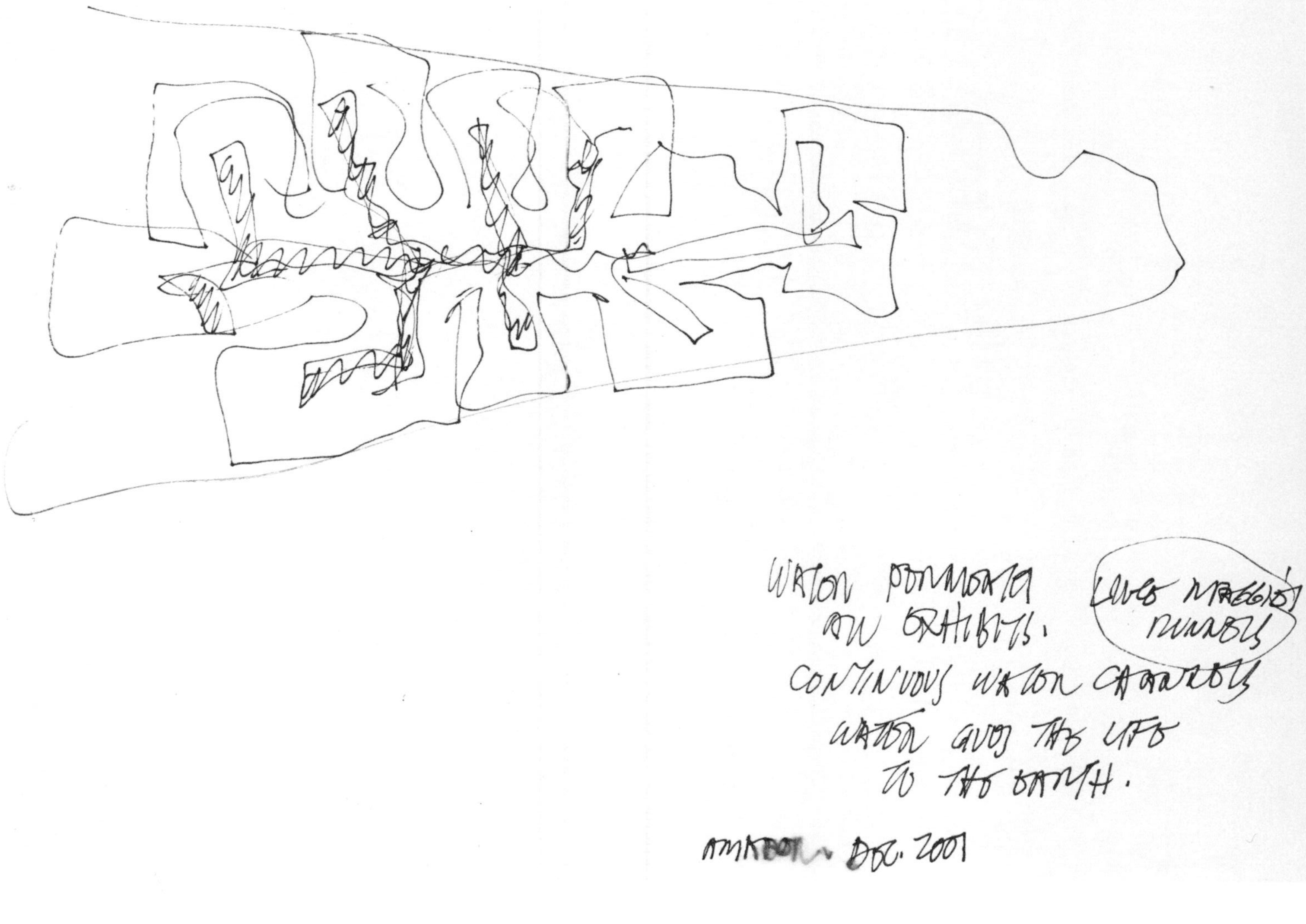

CORE MAGRID
DUNES

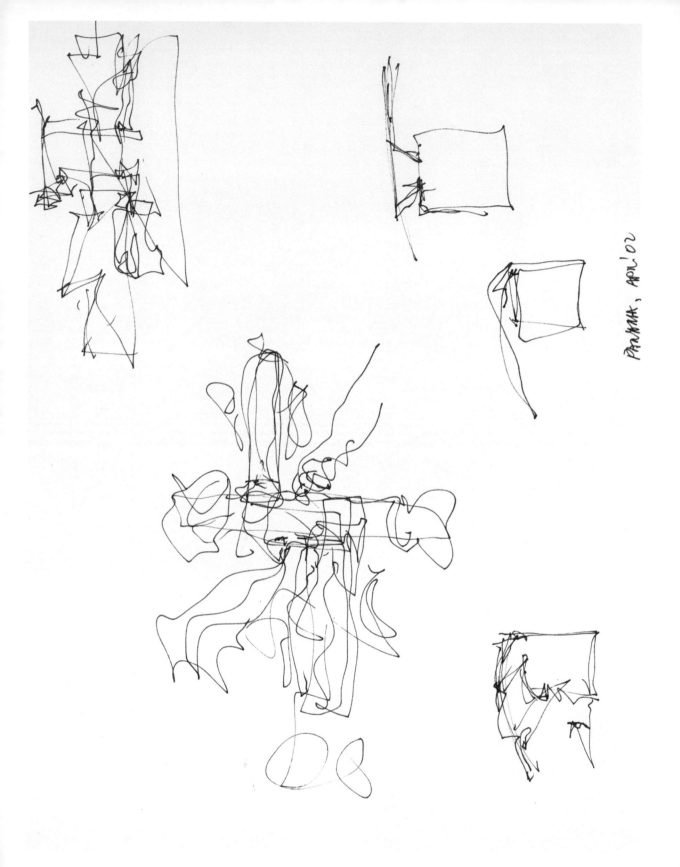

PRAGUE, APR'02

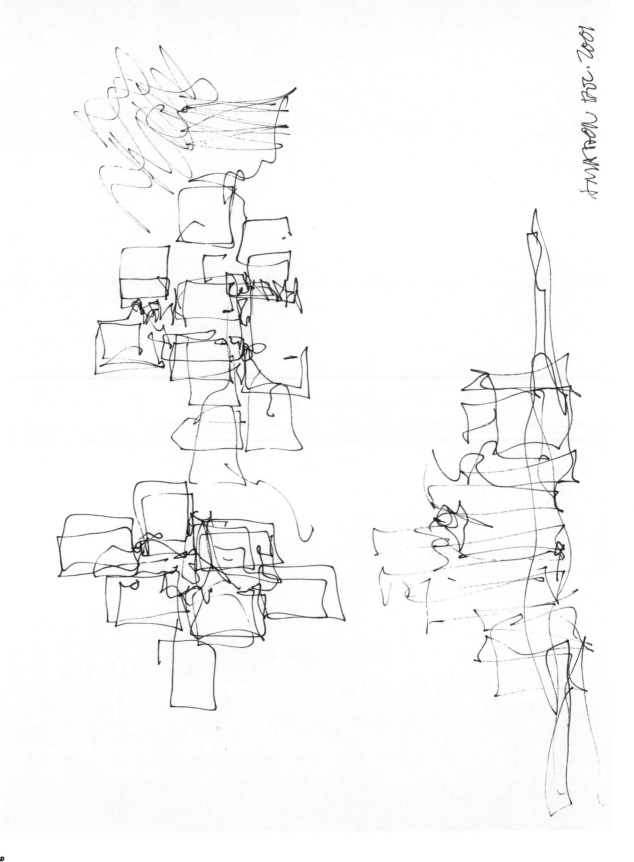

AVIATION INST. 2001

D28.06

M28.06
11.30.02

M28.07
11.30.02

M28.08
11.30.02

M28.09
11.30.02

M28.10
11.30.02

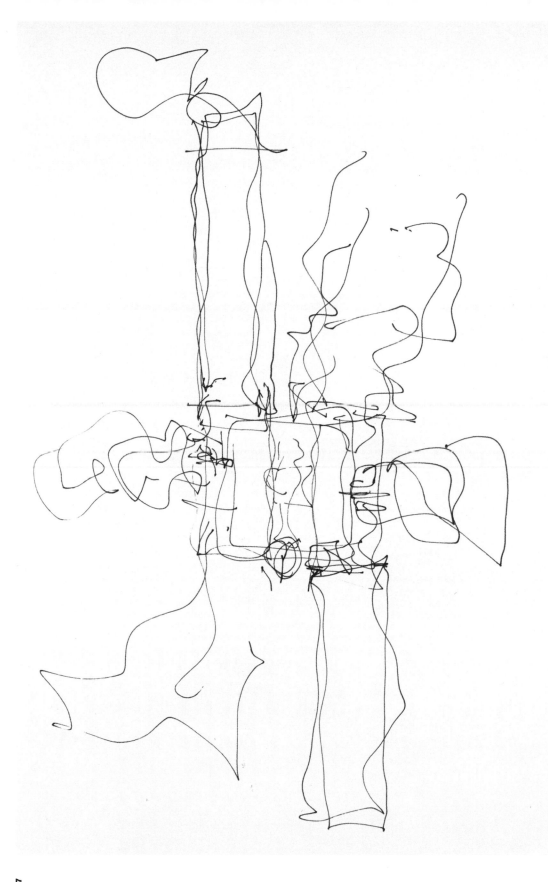

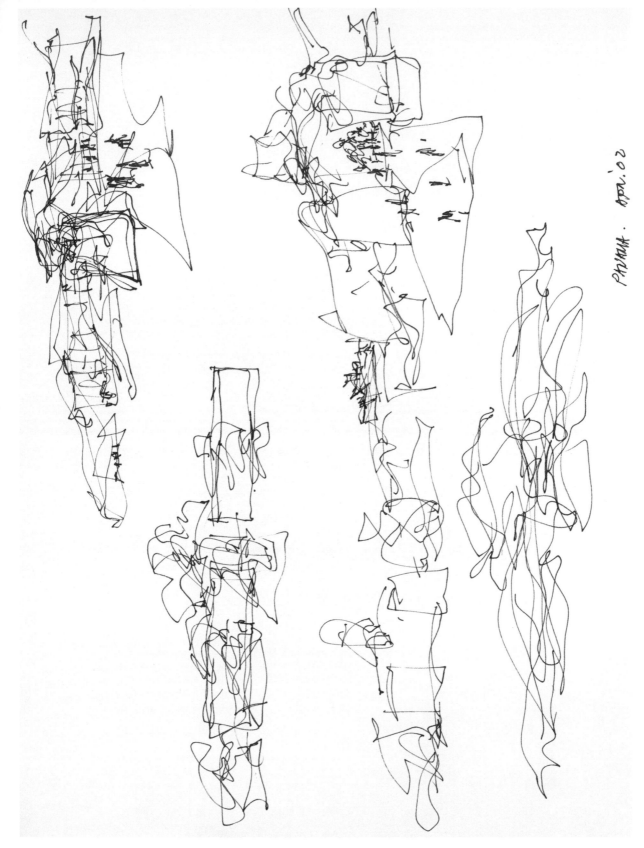

PARAMH. apri.'02

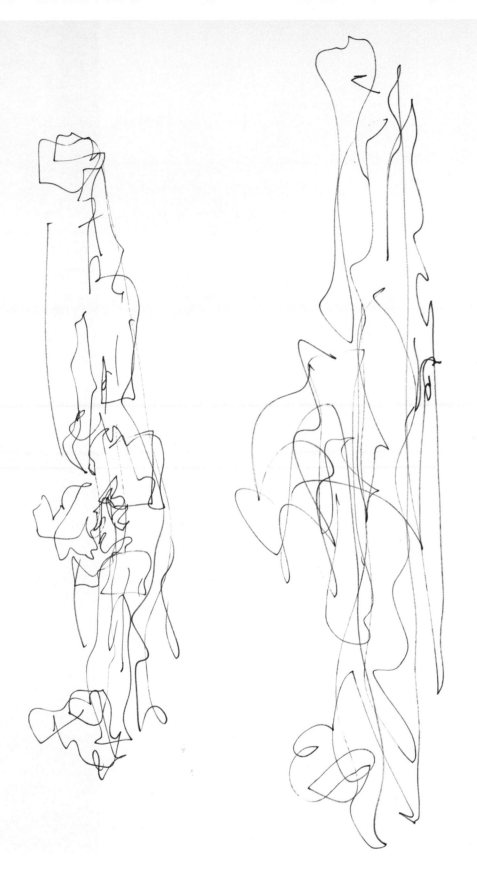

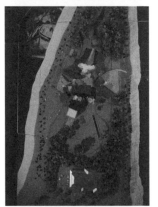

M28.11
01.28.03

M28.12
01.28.03

M28.13
01.27.03

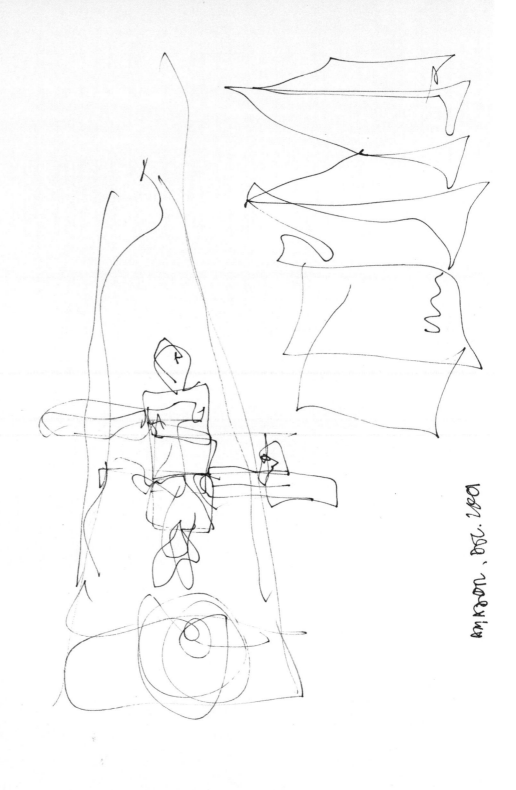

Ankara, Dec. 2001

D28.11

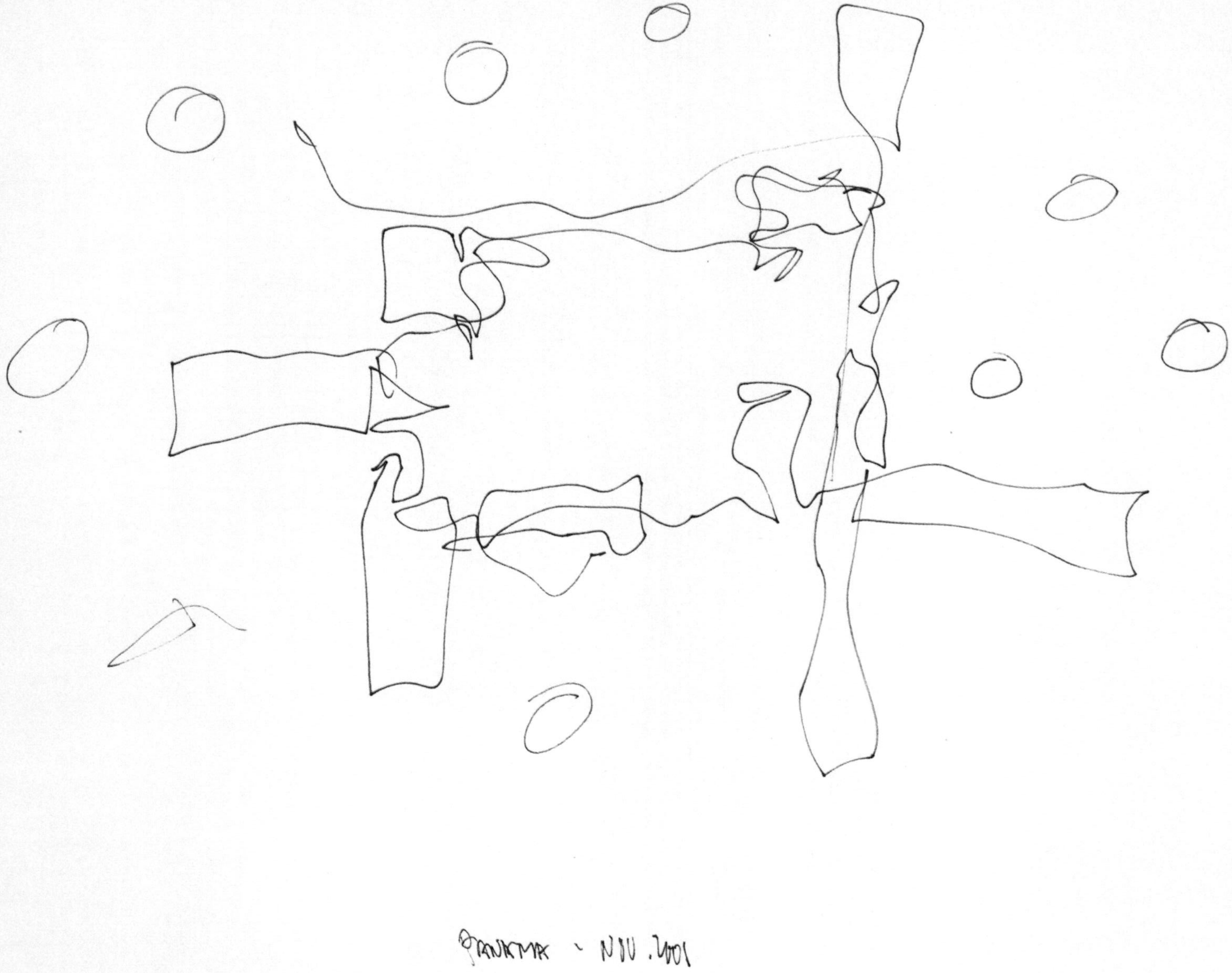

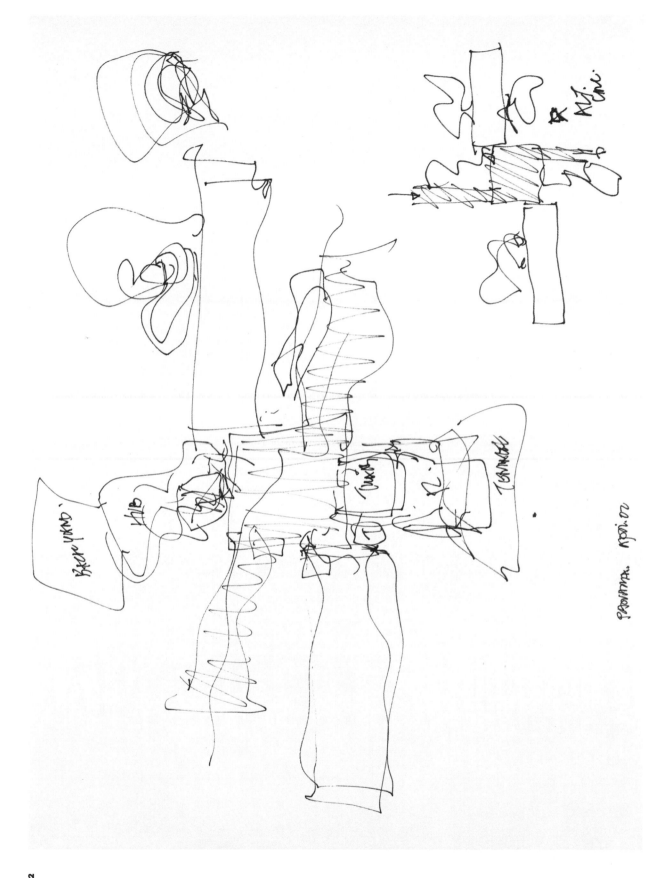

PANAMA, O ZAPU

PLAN.

Phoenix Mar. 02

Project 29

The Lewis Library

Princeton University,
Princeton, New Jersey
2002–

The Lewis Library
Princeton University,
Princeton, New Jersey

Design: commenced 2002
Construction: commenced 2004
Status: expected completion 2006
Number of drawings illustrated: 15

Supported by a gift from Princeton
alumnus Peter B. Lewis, the new Science
Library at Princeton University is a
five-story, 85,000-square-foot building
featuring a central tower with bold,
curved shapes and accompanying wings.
In addition to the library, the building will
house classrooms, study areas, and
a café. The main entrance is approached
via a series of new walkways, while
the building itself is designed to reflect its
context. The tower is two-thirds of the
height of the adjacent Fine Tower;
the wings reflect the design of the nearby
Center for Jewish Life, while the brick
base mirrors the bricks of nearby
Prospect Avenue buildings.

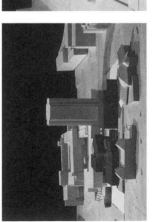

M29.01
09.02

M29.02
09.02

D29.01

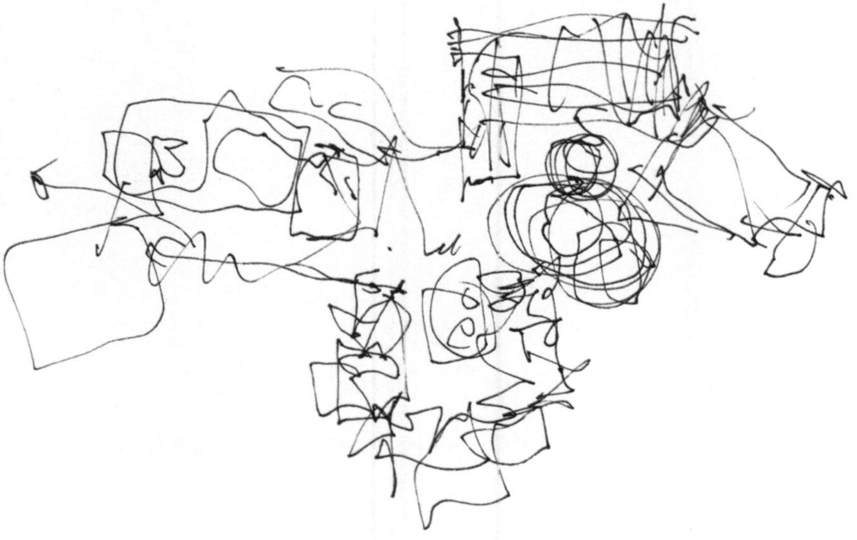

M29.03
07.08.02

M29.04
07.12.02

M29.05
07.16.02

PENINGTON avy, '02

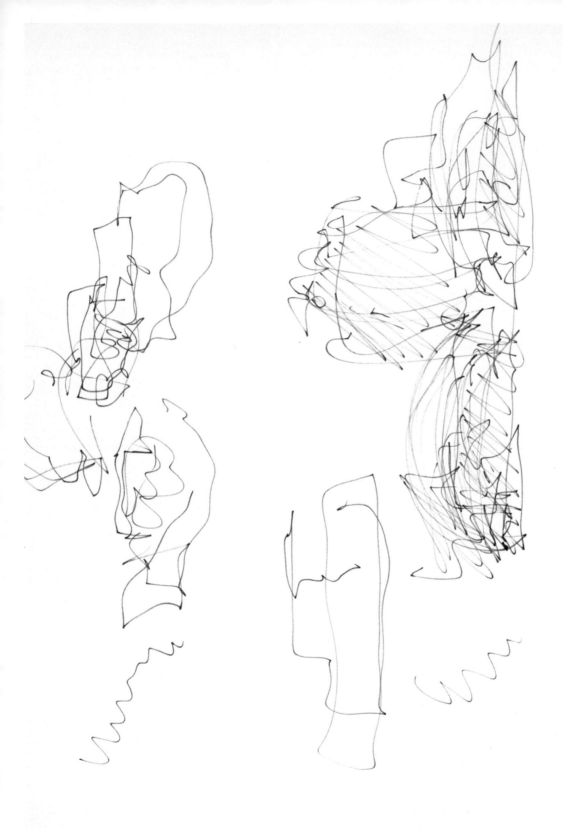

The problem with Princeton is that we got onto that Jerusalem shape and couldn't get off it for the tower, the main part of the Science Library. We made the mistake of showing that shape to the client and they didn't want to get off it either. There was a big budget crisis that finally changed their minds, and we just beat ourselves up until we were able to move on.

There was a point at which we completely abandoned the whole design and started over. I bet that when Frank got to the end of this process he didn't draw the final design, because it happened really fast. Usually when Frank "gets" it then it's kind of over for him. He moves on. cw

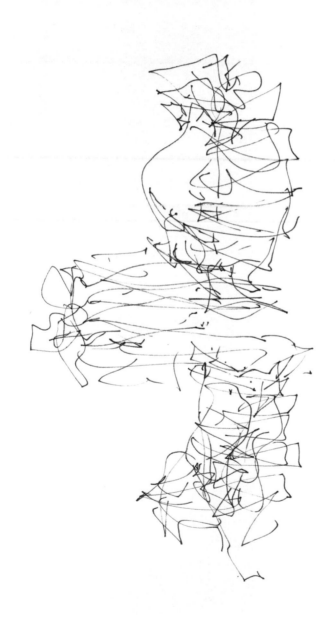

PAINTING. 5th July. '05

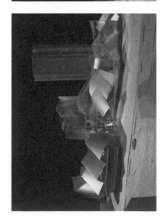

M29.06
09.04.02

M29.07
09.05.02

M29.08
11.02.02

PRINCETON - MAY'07

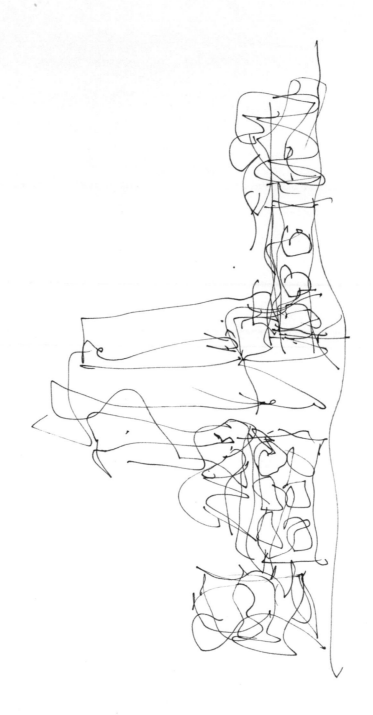

Princeton, Stay, Arr. '02

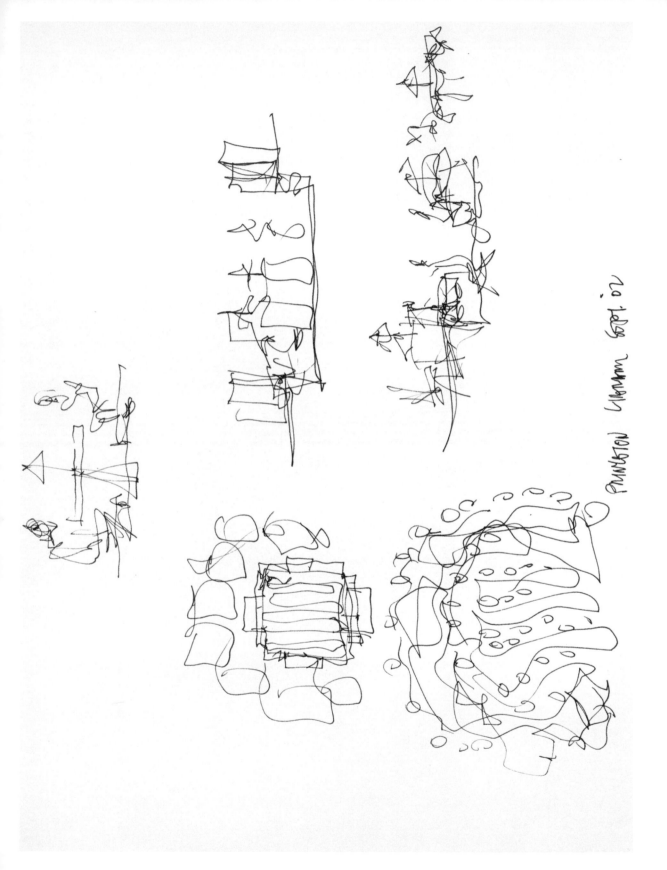

PRINCETON University Sept. 07

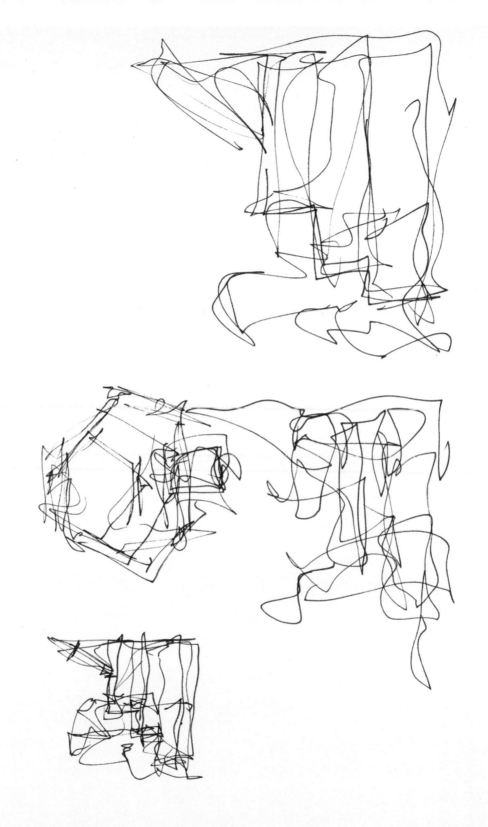

Henry James once said that creativity was like poking a stick into a big, deep hole, and occasionally bringing to the surface something irrelevant, which shouldn't be questioned. I agree with that. I also feel that in our culture, maybe, too much emphasis is placed on individuals, and not justifiably. One person does one's own work, and a lot of people are making work and putting information on the table. And so I don't feel that the work I have to show is necessarily a polemic or something for everybody to use. It's mostly my own searchings. FG

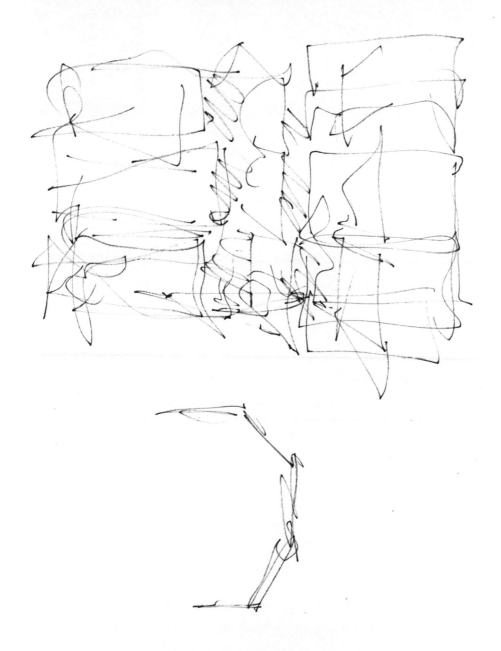

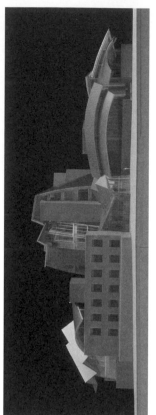

M29.09
07.25.03

M29.10
07.25.03

536
—
537

PRINCETON, NOV.'03

D29.14

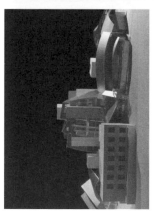

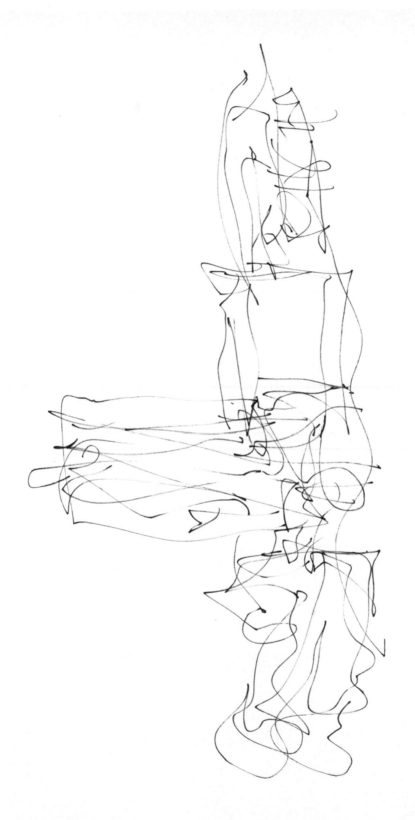

Boulevard St Michel, Paris '02

Project 10
Condé Nast Cafeteria
New York, New York

Design Architect—Gehry Partners, LLP
Design Partner—Frank Gehry
Project Designer—Edwin Chan
Project Architects—Christopher Mercier,
Michelle Kaufmann
Job Captain—Leigh Jerrard
Project Team—Kamran Ardalan, David Nam,
Rick Smith, Bruce Shepard, Kristin Woehl,
Julian Mayes, Douglas Glenn

Project 11
DZ Bank Building
Berlin, Germany

Design Architect—Gehry Partners, LLP
Design Partner—Frank Gehry
Project Designer—Craig Webb
Project Architects—Marc Salette, Tensho Takemori
Project Team—Laurence Tighe, Eva Sobesky,
George Metzger, Jim Dayton, John Goldsmith,
Jorg Ruegemer, Scott Uriu
Model Builders—Jeff Guga, Michael Jobes,
Kirk Blaschke, Nida Chesonis, Tom Cody,
Leigh Jerrard, Tadao Shimizu
Computer Modeling—Rick Smith, Bruce Shepard

Executive Architect—Planungs AG/Neufert Mittmann Graf
Project Manager—Michael Heggemann
Project Team—Achim Hauser, Johannes Wilberz,
Masoud Afchar

Structural Engineers—Ingenieur Büro Müller Marl GmbH:
Thomas Frankenstein, N.C.P. Nagaraj
Structural Engineers—Schlaich Bergermann und Partner:
Dr. Jörg Schlaich, Dr. Hans Schober, Thorsten Helbig,
Dorothea Krebs, Andrea Kratz
Mechanical/Electrical Engineer—Brandi Ingenieur GmbH:
Burkhard Feimann, Niels Wehlau, Peter Johanni
Façade Consultant—Planungsbüro für
Ingenieurleistungen: Klaus Glass, Karl Spanier
Lighting Consultant—A.G. Licht: Wilfried Kramb
Elevator Consultant—Jappsen & Stangier Berlin GmbH:
Hans Jappsen, Matthias Kramer
Acoustician—Audio Consulting Munich: Michel Schreiber
Audio-Visual Consultant—R.R. Ingenieurbüro für
Gebäudetechnik: Ralph Ammelung
Kitchen Consultant—Ingenieurbüro Schaller:
Ernst Schaller
Fire Safety Consultant—Technische Prüfgesellschaft
Lehmann: Klaus Kieke

Project 12
Peter B. Lewis Building
Weatherhead School of Management, Case Western
Reserve University, Cleveland, Ohio

Design Architect—Gehry Partners, LLP
Design Partner—Frank Gehry
Project Partner—James M. Glymph
Project Designer—Edwin Chan
Project Architect—Gerhard Mayer
Project Team—Rachel Allen, Thomas Balaban, Steven
Brabson, Henry Brawner, Susannah Dickinson, Heather
Duncan, Matt Fineout, Bryan Flores, Craig Gilbert,
Douglas Glenn, Douglas Hanson, Thomas Kim, Kurt
Komraus, Jason Luk, Colby Mayes, Julian Mayes,
Christopher Mazzier, Sy Melgazo, Frank Medrano,
Robyn Morgenstern, Brian Papke, Yanan Par,
Jonathon Rothstein, Marc Salette, Christian Schulz,
Frank Sheng, Rick Smith, Derek Soltes, Karen Tom,
Friedrich Tuczek, Frank Weeks, Adam Wheeler,
Brad Winkeljohn, Nora Wolin

Structural Engineer—DeSimone Consulting Engineers:
Vincent DeSimone, Derrick Roorda
Mechanical/Electrical/Plumbing Engineer—Bard:
Rao + Athanas: Ted Athanas, Mark Octeau, Ron Parsley,
Mark Suchocki, Jim Wilson
Civil Engineer—Euthenics: Richard Wasosky
Code Consultant—Rolf Jensen & Associates:
Nate Wittasek
Acoustical and Audio-Visual Consultant—McKay, Conant,
Brook: Dave Conant
Vertical Transportation Consultant—HKA: Daryl Anderson
Smoke Exhaust Simulation Modeling—RWDI: Ray Sinclair
General Contractor—Hunt Construction Group: Dan Seib

Project 13
Richard B. Fisher Center for Performing Arts
Bard College, Annandale-on-Hudson, New York

Design Architect—Gehry Partners, LLP
Design Principal—Frank Gehry
Project Designer—Craig Webb
Project Architect—John Bowers
Project Team—Suren Ambartsumyan, Guillermo Angarita,
David Blackburn, Kirk Blaschke, Earle Briggs,
Nida Chesonis, Matt Fineout, Sean Gale, Craig Gilbert,
Tim Gudgel, Jeff Guga, James Jackson, Julian Mayes,
Chris Mazzier, Frank Medrano, John Murphey, David
Pakshong, Yanan Par, Lynn Pilon, David Rodriguez,
Tadao Shimizu, Karen Tom, Jose Catriel Tulian, Mok Wai
Wan, Yannina Manjarres-Weeks, Adam Wheeler,
Brad Winkeljohn, Nora Wolin, Brian Zamora

Project 14
Hotel at Marques de Riscal
Elciego (Alava), Spain

Design Architect—Gehry Partners, LLP
Design Partner—Frank Gehry
Project Partner—Terry Bell
Project Designer—Edwin Chan
Project Architects—Richard Barrett, Andrew Liu
Project Team—Guillermo Angarita, Colby Mayes,
Joejohn McVey, Jonathon Rothstein

Executive Architects—IDOM, César Caicoya Gómez-
Morán Architecture: Fernando Pérez Fraile (DE), José
Sáenz de Argandoña Zatarain, Alberto Minguez Ropiñón,
Silvia Solá Santaolalla, Ana Lorena González Morales
Structural Engineering—Javier Gómez Corral, Miles
Shephard, Karl Blette, Miguel Angel Frías Villafruela,
Eduardo Sáinz de la Encina, Juan Ignacio Lesarri,
Shyamala Duraisingam
Mechanical Engineering—Francisco José Sánchez Aguilar
Budget Control—Javier Dávila de Eusebio, Iñaki Fuertes
Cajigas, Belén Usechi Carnicer, Julio Piedra García,
Juncal Aldamizechevarria, González de Durana
Geotechnical—Victor Sancho Villasante
Drafting—Iñaki Zabala Ciarsolo, Imanol Eizmendi Iraurgui
Project Assistant—Sonia López-Gómez Martinez
Project Revision—Javier Aja Cantalejo
Glazing Consultant—Umaran Scoop
Woodworking Consultants—Carpinteria Felix Landa,
Ludwig Seufert GmbH
Lighting Consultant—A.G. Licht
Kitchen Consultant—Comercial Hostelera Del Norte SA
Plasterwork Consultant—Kooplad

Project 15
Le Clos Jordanne
Lincoln, Ontario, Canada

Design Architect—Gehry International, Inc., Architects
Design Partner—Frank Gehry
Project Partner—James M. Glymph
Project Designer—Edwin Chan
Project Architect—Earle Briggs
Project Team—Tomas Dubuisson, Alexander Fernandez,
Jeff Garrett, Ali Jeevanjee, Leigh Jerrard, Frank
Melendez, David Nam, Diego Petrate, Zohar Schwartz
Structural Engineer—Yolles Partnership
Electrical Engineer—Mulvey + Banani Internation, Inc.
Mechanical Engineer—The Mitchell Partnership, Inc.
Code Consultant/Fire Protection—Leber Rubes
Landscape Architect—Janet Rosenberg & Associates
Planning Consultant—BLS Planning Associates

Project 16
Maggie's Center
Ninewalls NHS Hospital, Dundee, Scotland

Design Architect—Gehry Partners, LLP
Design Partner—Frank Gehry
Project Partner—James M. Glymph
Project Designers—Michael Cranfill, Craig Webb
Project Architect—Tomaso Bradshaw
Project Team—Saffet Bekiroglu, Meaghan Lloyd,
Colby Mayes, Joejohn McVey, Wai Wan Mok, Jose
Catriel Tulian, Bryant Yey

Executive Architect—James F. Stephen Architects:
James Fred Stephen, Douglas Reid

Project 17
Samsung Museum of Modern Art
Seoul, Korea

Design Architect—Gehry Partners, LLP
Design Partner—Frank Gehry
Project Partner—James M. Glymph
Project Designer—Edwin Chan
Project Architect—Douglas Hanson
Project Team—Kamran Ardalan, Richard Barrett, Nida
Chesonis, Douglas Dahlkemper, Alex Gentile, Bo Sook
Han, Leigh Jerrard, Yannina Majarres-Weeks, Brent
Miller, David Nam, Jay Park, Charles Sanchez, Bruce
Shepard, Rick Smith, Derek Soltes, Scott Uriu, Mok Wai
Wan, Jeff Wauer, Frank Weeks, Adam Woltag, Brian Yoo
Executive Architect—Samoo Architects & Engineers

Project 18
MARTa Herford
Herford, Germany

Design Architect—Gehry Partners, LLP
Design Partner—Frank Gehry
Project Partner—Terry Bell
Project Designer—Edwin Chan
Project Architect—Kamran Ardalan
Project Team—Reza Bagherzadeh, Cara Cragan, Sean
Gale, Sean Gallivan, Ali Jevanjee, Michelle Kaufmann,
Kurt Komraus, Andy Lui, Diego Petrate, Beat Schenk,
Rick Smith, Hiroshi Tokumaru, Catriel Tulian
Executive Architect—Archimedes GmbH
Principal-in-Charge—Hartwig Rüllkotter
Project Team—Stefan Hoffmann, Birgit Bastiaan,
Jürgen Beinke, Thomas Vollbracht

Structural Engineer—Bollinger + Grohmann
Mechanical Engineer—Construct
Lichting Consultant—A. G. Licht

Project 19
Walt Disney Concert Hall
Los Angeles, California

Design Architect—Gehry Partners, LLP
Design Partner—Frank Gehry
Project Partner—James M. Glymph
Project Designer—Craig Webb
Project Manager—Terry Bell
Project Architects—David Pakshong, William Childers, David Hardie, Kristin Woehl
Senior Detailer—Vartan Chalikian
Project Team—Andrew Alper, Suren Ambartsumyan, Larik Ararat, Kamran Ardalan, Herwig Baumgartner, Saffet Bekiroglu, Pejman Berjis, Rick Black, Kirk Blaschke, Tomaso Bradshaw, Earle Briggs, Zachary Burns, John Carter, Padraic Cassidy, Tina Chee, Rebeca Cotera, Jonathan Davis, Jim Dayton, David Denton, Susannah Dickinson, Denise Disney, John Drezner, Nick Easton, Manoucher Eslami, Craig Gilbert, Jeff Guga, Vano Haritunians, James Jackson, Victoria Jenkins, Michael Jobes, Michael Kempf, Thomas Kim, Kurt Komraus, Gregory Kromhout, Naomi Langer, Meaghan Lloyd, Jacquine Lorange, Gary Lundberg, Michael Maltzan, Gerhard Mayer, Christopher Mazzier, Alex Meconi, Emilio Melgazo, George Metzger, Brent Miller, Julianna Morais, Rosemary Morris, Gaston Nogues, Jay Park, Diego Petrate, Vytas Petrulis, Michael Resnic, David Rodriguez, Christopher Samuelian, Michae J. Sant, Michael Sedlacek, Robert Seelenbacher, Matthias Seufert, Dennis Shelden, Bruce Shepard, Tadao Shimizu, Rick Smith, Eva Sobesky, Suran Sumian, Randall Stout, Thomas Swanson, John Szlachta, Tensho Takemori, Laurence Tighe, Hiroshi Tokumaru, Karen Tom, Jose Catriel Tulian, Dane Twichell, William Ullman, Monica Vaiterra-Day, Mok Wai Wan, Yu-Wen Wang, Eric Wegerbauer, Bobbie Weiser, Gretchen Werner, Adam Wheeler, Tim Williams, Nora Wolin, Bryant Yeh, Brian Yoo, Brian Zamora

Structural Engineer—John A. Martin & Associates, Inc.
Mechanical Engineers—Cosentini Associates, Levine/Seegel Associates
Electrical Engineer—Frederick Russell Brown & Associates
Acoustical Consultant—Nagata Acoustics, Inc.: Yasuhisa Toyota
Acoustical Isolation Consultant—Charles M. Salter Associates, Inc.
Theater Consultants—Theatre Projects Consultants, Fisher Dachs Associates
Fire Protection Engineering—Rolf Jensen & Associates, Inc.
Civil Engineer—Psomas & Associates
Accessibility Consultant—Rolf Jensen & Associates
Exterior Wall Consultant—Gordon H. Smith Corporation
Elevator Consultant—Lerch-Bates North America, Inc.
Building Maintenance Consultant—Citadel Consulting, Inc.
Garden Design Consultant—Melinda Taylor Garden Design
Landscape Architect—Lawrence Reed Moline Ltd.
Organ Builders—Rosales Organ Builders, Inc., Glatter-Gotz
Graphics Consultant—Bruce Mau Design, Inc.,: Adams Morioka
Lighting Consultant—L'Observatoire
Waterproofing Consultant—D7 Group, Inc.
Security Consultant—Con-Tech Consultants
Food Service Consultant—Cini-Little International, Inc.
Environmental Management—Sapphos Environmental
Audio Consultant—Engineering Harmonics
Hardware Consultant—Finish Hardware Technology

Project 20
The Ray & Maria Stata Center
Massachusetts Institute of Technology, Cambridge, Massachusetts

Design Architect—Gehry Partners, LLP
Design Partner—Frank Gehry
Project Partner—James M. Glymph
Project Designer—Craig Webb
Project Architect/Project Partner—Marc Salette
Assistant Project Designer—Rachel Allen
Assistant Project Architect—Larry Tighe
Assistant Project Architect—David Rodriguez
Core Project Team—Helena Berge, Henry Brawner, Vartan Chalikian, Christine Clements, Edward Duffy, Yono Hong, James Jackson, Thomas Kim, Jason Luk, Yannina Manjarres-Weeks, Frank Melendez, Emiliano Melgazo, Ngaire Nelson, Gaston Nogues, Yanan Par, Doug Pierson, David Plotkin, Derek Sola, Karen Tom, Steve Traeger, Monica Valtierra-Day, Yuwen Wang, Jeff Wauer
Project Team—Chris Banks, Christopher Barbee, Herwig Baumgartner, Saffet Bekiroglu, Tom Bessai, Tomaso Bradshaw, Tina Chee, Susannah Dickinson, Brian Flores, Raymond Gaetan, Craig Gilbert, Jeff Guga, Dari Iron, Michael Kempf, Kurt Komraus, Irwin Larman, Dennis Lee, Frank Medrano, Clifford Minnick, Robyn Morgenstern, Scott Nakao, Dennis Shelden, Bruce Shepard, Suren Sumian, Birgit Schneider, Gavin Wall, Bryant Yeh, Brian Zamora

Associate Architect—CANNON Design
Project Manager—Debi McDonald
Project Team—Christine Clements, Edward Duffy, Tom Tostengard, Frank McGuire, Nancy Felts, Karl Leato, Dave Ordonica, Julie McCullough, Peter Hefferman

Structural Engineer—John A. Martin & Associates
Principal-in-Charge—Trailer Martin
Project Manager—Ron Lee
Project Engineers—Les Cho, Martha Gonzalez, Marcello Sgambelluri, Jose Hebreo, Renie Beasley
Exterior Enclosure Structural Consultant—Martin/Martin & ABS: Steven Judd, Tait Ketchun, Kevin Wright, Michael Smith, Ken Peterson
Local Structural Engineer—CBI Consulting, Craig Barnes

MEPFP Engineer—Vanderweil Engineers
Principal- n-Charge—Joe Manfredi
Project Managers—Mark Aprea, John Daly
HVAC Engineers—Chris Schaffner, Matt Stone
Electrical Engineer—Robert Chaves
Plumbing Engineers—John Rattenbury, Jeri Sullivan
Fire-protection Engineers—Demetri Tsatsarones, Amy Hughes

Acoustical and Audio-Visual Consultant—McKay, Conant, Brook
Project P'incipal—David A. Conant
Project Manager, Acoustics—Michael P. SantaMaria
AV Design Supervisory Consultant—Randal B. Willis, P.E.
AV Support Supervisory Consultant—Timothy R. Waters

Exterior Enclosure Consultant—Gordon H. Smith Corporaton: Gordon H. Smith, P.E., S. 'Alex' Marton, A.I.A.

Landscape Architect—Olin Partnership
Principal-in-Charge—Laurie Olin
Associate—Keith McPeters
Project Manager—Yue Li
Landsca:e Designer—Annie Griffenburg

Civil Engineer—Judith Nitsch Engineering, Inc.
Chief Engineer—Stephen M. Benz, P.E.
Project Engineer—William Doyle, P.E.

Lighting Consultant—A. G. Licht: Wilfried Kramb, Klaus Adolph

Project 21
Corcoran Gallery & School of Art
Washington, D.C.

Design Architect—Gehry Partners, LLP
Design Partner—Frank Gehry
Project Partner—George Metzger
Project Designer—Edwin Chan
Project Architect—Tensho Takemori
Job Captain—Doug Pierson
Project Team—Laura Bachelde, Vartan Chalikian, Cara Cragan, Chris Deckwitz, Anand Devarajan, Matt Gagnon, Sean Gallivan, Jeffrey Garrett, Craig Gilbert, Tim Gudgel, Ana He ̄ton, Dennis Lee, Napoleon Merana, Julianna Morais, Tim Paulson, Christian Schulz, Zohar Schwartz, Karen Tom, Steve Traeger, Frank Weeks

Renovation Architect—Smith Group: Colden Florance, David Greenbaum, Elsa Santoyo, Thomas Lindbloom

Structural Engineer—John A. Martin & Associates: Trailer Martin, Chuck Whitaker, Ron Lee
Mechanical/Electrical/Plumbing Engineer—Cosentini Associates: Igor Bienstock, Mark Malekshahi

Project 22
The New York Times Headquarters
New York, New York

Design Architect—Gehry Partners, LLP
Design Partner—Frank Gehry
Project Partner—James M. Glymph
Project Designer—Edwin Chan
Project Architect—George Metzger
Project Team—Sean Gallivan, Matthew Gagnon, Ana Henton, Steffen Leisner, Christopher Deckwitz, Anand Devarajan, Jose Catriel Tulian, Michelle Kaufmann, Kamran Ardalan, Cara Cragan, Chad Dyner, Sean Gale, Eric Jones, Meaghan Lloyd, David Nam, Diego Petrate, Birgit Schneider, Zohar Schwartz, Brian Zamora

Associate Architect—Skidmore, Owings & Merrill: Samer Bitar, Peter Buendgen, Shashi Caan, David Childs, Scott Duncan, Michael Fei, T. J. Gottesdiener, Dale Greenwald, Donald Holt, Kaz Morihata, Simone Pfeiffer, Ursula Schneider, Marilyn Taylor, Tran Vinh, Ross B. Wimer

Structural Engineering—Skidmore, Owings & Merrill: William F. Baker, Hal Iyangar

Project 23
Ohr-O'Keefe Museum
Biloxi, Mississippi

Design Architect—Gehry Partners, LLP
Design Partner—Frank Gehry
Project Designer—Craig Webb
Project Architect—Jeffrey Wauer
Project Team—Saffet Bekiroglu, Jennifer Bruno, Michael Cranfill, Eric Jones, Joejohn McVey, Frank Melendez, Aaron Turner, Gavin Wall, Brian Zamora

Executive Architect—Guild Hardy & Associates Architects
Civil Engineering—Brown & Mitchell, Inc.
Structural Engineering—Morphy Makofsky, Inc.
Mechanical/Electrical/Plumbing Engineer—Schmidt, Dell, Cook & Associates
Landscape Consultant—Cashio, Cochran, LLC
Reed House Restoration Architect—James Dodds, A.I.A.